cornbread nation 3

P9-EMD-884

CORNBREAD NATION

John T. Edge, General Editor

cornbread
nation 3

Foods of the Mountain South

EDITED BY RONNI LUNDY

Published in association with the

SOUTHERN FOODWAYS ALLIANCE,

Center for the Study of Southern Culture,

University of Mississippi,

by the

UNIVERSITY OF NORTH CAROLINA PRESS

Chapel Hill

Andrew Carnegie Library,
Livingstone College
701 W. Monroe St.
Salisbury, NC 28144

© 2005 Southern Foodways Alliance,
Center for the Study of Southern Culture,
University of Mississippi
All rights reserved
Manufactured in the United States of America
Designed by Richard Hendel
Set in Minion types by Keystone Typesetting, Inc.
The paper in this book meets the guidelines for permanence and
durability of the Committee on Production Guidelines for Book
Longevity of the Council on Library Resources.

This volume of *Cornbread Nation* was underwritten,
in part, by a gift from the Atticus Trust.

Library of Congress Cataloging-in-Publication Data
Cornbread nation 3 : foods of the mountain South /
edited by Ronni Lundy.
p. cm.
"Published in association with the Southern Foodways Alliance,
Center for the Study of Southern Culture, University of Mississippi,
by the University of North Carolina Press."
ISBN 0-8078-5656-8 (pbk.: alk. paper)
1. Cookery. 2. Food habits. I. Lundy, Ronni.
II. Southern Foodways Alliance.
TX651.C665 2005
394.1'2'0975—dc22   2005017545

09 08 07 06 05   5 4 3 2 1

CORNBREAD NATION ANTHEM

Corn pone, spider bread, hush puppy, dog bread,
Ash cake, bannock bread, johnny cake, spoon bread.
Dish it up, pour it on, give it all you got;
Put the fatback in a cast-iron pot.

Richmond to Fort Worth, Davenport to Natchez,
Burly 'bacca fields to your snowy cotton patches;
No matter where you're headin' when the train leaves the station
You still take your supper in the Cornbread Nation.

Save a can of bacon grease, soak a bowl of beans,
Chop a yella onion, wash the grit off the greens;
Sift a little soda and some powder in the meal,
Pour in the buttermilk to get the right feel.

Hot water, cold water, doesn't really matter;
Don't work too hard when you're mixing up the batter.
Hot corn, cold corn, friends and relations
Sittin' at the table in the Cornbread Nation.

Up in Kentucky, where I was born,
Up in Kentucky, where the Colonel's in the corn,
They shake up the jar, look for the beads,
Take a little sip, no more than you need.

You can scrape it, you can chew it, you can roll it into dough.
You can sip it, you can brew it, you can let the liquor flow.
Hot corn, cold corn, friends and relations,
Sittin' at the table in the Cornbread Nation.

—Tim O'Brien

CONTENTS

cornbread Nation 3

Introduction

RONNI LUNDY

Come and listen to my story 'bout a man named Jed,
A poor mountaineer, barely kept his family fed.
—*"The Ballad of Jed Clampett"*

In the year 2003, members and friends of the Southern Foodways Alliance (SFA) turned analytical attention and copious appetites to the foods and traditions of the mountain South. Zealously we consumed vats of gold and glistening shuck beans mopped up with sops of brown-crusted, bacon-seasoned cornbread. We sampled apples (many of vintage origin, still grown in the hills and hollers) sliced fresh, or dried, cooked, and slathered between sorghum-sweetened layers of stack cake. We celebrated the holy transformation of humble pig into paradise-worthy slices of slow-cured, smoke- and salt-tinged country ham. We weighed the merits of rich and dusky fried apple pies versus sun-kissed peach ones. And we partook of the sacred corn of the region, not just in bread and kernels, but in the purest, potent-est distillations known to man and angels.

And when at last we were, as my mother would have observed, "like to founder," we leaned back from the table and began to discuss, debate, and imagine exactly what all this food might mean.

What does it say about the work ethic of a culture, for instance, when you discover that to make eight small servings of cooked shuck beans, someone has to plant, cultivate, weed, pick, string, and sew onto thread five pounds of green beans for drying?

How can you assert a purely Anglo-Saxon and profoundly isolated culture when you discover that those same shuck beans are a German creation and that the traditions of the region also include Italian, Swiss, African American, and Native American foodways? Not to mention oysters.

How do you hold to assumptions of ignorance when you see a list with dozens of native greens, berries, barks, and seeds that were turned into food and/or medicine? Or believe in traits of clannishness and hostility when you

1

hear the catechism of a Loaves and Fishes ethic that made friends and strangers alike welcome to mountain tables, that caused pork chops-enough-for-the-family to be reconfigured in the kitchen into a pork casserole that would provide as well for any and all drop-ins?

In other words, looking through the lens of real Southern mountain food—the methods of its growing, processing, and eating—we began to see a vivid picture of the region and its people that had little in common with their most prevalent and demeaning stereotypes. And we began to wonder where those stereotypes came from and why they were so tenacious. As is so often the case with the SFA, we discovered lurking under the dinner table an unexpected subject inextricably connected to the food above. In the past, meditations on the provenance of fried chicken and barbecue led us to impassioned explorations of the issues of food and race. At this conference we discovered that the visitor under the table looked suspiciously like class and the prejudices that accompany it.

Now it happened that in this same year we were honoring Bill Best as the Ruth Fertel Keeper of the Flame. You will read about him here in a piece by Sarah Fritschner that describes the work that earned Bill this most cherished SFA award: his heirloom seed bank of green bean varieties grown in the Southern mountains. Born in western North Carolina and having spent most of his life in Berea, Kentucky, Bill is a true man of the Appalachians, geographically and spiritually. He is a scholar and philosopher, as well as a husband of the land. In addition to farming, he was a professor at Berea College until his retirement a few years ago. He has made it his life's work to understand on many levels the impact of the dissonance between the truth of Southern mountain life and culture and the dismissive way it is perceived and portrayed by the dominant world "outside." In his writing on this subject, he draws often on the work of Carl Jung, and Bill's perceptions on the power of myth in the shaping of personal identity have been likened to those of Joseph Campbell. That Bill can explain some of these concepts in a story about the taste of his mother's tomatoes makes him our sort of people.

It was in a book of Bill's, *From Existence to Essence*, that I discovered a key to understanding why mountain ways have persistently been translated in such pejorative terms in larger American culture. Bill's explanation is complex and nuanced. My paraphrase is, perhaps unfairly, simple: For the last century and then some, the culture of America at large has been a culture of things. From its onset, the culture of the Southern mountains has been one of connection. Being intangible, the treasures of the latter are virtually invisible to the citizens of the former. Consequently, a life focused on fostering connection, as opposed to acquisition, might seem to the dominant culture, at best, quaint and anachronistic, at worst, ridiculous and perverse.

In other words, if you value a person most in terms of the number of things he or she has—cars, Cuisinarts, face lifts, cell phones—you will not value a person who has few things but is, instead, rich only in connection. If you see time as well spent only when it is spent in pursuit of things, you will see time as wasted when it is spent instead nurturing connection.

Consider the green bean: In contemporary American culture, the bean has little status (unless it is, of course, *haricot vert*, appearing in cameo star turn in a major production by a celebrity chef). In the contemporary kitchen, this bean is sometimes a matter of nourishment, but more likely just a color on the plate. Consequently, the beans we buy at the grocery store have been bred to minimize the amount of time we spend with them—commensurate to their insignificant value as "things." They no longer have strings. Heck, they barely have beans, so they can be cooked in a flash. In fact, we buy most of them in cans already cooked, or frozen and simply in need of heating.

In the mountain South, however, the green bean is the center of a network of amazingly complex connections. Beans are grown for nourishment, so the favored varieties have plump pods that are allowed to fill out with protein-rich seeds. The time it takes to simmer these, slow and low on a back burner, can be spent outside by cooks who are as connected to the earth and their garden as they are to the stove. These beans are bred for flavors and textures so idiosyncratic that Bill Best has acquired some 200 seeds of distinctly different characteristics. Mountain people name their homegrown varieties of green beans; some are linked to specific families, some belong to communities, some have names that suggest poetry or stories: Lazy Wife, Roan Mountain, Tobacco Worm.

Bush beans are grown commercially because they are easy to cultivate and pick. Pole beans are grown in the mountains because they taste better, and that alone is reason to justify the extra care. Corn stalks provide the poles traditionally, and the beans are connected to the health of the corn crop, providing nitrogen to the soil that corn depletes.

Mountain beans have strings. Ask anybody from the hills and they'll tell you that a bean with strings beats a bean without on flavor anytime. But those strings also provide connection. Women sit on the porch to string beans, a task that offers a cooling respite in a physically exhausting day of gardening, cooking, and housework. Grandmothers, sisters, aunts, and children are apt to join in, and the stringing becomes an occasion for conversation and community.

At canning time that community moves into the kitchen. More hands make the task go faster. And why buy lots of equipment? One canning kettle will do for an extended family of several households if everyone takes turns.

Threading shuck beans for drying was often a community project for the porch as well. Or it could be a special time between mother and child, as Billy C. Clark describes in his story "Leatherbritches." Originally dried for sustenance in the long, cold winters of the mountains, these labor-intensive beans are still prepared by mountain people today for their flavor, and also for their connection—to the past, or to the home that many mountain people have had to leave, looking for work.

When I left my home in Kentucky for the first time, moved out west, and spent my first Christmas alone, my homesickness was tended by my mountain aunts who sent a care package with a bag of shuck beans inside. I cooked those beans for the people who had befriended me in New Mexico, and a boy from Baltimore could not leave the pot, so delighted was he by their flavor, so fascinated by their history. He became my husband, the father of our child. Connection. Slender yet sturdy as the strings on beans.

All of this is the long way around to telling you that this, the third volume of *Cornbread Nation*, a compendium of splendid writing on the foodways of the South, has two themes. Up front and plainly, we devote the bulk of this volume to the foodways of the mountain South. Geographically, that region is defined as the Appalachian range beginning in Maryland and West Virginia and extending to the northernmost hills of Alabama, plus the Ozarks of Arkansas and Missouri. Culinarily, those borders extend farther to include eastern Texas, where many of the Anglo settlers came from the mountain South and the foodways still show it, and also the fingers of the hillbilly diaspora that stretched north into the factories of Ohio, Michigan, Chicago, Indiana, and south and east into the mills of the Carolina lowlands.

In these selections we hope to share with you visions of a culture that is not only rich in terms of its past but still strong in the present. You will travel from an eastern Kentucky sorghum stir-off attended by folksinger Jean Ritchie in the early part of the twentieth century to a couple of present-day restaurants in West Virginia, where a young writer ponders the meaning of the different cultures each attracts. Those of you new to the region will learn about pawpaws and papaws who hunt for possum. Those of you familiar with your own neck of the woods may be surprised, as I was, to travel to Helvetia, West Virginia, with Sally Schneider and discover the rich, Swiss-rooted traditions that form the foodways there. You will hear Adriana Trigiani describe growing up as an Italian hillbilly and Frank X Walker limn the truth of being born Affrilachian. You will consider food and its connections remembered, sometimes mourned, and more often recreated by the mountaineers of the hillbilly diaspora. At every stop along the way you will be welcomed to a table where the real food described is distinct and delicious, the food for thought sustaining. Don't be afraid to dig in. There is always enough to nourish us all.

Not all of the pieces in this anthology have to do with the mountain South, however. As West Virginia–born singer/songwriter Tim O'Brien notes in the lyrics to our organization's new national anthem, "No matter where you're headin' when the train leaves the station / You still take your supper in the Cornbread Nation." It was our intention from the outset that each edition of *Cornbread Nation* would showcase the best writing we could find to illuminate the foodways of the South at large. So here you will also journey to Cajun Louisiana with Rick Bragg, where he finds a cure for a broken heart at the communal tables of the boudin circuit. You will attend a syrup making and family reunion with self-styled cracker ecologist Janisse Ray; and ponder the secrets of geophagy, not to mention the political ramifications of methods of chilling iced tea, with Guy Davenport. If you read closely you will realize that these diverse geographic stories are linked by more than blue highways. Like our stories of mountain food, they are also, at heart, tales of connections that reach beyond the table and garden into the hearts of the individuals and communities they sustain. It is the power of such connections that have made food and foodways the most potent signifiers of what it means to be Southern and, as you will soon discover, what it means to be from the mountains.

It's because of these connections that I am sure that Jed and all his kin would, in fact, have been loathe to pack up and leave home when he came into all the money in the world. I also think the potency of connection is why, when CBS television put out a casting call in 2003, looking for a poor family from the Southern mountains to move to a mansion in California for a reality-based version of *The Beverly Hillbillies*, the company was barraged not with hordes of eager candidates but a flood of outrage and a well-organized media campaign from the natives, most particularly the folks at the Center for Rural Strategies.

Or, to put this concept in terms that a thing-centered world might better understand:

Jethro and Elly May's new ce-ment pond: $37,000
Granny's green felt dining room table: $4,500
The chance to hunt possum with your papaw or break cornbread with the cousins: Priceless.

So join us now as we take an armchair journey through the larders of the mountain South and points beyond. Sit a spell. Take your shoes off. . . .

Erratum: In error, *Cornbread Nation 2* presented two poems, "Roadside Table" by Michael McFee and "To the Unconverted" by Jake Adam York, in incomplete form. While the SFA and University of North Carolina Press regret the error, it is our pleasure to reprint each poem in full in this volume. You'll find them on pages 100 and 151, respectively.

planting the essential seeds
Corn & Beans

I Offer You a Gift

MARILOU AWIAKTA

Still of the night . . .
   moon on the wane
   sun deep in sleep.
Cricket, bird and wind lay low
as rhythms of earth and sky
   suspend
   prepare to turn.

Awake in the dark
   you know
   I know
We may not make it.
Mother Earth may not make it.
   We teeter
on the turning point.

Against the downward pull,
against the falter
of your heart and mine,
I offer you a gift
a seed to greet the sunrise—
   Ginitsi Selu
Corn, Mother of Us All.
   Her story.

Compass for Our Journey

MARILOU AWIAKTA

"SELU . . . Say-loo . . . Selu . . . Say-loooo. . . ."

Her name echoes through the centuries. But who is Selu? Knowing just her name is not enough.

She will speak for herself in the following traditional Cherokee story. Like Siquanid', who tells it, from my childhood I have found this story interesting.

For thousands of years, indigenous peoples of the Americas have formally recognized corn as a teacher of wisdom, the spirit inseparable from the grain. Through corn's natural ways of growing and being, the spirit sings of strength, respect, balance, harmony. Of adaptability, cooperation, unity in diversity. Songs of survival.

As a link to the spirit, many tribes long ago composed an Origin of Corn story, which they tell to this day. They designed the story to create a synapse in the mind, a lens in the eye, a drum in the ear, a rhythm in the heart. Listeners take the story in, think it through, and, when the need arises, apply its wisdoms to life. Although the stories vary in content from tribe to tribe, they have a spiritual base in common, which began when the People first cultivated maize from a wild grass. They perceived corn as a gift from the All-Mystery, the Creator, the Provider. In telling Selu's story to a general audience recently, a Cherokee medicine man established its spiritual base immediately. "In the beginning, the Creator made our Mother Earth. Then came Selu, Grandmother Corn."

Used in this ritual sense, "Grandmother" connotes "Mother of Us All," a spirit being who is eternally wise. And if the medicine man had been speaking his native tongue instead of English, the indivisibility of grain and spirit would have been apparent, for both are spelled s-e-l-u. Saying one evokes the other. In the Smoky Mountains of my homeland, the Cherokee pronounce the word "say-loo." In Oklahoma they pronounce it another way but with the same meaning.

Especially during the past decade, I've been seeking deeper understanding of Selu's wisdoms and ways of applying them to contemporary life, including my own. I invite you to share my path of thought to the place it has led me in the early 1990s—the cusp of the millennium, a time of upheaval and change for us all. Our compass for the journey is Selu's traditional story and its cultural context. To be accurate and useful, a Native American story, like a compass needle, must have its direction points.

The following version of Selu's story, thought to be very old, is rare in other ways. During the mid-twentieth century, Siquanid', an elder who lived in the lonely hills east of Tenkiller Lake in Oklahoma, told it to Jack and Anna Kilpatrick, distinguished Cherokee scholars, who spoke, read, and wrote their native language. Included in their book *Friends of Thunder*, this story, unlike many published versions that appear to be retellings from the English, was translated directly from the verbal text. Told in the unaffected, friendly manner in which the older Cherokee talk, it provides a word-portrait of Selu. To make a story relevant to listeners, details are sometimes altered. For example, Siquanid' substitutes guns for bows and arrows. Because Native American cultures relate wisdom to age, it is significant that Selu is a "very old woman."

At one time there was a very old woman who had two grandsons. These two grandsons were always hunting. They hunted deer and wild turkeys. They always had plenty to eat.

Later on, after many hunting trips, when they got ready to go hunting early in the morning, they were cleaning their guns. When their grandmother noticed that they were ready to go, she thought to herself, "They are getting ready to go hunting," so she went to them where they were cleaning their guns, outside the fenced-in yard.

When the grandmother came to them, they were busily cleaning their guns. She said to them, "I see that you are getting ready to go hunting," and they replied, "Yes. We are going to hunt deer today."

"Well, when you come back, I'll have the most delicious of dinners ready. I'm going to cook all of the old meat, and I'm going to put into it something they call corn and we're going to drink the broth from it," she said to the young men.

"All right," said the young men.

When they got to the forest, they wondered about the word corn that she had used. They didn't know what that was, and they wondered where she got it.

"I wonder where corn comes from?" they asked each other. "When we get home, we'll find out," they said. They killed a deer, shouldered it, and went home.

When they got home, they saw the large pot bubbling. They noticed that with the meat, corn in small ground-up pieces was boiling in there. (If anyone had ever seen it before, he would have known what it was; but then these boys had never seen it before.)

They asked their grandmother, "What is that that you have in the pot?"

"It is called grits."

They didn't ask her where she got it.

When they ate their dinner, the young men had the most delicious meal that they had ever had. After dinner they told their grandmother what a superb meal she had cooked. The grandmother was pleased.

"Well, tomorrow at noon we will have some more delicious food."

The next day they went hunting again, but they already had some dried turkeys. So the grandmother cooked these dried turkeys and cooked grits with them.

When they returned home that evening with their bag of turkeys, dinner was announced. With this meat were these grits, and the young men said, "This is the best meal that we have ever had." They thanked their grandmother again and told her that her food was delicious.

The grandmother was very pleased and said, "I'm so happy that you said what you did."

Next day they again went to the forest. While they were in the forest, one of them kept thinking about the corn. "This thing she calls corn . . . she said that today about noon she is going to start cooking again," said one to the other; and the other said, "Yes, that's what she said."

"I'll go hide around somewhere and see where she gets it if you want me to," said one.

"All right," said the other. "You had better go before she begins cooking."

So one of them went. This thing called corn was troubling this young man; so he hid behind the smokehouse and watched for his grandmother.

Later on the grandmother came carrying a large pan and went into the smokehouse. The young man peeped through a small hole. When the grandmother got into the smokehouse, she put the pan under where she was standing. Then she struck both of her sides, and when she hit her sides grits fell from every part of her body. They fell until the pan became full. When she came out of the smokehouse, she carried this pan of grits, dumped them into the pot, and began cooking them.

That's what the young man learned, and he went back to his brother and told him about it. When he arrived where his brother was, his brother asked him what he had learned.

He said to his brother, "This delicious food of Grandmother's that we have been eating comes from her body. She shakes it off from all over her body. She puts a pan under her. She strikes her sides, and it falls off her body and falls into the pan until it is full, and that is what we have been eating," he told his brother.

His brother said, "We really eat an unsavory thing, don't we!" So they decided that they would not eat any more of it when they got home.

When they arrived home, their grandmother had dinner ready. Again she had the same kind of food. They both didn't eat much.

"What's wrong? You're not eating very much. Don't you like me?" said their grandmother.

The young men said, "No. We're just too tired from walking so much in our hunting."

"But I think that you don't like me," she said. "Or maybe you learned something somewhere, and that's the reason that you don't want to eat," they were told.

At that moment the grandmother became ill. She knew that they had found out [her secret]. The grandmother took to bed, and she began to talk to them about what they should do.

"Now that I'm in bed, I'm going to die." (She told them all about what was going to happen in the future.) "When you bury me, you must put a large fence around me and bury me just right out there. Something will grow from right in the middle of my grave. This thing will grow up to be tall. It will flower at the top, and in the lower part will come out beautiful tassels, and inside of them will be kernels. It will bear two or three ears of corn with corn silk on them.

"This thing they call corn is I. This corn will have its origin in me.

"You must take the kernels off the cob and plant them. Store them away until spring. When spring comes, make spaced-out holes in the ground and put about two of the kernels in each hole. By doing this you will increase your supply—and it is surpassingly good food—and when it sprouts, it will go through the various stages of growth that you will have seen in this one of mine.

"Then it will bear corn that you can use, either to boil (boiled corn is very good to eat all summer long, while it is green) or in winter you can use it to make a meal."

"I will be the Corn-Mother," said the old woman (a long time ago, they said).

That's the injunction that the young men were taught to carry out. They thought about this deeply as they were burying her after she died. After they buried her, they made the fence; and all that summer [the corn plant] grew and bore corn just as she told them it would do, and when the corn became dry, they gathered it and took the kernels off the cobs.

Then again next spring they planted it. Then the two young men said, "It would be better if we each had a wife."

One of the young men said, "Let's just one of us get a wife. You get a wife, and I'll be a bachelor and live with you."

The other said, "All right," and left to search for a wife.

The young man said to the one who left to get a wife, "Just walk some distance over there, blow into your hands, and there will be a girl run to you."

So he arrived away off into the forest near a house, I believe. In that house was an old couple with a large number of young women. These young women were all outside playing. Some of these young women were frolicking about, and others were laughing and making a lot of noise.

The young man came quite near, blew into his hands, and whistled. One of the young women who was playing stopped and said, "I'm going to stop playing because someone is whistling for me," and left the group.

She ran directly to the young man. The young man said to her, "We'll marry, if it's all right with you."

She said, "All right." So they went to his home.

The young man told her that in the spring they would plant corn, and each year they would plant more and more of it. So when spring came, they used their hoes to make holes so that they could plant corn. They hoed and hoed and had a very large field of corn, and that was the beginning of there being so much corn. And they remembered what the old woman had said to them, "I will be the Corn-Mother," she had said. "Don't ever forget where I am buried," she had told them when she talked to them.

From this beginning there became so much corn that everyone in the world had some. They said that corn had its beginning from a human being, that the plant called corn started from a woman, and that when this man took a wife, they had such a huge field that they had much corn and much food to eat.

That's what I know, and that's the end of it: that's all.

Undoubtedly with a twinkle in his eye, Siquanid' tells the story in perfect harmony with its design to entertain, instruct, and inspire. Subtle as sunlight playing through forest leaves, humor backlights the depth of the Corn-Mother and her teachings—especially the law of respect—and makes them familial, accessible. Unavoidable. Run as fast as you can to any corner of the universe and the Law will be there waiting for you.

Even as a child I understood this lesson because the elders kept the story's direction points firmly in place. Throughout our mountain county, my grandfather was known to "have a way with corn," meaning he grew it exceptionally well. Early one morning I was helping him pick green corn for lunch. My grandmother had told us when to go, because she was doing the cooking. To

MARILOU AWIAKTA

keep its best flavor, she said, the corn had to be pulled before the sun warmed it—and cooked the same day. Making a good meal is hard work, so when she said, "Go," we hopped to it. Since I was too short to reach the ears, I held the basket. A question had been on my mind, and I broached it through the familiar story.

"Papa, was Grandmother Selu mad at the boys for spying on her?"

"She wasn't mad or mean-spirited. She just told them how it is. Way back in the beginning of time, the Creator put the Law in Mother Earth and all she gives us. If you take from her, you have to give back respect and thankfulness. If you don't do that, why then she quits giving. So when the boys were disrespectful, Selu had to leave. That's the Law."

Circling the conversation closer to the mark, I said, "But the boys didn't mean to hurt her. They just wanted to know. . . ."

From Papa's smile, I knew he had caught my drift. We'd just reached the bare spot in the corn row where several weeks earlier he'd caught me digging up germinating seeds to see if they were growing. He'd explained why the seed had to die by showing me the tiny taproots broken off and the hair-fine ones that were also damaged. "You can't spy on a corn seed—or any other seed—when it's doing its private work," he'd said, calling up Selu's whole story with that one word, "spy."

"And Selu gave her grandsons another chance. She told them how to show their respect by taking care of her. Then she changed to her other self and came back as a corn plant to see if they would do it. When they did, there was plenty of corn for everybody. They were smart boys. They didn't have to be told but once." His glance said, "A word to the wise is sufficient."

And that was my unspoken question as Papa and I gathered the corn together. Had he noticed that I'd learned my lesson? As we moved on down the row, Papa said, "Yessir, this corn looks real good. There'll be plenty for everybody." Knowing he was answering the question I was thinking as well as the one I was asking made me feel good, like the rich earth on my bare feet and the scent of hot sun on the plump, milky sweet ears I laid in the basket. In natural ways like this, the elders plant a story such as Selu's in young minds, where one day—maybe years later—it will bear fruit.

When I tell Selu's story to a general audience, some people are disturbed because Siquanid' says the grandsons used guns. How can the story be authentically old if modern weapons are in it?

The inquiry is usually earnest and respectfully asked. I've gradually realized that it signifies a basic cultural difference. American society (and Western society as a whole) is so oriented toward science, technology, and legality that a discrepancy in a fact calls the validity of what is being said into question. If the facts are wrong, how can the statement be true? But the arts are not about facts. They are about creating images and mental connections.

I'm always glad when the subject of guns comes up because it underlines the necessity of keeping the story's cultural context—its direction points—in place. Revealing spiritual truth, not facts, is the purpose of Selu's story, which the storyteller keeps alive and current by adapting details, such as guns, to the times. Long ago the grandsons may have been sharpening arrowheads or restringing bows. Locations are varied also. Sometimes Selu goes into a smokehouse, other times into a hut. In one often-told version of the story, Selu lives with her husband, Kanati, the Lucky Hunter, and the boys are their sons—one by blood, one by adoption. What cannot be changed are the spiritual base and the spine of the story, which include Selu's identity, the grandsons' (or sons') disrespect, the consequences of it, and Selu's teaching of how they can restore harmony for their own good and the good of the people. Used as it was originally designed, the story is a timeless and reliable compass to right relationships with Mother Earth, with the human family, and with oneself.

Take away its cultural context, cut out its spiritual heart—as many people do who are unaware or unmindful of Native storytelling tradition—and instead of a compass, you have an archaic legend of "How Corn Came to the World." A literary play-pretty in which an old woman, quaintly calling herself the Corn-Mother, teaches her grandsons a lesson in respect. A thoughtful person might draw some interpersonal wisdoms from the story, such as "respect your elders," or "share good things with others," or, perhaps, "you must take care of seeds to make them grow." Important lessons certainly, but it wouldn't take years to grasp them. The surface mind can do it. And a legend carries no spiritual imperative to change one's behavior. It simply suggests a lesson one might take to heart.

With extraordinary precision, the Cherokee medicine man sets the story to its fixed point, the constant to which all other points relate and from which all life and wisdom flow: *"In the beginning, the Creator . . . "* Through this source, all that exists is connected in one family. Traditionally, the philosophic magnetic direction is East, the direction of triumph and the deep red light that immediately precedes the rising of the sun, which the Cherokee says is "impregnated with miraculous creative power." East is the heading for hope and determination and life.

The story of *Ginitsi Selu*, Corn, Mother of Us All, faces east. What does the story mean?

"Think it through," the elders advise, but they mean a special kind of thinking. And this is a crucial cultural difference. In Western culture, thought is a function of the mind; feeling a function of the heart. Rational thought is generally considered superior to feeling (emotion), which may deceive. The soul is a third entity.

In *Walk in Your Soul*, Jack and Anna Kilpatrick emphasize that the word they translate as "soul" could just as fittingly be rendered as "mind" or "heart." All derive from the verb stem *da:n(v)dh* ("to think purposefully"). The soul is conceived to be in the heart. To "walk in your soul" is to think purposefully from the center of your whole being. It is this kind of thinking, not intellect, that perceives wisdom. Through the centuries, sages of many cultures have taught a similar principle, and in their search for balance and wisdom, people of many races have communed with nature. For indigenous people, this communion has also been study, for nature contains the Original Instructions, the laws.

To think from the center of one's being has always been easier in the solitude of mountain, plain, desert, or sea. To do it on the freeway is a different matter. Or in the subway, airport, train station, or shopping mall. At the office, the telephones ring, computers click, the fax machine rolls relentlessly. These machines are in many of our homes also, along with the inexorable voice of television, which at regular news intervals spins us "around the world in thirty minutes." Although technology undeniably helps us, it also drives us, creates a feeling of being whirled faster and faster until we fear we'll be flung off into space.

How remote Selu seems in this world. How inaccessible her singing.

And yet, corn is almost everywhere in America—in our fields, in our food. Through its by-products, it is even in many machines. And where corn is, the Corn-Mother is also. "This thing they call corn is I," she said. Through her story, which creates a spiritual dimension of mind, eye, ear, and heart, we can perceive the Corn-Mother and her wisdoms. She teaches by precept and example. One wisdom immediately apparent is strength. *Ginitsi Selu* faces life as it is.

Other wisdoms, which we can see in the corn as it grows, are balance, harmony, adaptability, cooperation, and unity in diversity, centered in the law of respect. . . .

Americans eat corn everyday—in fresh kernels, meal, syrup, and oil. What if every time we encountered the grain, we remember the Corn-Mother—the law and wisdoms embedded in her story? What if we connect this law and wisdoms to kindred ones in other spiritual traditions we hold? What if we then create new harmony in ourselves, with each other, and with Mother Earth? What if this result was the intent of the Original Donor of the gift, seven thousand years ago?

Cornbread Communion

SHERI L. CASTLE

A confederacy of old men gathers outside a small, silent gristmill. They started work at this mill as young men, just boys really. They milled wheat and corn for families across the county. Over time, the work trickled away, and they conceded that a business must offer a service people need, not one they only remember. Now they sometimes start up their mill because as young men they were millers and mechanics. When they step inside, they return to that time again.

Old French men have croissants and cafés. Old Italian men have ciabatta and bocce. These old men of Watauga County have cornbread and a mill.

The mill sits in a meadow on the bank of Grassy Creek in Watauga County, high in the Blue Ridge Mountains of North Carolina. The creek burbles and bounces against the stone foundation of the mill house. The water ripples like the ruffled hem of a skirt. The stones came from the creek itself. The dark plank walls from the surrounding woods. Despite its age, the mill is stately and solid. It stands firm against the backdrop of indigo hills and golden fields.

The men rouse the machinery. The mill sputters and stutters until they coax it into fluency. They've come together to grind some meal, just enough to take some home, put a few sacks out for the occasional tourist, and enough to make cornbread tonight.

The stones waltz the corn into meal. The air above the hopper begins to fuzz with dust dancing in the sunbeams coming through the windows. Over the years, broken panes have been replaced, so the windows display a timeline of glass. The original panes are thick and creamy, some are thin and flinty, the newest are lightly tinted blue. These subtle stained glass windows speckle light throughout the mill.

The mill smells musty, like the inside of a drawer in a grandmother's sideboard that's opened only when someone needs the good napkins. The machinery smells like silver that's just been polished, clean and metallic. The scents aren't pungent; they're soft and cumulative, as though the mill has been wearing the same perfume for a long time.

While two men tend to the grinding, another man begins to cook. The rest of the men settle in to talk about the weather, politics, and the like. Most members of this confab stand sturdy with their hands in their pockets. A knot of older gentlemen sit with arms crossed loosely. They cock their heads to hear a bit better and nod in agreement with the truer tales. The men throw their heads back in laughter. At times they sit quietly and watch the mill at work. They gaze with the awe and wonderment of curators in the museum, hikers in the wilderness, believers in the chapel.

The cook takes a cast-iron skillet down from a nail. He cooks on the woodstove. He knows how to control the heat with the types of wood he uses. Locust for intense heat, oak for gentler heat, and cherry for the pleasure of its smell. If the oven gets too hot, he can nudge the temperature down by propping its door open with little wedges of wood of varying thickness, little doorstops between hot and cool.

When the oven is hot, the cook puts a generous knob of bacon grease in the skillet and sticks it in the oven to heat while he makes the batter. He contends that a cup of clean, white bacon grease sitting by the stove is the hallmark of any good cook.

He unties the string from around the neck of a meal sack and sifts the right amount through his fingers into a bowl. He stirs in a little leavening, eggs, and enough buttermilk to make it all moist. When the skillet is smoking hot, he pours in the batter. It hits the shimmering grease with a fierce sizzle and a sharp smell of raw cornmeal leaps up.

Cornbread loves a seasoned cast-iron skillet. When asked about his skillet, the cook tells that it was his mama's and that he's mighty proud to have it. He offers a little advice: Take good care of a skillet that's seasoned right. Don't ever wash it, just wipe it with a clean cloth. Most of all, he always says, no matter how old you are, make sure your skillet is older.

If he hears that you don't have a seasoned skillet, he sighs and looks at you as if to say, "Sorry about your lack of inheritance, but if you start now, at least you'll have something to leave your children."

The cook knows the cornbread is done when it starts to smell like roasted corn. He turns out the crusty, steaming brown cake onto a plate and cuts it into generous wedges. The crust is thick and crunchy, the inside tender and fragrant. He splits the wedges and lavishes them with butter. Rivers of melting butter etch into the crumbs. The cook calls the men to the table. They sit and pass the plate from one to another.

Two Grandmothers

TONY EARLEY

In 1947 the rural electrification initiatives of the New Deal finally staggered up to the farmhouse in Polk County, North Carolina, where my grandmother Clara Mae Ledbetter lived with my grandfather, their three children, his parents, and a constantly rotating assortment of spinster aunts and decrepit bachelor uncles. Within days of the lights' coming on, traveling appliance salesmen, following the newly strung power lines, began pulling into the yard in mud-spattered, late-model cars. Soon Granny owned an Electrolux vacuum cleaner (which she did not need), a Maytag wringer washer (which she did), and a squat Frigidaire refrigerator, whose spacious freezer compartment proved to be the single tool she needed to establish herself as a genius, at least among the handful of farm families that orbited the Rock Springs Baptist Church.

The miracle of an electric freezer allowed Granny to "put up" corn for consumption all year long, to preserve those glorious few days in late summer when the sugar level in certain varieties of newly ripened corn approaches the narcotic. I've seen more than one person close his eyes and moan upon tasting a mouthful of Granny's corn. My great-grandfather, I'm told, began to demand it for breakfast once the freezer assured him of an adequate supply. Mobs with paper plates formed around it at church picnics, impatiently waiting for the preacher to finish the blessing. In short, my grandmother's corn was the single best-tasting food I've ever put into my mouth, or ever expect to.

Cut from the cob and frozen into plastic pint containers, Granny's corn resembled the common creamed corn you might find in a school cafeteria, but it contained neither added sugar or milk. As with any work of art, the qualities that made it extraordinary remain steadfastly ineffable. You can mimic the motions that she used to conjure up her masterpiece, but not the results. Granny planted a certain variety of corn (always Golden Queen) in a certain red-dirt upland field, and hoed, fertilized, and harvested it according to accepted gardening practices. The techniques she used to prepare the corn for the freezer, and later to cook it, also met the community norms.

The secret of Granny's corn, I suspect, lies instead somewhere in the patience and labor that it took to produce even a single helping. At her peak, Granny was never able to put up more than sixty or so ears a day. She pulled the corn in the morning, as soon as it was light enough to see. (My father says that early morning is the time when the sugar content of the ears is highest, but Granny did this primarily because she wanted to get the corn, which she had to cook in a kitchen without air-conditioning, into the freezer before the heat of the day set in.) After shucking the ears, removing the silk with an old toothbrush, and washing them, she blanched the corn by boiling it for three minutes then dropping it into a pan of ice water. She made sure that she cut and scraped only the sweetest parts—the tips of the individual kernels and the pulp inside—from the cob. The husks of the kernels she left behind. Five dozen roasting ears generally yielded only ten pints of Granny's corn. If the whole family came to dinner, it took five pints to feed us.

Granny moved into the farmhouse at Rock Springs when she was a nineteen-year-old bride, in 1933, and lived there until December 2002, when she fell and broke her hip at the church Christmas pageant. She has resided since then in an assisted-living facility. When I visit her now, she talks mainly about returning home, though she knows that she isn't likely to. What she misses most is the work. She still marks time by the seasons of labor that she followed for almost seventy years—when to break ground in the garden, when to plant or harvest each vegetable, when to can green beans or tomato juice, or freeze peaches or field peas. Though she found a solace in the work itself, her labor always resulted in comfort or pleasure or sustenance for someone else as well: a clean house, daffodils or irises or lilies blooming in the yard, a steaming bowl of corn circling the big table in the dining room during Sunday dinner. The only praise one usually receives for such a life is necessarily local and private, though in a perfect world perhaps it wouldn't be. The last time I tasted my grandmother's corn was Thanksgiving 2002, and I took it for granted that there would be another bowl come Christmas. I would not have said so at the time, but I now realize that love, in its most selfless form, tastes like sweet corn made by an old woman working at daybreak, during the hottest part of the summer.

My grandmother Earley was a tiny, fierce woman, equally capable of great love and great hate. She loved my father, her baby, exorbitantly, but swore on his wedding day that she would never forgive my mother for marrying him. And she didn't. She stopped attending Rock Springs before I was born because someone insulted her in the churchyard. She did not return until I was in junior high school. But she was a devout Christian, acknowledged in the community to be a woman to whom God spoke. People brought her questions for God to which they especially needed answers. When she was troubled she prayed without ceasing, until God's will became clear in her mind. If she could not get an answer, she ran everyone out of the house, as if their presence interfered with God's signal beaming down, and climbed into the closet, where she prayed for hours in the dark and the quiet. Other times she went off into the woods along the creek and knelt in the laurel until God gave her a word she could repeat when she opened her eyes.

She spent most of her life on a red, upland farm, a mile down the ridge from Rock Springs, frustrated by my grandfather's lack of ambition. Paw-paw found God's provision for them enough, while his willingness to settle for their life as it was infuriated Granny. On their farm they kept a small flock of chickens, a mule, a pig, and a milk cow; they fed the livestock and themselves on what they grew in the fields. They worked a small patch of cotton to earn money for things they could not grow or make. My father and uncles worked with them in the fields to save anything that made them richer, or even better off, than they had been the year before. A sick pig, or a blight in the potatoes, or a drop in cotton prices was all that ever separated them from hard times. Granny prayed constantly to keep their small world intact.

One fall day when my father was a boy, the wind turned bitter and cold several weeks early. When the sun set behind the mountains, the air bristled with frost. Granny hadn't picked the green beans hanging on the vines in her garden. The beans she canned each fall were the only green vegetables the family had to eat until the following spring. That year the early frost caught her unprepared, and she simply ran out of time. The sky was clear and purple above the black mountains when the family came in from the fields. Paw-paw brought in an armload of wood and started a fire in the stove. Granny paced around and around the living room. She could not accept losing her beans. She told Paw-paw she had to talk to God. She walked out of the house and down across the pasture toward the woods in the twilight. She came home several hours later, stiff and shivering cold, and announced that God said he would give her one more day.

The next morning Dad watched his breath steam in front of his face as he dressed in his room. Outside, the frozen world sparkled in the new sun, and the grass crunched under his feet as he walked with Granny up the path to the garden. Everything in the garden was dead, had been burned by the frost, except Granny's beans. The bean rows drew vivid, green lines across the white field. Granny picked every bean in the garden that morning and canned them that afternoon. That night another frost settled onto the ridgetop and killed the stripped vines. "Now let me tell you something," my father says, "I saw that."

A Man and His Beans

Here's what a green bean is: A green bean is something that is long—sometimes ten inches long. It has beans inside that might be white, or mottled brown and taupe, or bluish black, or a mix of white and black and brown, or other colors. Most important, when the beans inside are mature, the green outside isn't too tough to eat. But they can be left on the vine to dry, and the beans inside can be harvested.

Old-fashioned green beans, the kind that grew before commercial seed sellers got ahold of them, aren't uniformly long and perfectly straight with uniform green color. They can't be picked by machine. And they aren't Blue Lake beans, the pride of the supermarket produce bin.

They have names like Lazy Wife bean and the Dois Chambers greasy cut-short bean, the Nickel bean and the Tobacco Worm bean. They come from Estill and Leslie Counties, Kentucky, from Haywood, North Carolina, and from sundry points in Ohio, Tennessee, and West Virginia. Certain beans become "shucky beans," those that are dried and cooked, bean and dried hull together. Some are butter beans of various colors.

You can learn all this from Bill Best, a Madison County, Kentucky, farmer who collects heirloom beans. Now he's "getting up close to 200 varieties," growing more than a dozen to sell fresh at the farmer's market, almost a dozen more to sell as seed, and saving the others in plastic bags, glass jars, and old cottage cheese containers until he has time to grow them and see what they yield.

Samples of many are kept in small Ziploc bags, labeled and held together on a chain. He can flip through them like charms on a bracelet, describing the significance of each one, and maybe who sent it to him and why.

Others more recently acquired—a few beans sent with a note in an envelope or handed to him at the farmer's market—are less organized in boxes and bags. As he sorts through them slowly, he stops and stares at each one. It's sometimes as if he's seeing them as children, as little beings with so much potential and so many secrets.

These beans come to him from nearly everywhere. Best's aunt gave him a set, 90 percent of which are white, with a few black and a few brown among them.

"They never made any attempt to separate them, and I probably won't either," says Best, holding the calico mixture in his hands. He thinks the seed has been providing beans at least 120 years.

The sixty-nine-year-old Best, a retired administrator from Berea College, has always gardened. Growing up in the western North Carolina mountains, his parents were subsistence farmers. His father grew a little tobacco to make money for taxes, raised corn for the hogs and hay for the cattle. He traded eggs for coffee, sugar, and sweets.

His mother raised a garden, where Best grew up working along with his sisters. When he moved to Berea more than thirty years ago, he started his own garden to raise vegetables for sale. On a visit home, his mother handed him some of her greasy beans. " 'Here,' " he recalls her saying, " 'I have these seeds you need to keep going.' " Greasy beans, Best explains, are beans that grow without fuzz on the outside; their slickness was referred to as greasy, then creasy, and sometimes crease.

He grew them. The tall vines produced a bean that got knobby when the beans matured. He could sell them easily at the Lexington farmer's market, which he helped start thirty-two years ago. "People from eastern Kentucky really like the greasy bean," he says. "Then the horsy set started buying greasy beans." He always sells out early.

"The greasies are the premier, and even the bugs know it," he says. Other descriptive terms for beans include "cut-short," which means the beans are so crowded in the pod that they are blunted and squared off, and "cornfield" bean, which describes a plant that climbs up the stalks of field corn—it applies to most heirloom beans.

A 1988 article in the *Rural Kentuckian* about his garden-growing family hit a nerve, says Best. Though the two-page article only dedicated three paragraphs to his mother's greasy beans, Best received eighty-six letters and several visitors from six states, many of them asking for seed.

Until the article came out, he says, "I thought I was the only one frustrated by the current state of fruits and vegetables."

The current state, says Best, is of food that can be grown, harvested, and sold cheaply. It results in beans that, grown to maturity, are too tough to break and too tough to eat. "You can make shoestrings or something, but they can't be broken."

He blames the state of beans on the seed industry's wanting to make a profit by developing stringless varieties such as Blue Lake. In the middle of the last century, says Best, half runners were a popular all-purpose bean that "caught the attention of commercial seed producers," who "decided to toughen the bean for shipping and shelf-life purposes."

So while many of us bemoan the state of supermarket tomatoes, Best focuses on beans. "The tomato is a glamour vegetable," he says. "Beans are a peasant food, and I'm a peasant, and I collect them from my fellow peasants."

Best specializes in beans of southern Appalachia, he says, "because there are so many, and there are so few that have been collected."

Beans cross-pollinate easily, so it's not uncommon for one family to be growing a bean that is significantly different from that of another family in the next relatively isolated "holler" or down the road. Families often name their beans—Lazy Wife, Fat Man. Best has named his variety "Rogue Mountain," and he describes it as "big, plump, and tender."

Tender is the operative word for all of Best's beans. He steers clear of commercial beans, trying to avoid "tough genes." When his beans are mature, they are large—sometimes ten inches long—they may be crooked or hooked, and they are bulging with beans. And they require stringing. "What you see being sold in stores is bean hulls."

Best has made his beans available to other farmers, including those who "compete" with him at the Lexington farmer's market. "I need to get these out both from a genetics point of view and a nutritional point of view. There is such diversity in the genetics of the bean."

In 2003 Best was recognized for his efforts to save these bean varieties at the Southern Foodways Alliance annual symposium in Oxford, Mississippi, where he received the Ruth Fertel Keeper of the Flame award. Recipients are "unheralded tradition-bearers of Southern foodways," according to the organization, but to his loyal customers at the farmer's market, Best is just a man who knows beans about beans.

Leatherbritches

. . . .

BILLY C. CLARK

She had been watching the sky for days now looking for a sign. A change in the weather had come. There was a chill in the wind, and it carried moisture with it. The sky was as gray as the feathers of a mockingbird. There had been forecasts of cold weather and the possibility of a first snow. But I knew by her searching that she had chosen to follow signs that had been passed down to her by heritage, a heritage that came from her beloved Kentucky hill country. A heritage akin to a birthright.

And then one evening, when the wind had settled as silent as a sunset and flakes of snow fell as soft as bird down, she said to me:

"I'll put us a mess of Leatherbritches in the kettle to soak tonight. I'll need a piece of smoked side bacon to season and enough cracklings for cornbread. Soft cracklings, mind you, shed of skin."

To Mom and most of the hill people of the Big Sandy Country, the first mess of Leatherbritches was a yearly ritual that took place with the coming together of two ingredients: the right green bean and the coming of the first snow. Bean-wise, Leatherbritches could only come from a green bean that had strings. Stringless green beans were not considered worth planting in the hill country and were never tolerated. Not then, not now, by true hill country people. Of the string green beans, the mountain White Half Runner has forever been the favorite. The Striped Cornfield Bean and the Old Homestead (Kentucky Wonder) come after. But all three have strings. The last two are strictly pole beans, with the half runner grown either as bush or pole bean, depending on the preference of the grower. On poles it will grow about half the length of the other two. Thus the name.

In a family of ten, Mom and I were the only ones who "took natural to the land." Me, she said, from the time I was hip-carrying size and she could set me in a furrow for safekeeping while she grubbed out food that we ate in the spring and summer, and put up for the winter by either pickling, drying, or canning.

Our land was plowed each spring by a man by the name of Jess Puckett. He was very old, and his back was curved like a hunter's horn. He had a mule that he plowed with named Maud and he brought with him a hillside turning plow that had a spider and coulter on it. He also brought an A-harrow that he had made from wood and railroad spikes and used to level plowed ground. And from an early age I was allowed to ride the harrow since my weight, he said, helped hold it to the ground and I was less work than trying to put a log on it. Plowing or dragging, he never gave the old mule a moment's peace. Cracking a long rawhide whip over her head, he called upon supernatural powers to do her in and cursed her with words that would get you a whipping but that I could not find the meaning of anywhere. That is until I was old enough to learn that words like that were the heritage of hill country people. I mean, whenever you needed a word that you couldn't find to fit the occasion, you just made one yourself. I also learned after I was old enough to work a mule myself that a mule was probably greater incentive for making new words than anything else in the hill country. But I learned something else about a man and his mule, too. I learned of the special bond that was unbreakable between them. Even between Jess and Maud. For Mom had told me the story of how when the timbers were still big enough up the hollow behind the house to be worth cutting and mule-dragging out, she used to watch Jess stand beside old Maud at the mouth of the hollow with a great log still shackled to her to let her "blow" and cool in the wind that forever came down the hollow. Maud would be frothing at the mouth from the bit, and her hide would be lathered with foam-sweat from pulling the log. She stood quivering her hide to shake off the flies that settled on her. Mom had heard him curse her in one breath and then whisper pretty words to her in another while he gave her a handful of soaked corn to eat because she was so old that most of her teeth were gone.

Mom laughed. "Ways of menfolk," she said. "Harnesses you to work and figures to wipe it out with a handful of soaked corn."

Mom preferred to raise her half runners on short poles. They bore longer and kept their beans off the ground where they were less apt to rot, especially during wet weather. They were also much cleaner. And that was most important when it came to making Leatherbritches since they were never washed before being strung to dry. My job was to get the short poles. And since Mom generally raised a few teepees of Kentucky Wonders for pickling, I needed to get a few long poles, too. Poles usually six or seven feet long from the ground up.

I always got the poles from inside the mouth of the hollow from a sassafras grove that grew on the side of one slope. The tall, slender poles grew like cane, were easy to cut, and would hold well without rotting. Old men claimed that a post-sized sassafras that had been barked would stand seven years as a fence post.

The hollow behind the house was the longest, deepest, and darkest hollow gouged out of the hills at the mouth of the Big Sandy Country. Squeezed by hills on either side, the hollow itself was not much wider than a tramroad. On either side, the slopes were ridged as keen as plow points and, looking up, appeared high enough to furrow clouds. From these ridges, looking down, the hollow looked no broader than a finger. Scary to look down! But even more scary, I thought, to be standing in the hollow looking up! For the ridges appeared to bend inward threatening to fold over you. And high up old cedars, twisted by winds and whitened by time-death, still clung to cracks in sandstone rocks with gnarled and feeble roots, roots that if whittled on with a pocketknife still held the beautiful red heartwood that old-timers said would remain for eighty years after the death of the tree. Crows cawed their lonesome songs from ridge to ridge, from cedar to cedar, and turkey buzzards circled above, always searching for something below. And with a boy's imagination, it didn't take much to figure a maybe-what. There were too many scary tales about buzzards to suit me!

Going inside the hollow early of a morning to gather the poles, a fog had generally settled there, and it hung from the limbs of trees like a ghost-wash. As the morning grew old a meager sun came to wring the ghost-wash like the hands of an old woman, and I stopped to listen to it drip, dripping on the underbrush below. Scary and like the tick, ticking of a clock. Moss quilted much of the lowland, and, over the mouth of played-out and now-deserted coal belly mines, ice hung like white beards of old men and remained there long after the thaw outside the hollow. What sun there was so early in the spring was as meager as a miner's lamp.

While many of the green beans we raised were eaten fresh, they only served as a prelude to Leatherbritches. Mom's favorite; my favorite! Beans that were used for Leatherbritches were pulled from the vines late in the season when the bean itself inside the shuck was full. Coming just ahead of the first frost, some of the beans had started to dry and had turned a beautiful, almost transparent brownish yellow. And so the vines held drying beans, green beans, and especially if poled, blooms with a promise they could not keep.

Often Mom and I would pull the vines ahead of frost and doodle them in the yard where we hunkered and stripped the beans from the vines. Pinching off the ends of each bean, we pulled the strings "one down the back, one down the belly," I can hear Mom cautioning even today. Mom preferred, generally, to leave the green bean full-length for threading and under no circumstances broken more than once.

I can still see my mother today, her beautiful hair dancing in the wind while she lifted a sewing needle to catch sky-light so she could see to thread the eye with thread she had end-shaped with her teeth and wet with her lips. I can still hear her cautioning me to be sure to sew between beans in the shuck. Once dried, thread through a bean was almost impossible to pull out. We sewed the beans into long strings, beading them every few feet with a hot pepper to keep the weevils away. And once threaded, we hung the long strings of beans from the edge of the porch ceiling to dry in the wind and sun. We hung so many that the inside porch was screened off. And you could sit behind the strings on the floorboards of the house and watch as they wind-danced like snakes. The beans would remain on the strings until they had dried to a fraction of their original size. And then they were stripped off the strings and brought inside for winter storage.

To cook, the Leatherbritches were first soaked overnight in a kettle of water, then rinsed and cooked over a low heat the next day until fork-tender. The amount of beans to cook required a cautious and practiced eye, for once touched by water and then heated, Leatherbritches returned to their normal size. And so a mistake here could amount to a boiling over of more beans than pots to hold. The hill country abounded with stories of these mistakes, generally attributed to young brides wanting to please their husbands with their first mess of Leatherbritches fixed away from the watching eyes of their mothers. The mistake made, the best they could hope for was a secret kept. But there were never secrets kept in the hill country, only embellishments added.

Not only was it my job to select enough cracklings for the crackling cornbread, but it was also my job, from an early age, to earn them, for we did not raise hogs. But an old German who lived in the head of the hollow behind the house did; he raised both hogs and hounddogs. Little ones, middle-sized ones, big ones, and in-betweens. He was called Old German because it was said that he was as old as the hills and that his nationality was German, and you could tell that because he spoke with a German accent, although no one I ever knew could tell you what a German accent was supposed to sound like. Truth was, he had a name that you couldn't have pronounced without knowing German, which no one around did, and no one was willing to gamble on a try. Sam Stumbo, who had worked on and off for him more than anyone else, said that the Old German didn't take lightly to having his name mispronounced and that he had creased some poor man's hair some years back with a slug from a hog rifle for doing just that. While some doubted the story, no one cared to find out for sure. I mean, most figured Sam didn't know everything. Asked once where Germany was, he thought for a while and said, "Well, it ain't around here."

It was simply reckoned that there was really no need to call him anything anyway. Better to just nod and agree with whatever he said as well as to do whatever he asked, in particular, I figured, if you worked for him on and off, which I did to earn cracklings, smoked slab bacon, and the sort, as well as a hounddog pup he held out with a promise, a promise I worried much of the young years of my life about but was afraid to go for a cure and ask.

My job with him amounted to a number of things: feeding hogs as well as helping to raise the feed they ate, making crackling mash to feed his hounds as well as crackling mash to sell to his hunting friends. And when the weather turned cold enough for meat to keep, since the only refrigeration around was ice boxes, my job was to also feed the fires once the hogs were killed so that they could be scalded for scraping. In between feeding the fire, I scraped the hogs with a sharp grubbing hoe alongside three or four men who worked for him and also hunted with him. And while I scraped, I saw each hog drop from the slug of the hog rifle hit between the eyes. I saw the old men drop and wrestle the hog while they slit its throat with a knife they called a pigsticker and then catch and drink their fill of the red, hot blood that poured from the slit. Claimed it thickened their own blood to shield against the cold.

After the hogs were scraped and gutted, I cut the fat off them into small chunks and dropped them into a large iron kettle with a fire underneath that I also fed. I stirred the fat to render lard and took payment in cracklings to take home. Cracklings were the residue left from rendering lard and to me the tastiest meat on earth, especially with a little lean meat left on. At best, my take would be cracklings, side bacon that I helped smoke with hickory wood I carried from the slopes, hog heads, pigs' ears, and tails. All of which Mom loved, and except for the smoked side of bacon and cracklings, I tolerated. As a bonus, the Old German allowed me over the winter to sit around the foxfire that I also fed with him and the old men who hunted with him to listen to their hounds and dream of owning my own hound one day, one that would lead the pack.

But many times, too tired to join them along the ridge after work, working often from daylight until just this side of dark, I went home by way of crossing the ridge, which saved me more than a mile by not following the hollow out. And most times with my face flushed red by standing over and stirring the hot kettle of cracklings, rendering them for feed and lard, I stopped and looked down off the slope. The embers of the fire seemed no bigger than the glow of a lightning bug. On the ridge the wind was almost unbearable, foretelling of a season better to slip away from. Picking my way through briars and brush, along this lonesome ridge the first words of slipping away came: came in the form of a sonnet. The beginning was then, the ending was later. I called it "Creeping from Winter":

BILLY C. CLARK

Summer is gone and I along this clay
Path pause to watch the hills in winter's mood,
Wind-stripped the naked trees have shook away
My season and now doze in solitude.
Low on the slopes redbud and dogwood bend
From winter's touch, the trailing arbutus
And creeping phlox have sneaked to earthen dens
Leaving their wrinkled trails on frozen crust.
The hills are silent now, and like grey eyes
The mountain rocks are free from summer's green,
Exposed to brightness of a cloudless sky
They blink their freedom from the deep ravine.
I pause to watch, dreaming the while to creep
Away with summer, and from winter sleep.

And from the stirring of a second kettle that held water, cornmeal, and cracklings to make mash for hounds to eat during the winter and on into summer, I gained yet another sonnet that I called "Night of the Singing Hounds":

From high the ridge the hunters stop to play
Cow-horn music to low-singing hounds,
Foxfire ash-covered as the hound of the day
Slow-trails the rugged land mouthing no sound.
The song of horn houndtalks an ended night
A ritual song of fox, hound, horn, and men;
Frost-spun the scent of fox is cocoon-tight
To frozen earth that hounds no longer wind.
From high the ridge sore-footed Walkers lag
Their masters down a narrow cow-made trail,
Mute to all boastful talk and hounddog brag
Of bugled voices now on mountain stale.
Night-singing hounds sight-trailing homeward men,
Dreaming of crackling mash and burlap den.

The promise of the Old German for a hounddog pup of my own was never fulfilled. Cracklings for Mom's cornbread were. I am not certain that I would have been willing to trade the latter for the first. Others raised hounddogs that were just as good hunting-wise as the Old German's. But no one cooked a mess of Leatherbritches and crackling cornbread as good eating-wise as Mom.

Beating the Biscuits in Appalachia
Race, Class, and Gender Politics of Women Baking Bread

ELIZABETH ENGELHARDT

Throughout my childhood, to celebrate Christmas, my extended family gathered at my grandmother's house for breakfast. Each year, with my scrambled eggs and grits, I ate my grandmother's biscuits with apple jelly canned by my aunt and uncle. When I was twelve, my grandmother taught me to make biscuits. Sifted flour, milk, baking powder, soda, some salt, and lard (vegetable shortening, these days) in mathematical proportion—measured carefully by me, eyeballed from years of practice by my grandmother—all are baked in a hot oven until fluffy and flaky. Biscuits are a deceptive recipe; they may be short on ingredients, but they are long on touch. I may know her recipe, but I am still working on the touch; every time I move, I have to learn a new oven, and I keep practicing my skills. To celebrate the New Year, I fixed for myself a dinner of collard greens, hoppin' john, and a skillet of cornbread. My mother made cornbread for dinner regularly; in fact, I cannot remember when I first ate it. I have been working on my cast-iron skillet to perfect its seasoning; my mother seems to be able to make good cornbread in any pan that comes to hand, but this is a trick I have not learned. That New Year's menu should bring me luck throughout the year, so perhaps good biscuits and cornbread will follow.

Talking about the food we prepare and eat to celebrate our chosen holidays can help women understand the differences and similarities between us. Having told you about cornbread, collards, apples, black-eyed peas, and biscuits, you might place me—correctly—as from the southern United States. Depending on what you know about local crops, the combination of apples and cornbread might even help you deduce that I am specifically from the southern Appalachian mountains. Two of these foods, however—the biscuit and the cornbread—have shifted in meaning over the course of the twentieth century. Today they are, at least for Americans of European and African descent, both primarily Southern foods, hallmarks of down-home or country cooking, and sources of nostalgia for "simpler" times. But when the nineteenth century turned into the twentieth, they had very different and distinct meanings. To some observers, one was a mark of high culture, modern hygiene, and progressive woman-hood. Biscuit baking demonstrated class consciousness, leisure time for women, consumer-marketed equipment, and nationally standardized consumption. Cornbread, on the other hand, symbolized ignorance, disease, and poverty. It could be made with locally produced ingredients, equipment made at home, and brief moments of time seized between other work; even at the turn of the century, it was regionally identified and nationally disparaged. A social history of class, race, and gender hides in the different recipes and uses of cornbread and biscuits. Diaries, fiction, memoirs, and recipe books help us tease out that social history of women, beaten biscuits, and cornbread.

The 1890s until the 1920s were the heyday of the Progressive Era—a time of settlement houses, "New Women," public libraries, anti-tuberculosis campaigns, "Lifting as We Climb," temperance, and, of course, suffrage. Regionalist women's writing enjoyed great success; many local color authors chose Appalachia as a setting for their fiction. Although university education for select women emerged out of the 1860s and 1870s, a national consensus about what women would do with their educated lives remained elusive. Women like Amelie Troubetzkoy, Emma Bell Miles, Grace MacGowan Cooke, and Maria Louise Pool chose careers in writing. Margaret Morley combined writing with the scientific practice of being a naturalist.

Other women became teachers and activists; one of those was May Stone. In 1884 Kentucky native Stone entered Wellesley College, scarcely nine years after it opened. Despite leaving college a year before she was to graduate, Stone gained entrance into the group of socially conscious, educated women looking for careers. She found hers in her participation first in women's clubs and then in the "mountain work" they sponsored in eastern Kentucky. By 1900, the nation's women's clubs were working to found parks, clean up the water, battle illiteracy, get children out of factories and into schools, and expand libraries. Working with her friend Katherine Pettit, May Stone established libraries, taught elementary school, facilitated girls' applications to college, and planted trees. When the opportunity arose, both women left for a lifetime of work in Kentucky's Appalachia. Pettit and Stone were middle-class, white, educated women who came to Appalachia with the idea of helping the less fortunate Appalachians; each stayed for the rest of her life. They were not alone in their efforts; dozens of similar women came to Appalachia. Some, such as Lucy Furman, combined their activism with writing. All were ready to help the Appalachians. That "help" often took the form of cooking lessons.

One of the most well known experiments run by Progressive women in Appalachia was Pettit and Stone's Hindman Settlement School. Their challenge was to translate the settlement house model used by Jane Addams in urban Chicago to rural Appalachia. The journals Pettit and Stone kept were used for fund-raising; today, republished by Jess Stoddart as *The Quare Women's Journals*, they give us a picture of the school's early lessons in "domestic science." By Pettit and Stone's own account, they were summoned in 1899 by a letter sent from the Reverend J. T. Mitchell to the State Federation of Women's Clubs in Kentucky. Although Stone and Pettit educated both men and women, cooking lessons for women were a core element of their mission from the beginning. Reverend Mitchell requested they "conduct . . . meetings of wives, mothers, housekeepers, young ladies and little girls. Lectures and lessons in cooking and home-making should be made particularly enthusiastic and then the intellectual and moral features can be made interesting." Not only were women defined by Mitchell, Pettit, and Stone in the restrictive categories of wife, mother, and housekeeper before all others, but also cooking and home-making were presented as the path for Appalachian women to follow to reach the intellectual and moral positions occupied by Pettit, Stone, and their teachers.

Evidence from letters, diaries, and fiction suggests that the teachers began the enthusiastic lessons by targeting the staple food of mountain residents, corn-bread. They sought to replace it with what they considered a more healthful, appropriate, and civilized alternative, the wheat-based biscuit and light bread. Corn was, of course, not the only characteristic ingredient used by Appalachian cooks; the teachers could have targeted wild berries, ramps (unique, pungent onions), or mountain trout, for instance. They could have focused on the particular type of soft wheat flour that today is favored by Southern bakers, and for which Knoxville, Tennessee, an Appalachian city, was becoming known through companies like White Lily Flour. Distinctions between soft wheat and Northern or Midwestern hard wheat do not even appear in the writings of women like Pettit and Stone; reading their journals, one is left with the impression that Appalachian families were completely ignorant of the finer points of baking.

In fact, choosing to focus simply on corn was a politically savvy decision on the part of the women activists. Scholars such as Mark McWilliams have shown that, in the earlier colonial period of the United States, eating corn distinguished the new nation from Britain. Corn declared one's allegiance to the new country as effectively as throwing tea into the harbor. By the mid-1800s, in the Northeast and coastal population centers in the South, corn was no longer such a mark of national pride. But it had become a nostalgic symbol of America, and that made corn a particularly useful choice for the women going to Appalachia to teach. Pettit, Stone, and other Progressive women in Appalachia were in fierce competition for limited philanthropic money; portraying cornbread-eating Appalachians nostalgically as "our contemporary ancestors," to use the term of the day, made them worthy (and needy) American subjects for funding—and, thus, let the Progressive women set forth with their lectures and lessons in cooking.

Early in their journals Pettit and Stone reported as a success that "Mrs. Green and two girls came and wanted to learn to make light bread, but it was so late that we taught them how to make good soda biscuit instead." The Hindman women considered the preparation of soda biscuit, using wheat flour and baking soda, and light bread, using white wheat flour and yeast, worthy of being taught. My grandmother's biscuits resemble the soda biscuits Pettit and Stone describe; their light breads preceded store-bought bread loaves. But more appropriate for the mountain women, judging by its appearance in Pettit and Stone's journals, was the beaten biscuit. This was the recipe they crowned as the height of domestic achievement. For a special occasion, Katherine Pettit noted she was "up earlier than usual this morning to make beaten biscuit for Miss McCartney's luncheon." She and Stone were pleased when native mountain woman "Ida Francis . . . walked down with a pint of flour to learn to make beaten biscuit for her sick brothers." For other families, Pettit and Stone "promised to send them some beaten biscuit and go Wednesday to show the mother how to make them." So important was the beaten biscuit to their efforts that contemporaries looking to criticize the Hindman women focused on the biscuits to do so: they derided the entire project as the "beaten biscuit crusade."

Only when we examine the recipe for beaten biscuits do we begin to understand why Katherine Pettit had to get up early to prepare them. Bill Neal, in his *Southern Cooking*, writes that the beaten biscuit involves flour, salt, sugar, lard, and cold water. He lists the necessary equipment as a mixing bowl; blending fork; wooden spoon; mallet, cleaver, or rolling pin; biscuit cutter; and baking sheet. It is also apparent that anyone cooking this recipe needs a way to regulate the temperature for baking (such as an oven) and a board or flat table that is sturdy enough for the beating process. In 1913, in her cookbook *Dishes and Beverages of the Old South*, Martha McCulloch-Williams claimed that, for the perfect beaten biscuit, "householders, and especially suburban ones, should indulge in the luxury of a block or stone or marble slab—and live happy ever after." These perfect blocks, stones, or slabs are crucial because what distinguishes the beaten biscuit is that not only is it mixed in a bowl and kneaded on a board (Neal suggests twenty-five strokes), but it is also beaten with the mallet on a hard surface. Neal calls for at least 300 strokes for family and 500 for company. As my godmother suggested when I told her I was writing this chapter, the beaten biscuit is nothing like a good cathead biscuit (in other words, each one as big as and as fluffy as a cat's head) that we might long for today. The Hindman women's beaten biscuit had no leavening and thus was much more like today's crackers or an unsweetened English biscuit.

Reading Katherine Pettit and May Stone's journals today, one might think that the mountain women cooked no bread at all until Progressive activists came along to teach them. In fact, as most of the local color fiction about Appalachia (written both by women from the region and elsewhere) makes clear, Appalachian women baked plenty of bread. The action in Maria Louise Pool's 1896 novel, *In Buncombe County*, centered on the visit of two white, upper-class women tourists to the mountains outside of Asheville, North Carolina. One of these women observed upon watching two mountain girls fix dinner, "They mixed a pone and set it down in its kettle by the fire; they called it 'making bread.' " This was not wheat bread. Instead, these characters, and Appalachian women in general, cooked cornbread. And corn pone, and hoecake, and dog bread, and hush puppies, and corn fritters, and spoon bread. The basic ingredients of all of these recipes—cornmeal, buttermilk, lard, and salt, occasionally embellished with an egg or two and additional (although not strictly necessary) leavening—need only a bowl and spoon and a source of heat. Unlike biscuits, cornbread can be cooked in a variety of conditions—over an open fire or in an oven—and in a variety of containers—a skillet, Dutch oven, or the proverbial "hoe."

Although these are just a few variations of the basic recipe, almost all of the cornbreads can be mixed in the time it takes to heat a skillet. Unlike in other parts of the South, most Appalachian cornbreads, as my mother puts it, have hardly any flour or sugar added. Tommie Bass, from northeast Alabama's mountains, recalled for his memoirs, *Plain Southern Cooking*, his mother's basic recipe: "When mother made cornbread, she added baking soda, not always. It was about a teaspoonful to a cupful of meal. And she added a little salt and sugar and buttermilk, to make a thick batter. Then she melted a little grease (lard) in the hot skillet, and drained that into the batter. And she put a little dry cornmeal in the hot skillet, and put it back on the stove." He continued, "When the dry cornmeal was brown, she knew the skillet was hot enough to pour in the batter. She put the skillet of batter in the stove and cornbread would just swell up, you know, and become just as light as it could be." It is an adaptable and forgiving recipe.

Other writing of the era gives us a sense of the creativity and flexibility of cornbread baking in Appalachia. Tennessee author Grace MacGowan Cooke's 1907 short story entitled "The Capture of Andy Proudfoot" tells the story of a Northern, Irish bounty hunter searching for and then helping a mountain man. Cooke mentioned meals of corn pone and fish that Andy and his potential captor ate in a mountain hideaway. At most, Andy and his captor had camp equipment; their cornbread had to be cooked over an open fire. If they had milk or eggs, they stole them. Theirs was probably a very simple combination of meal, water, and lard. Margaret Morley described such a recipe in her 1913 naturalist text about the areas around Asheville, North Carolina, *The Carolina Mountains*. A mountain man said to her, " 'Stoves? . . . I ain't never owned a stove and I don't never aim to. I don't see no use in stoves noway. I wouldn't have one in the house. You can't bake bread in a stove. I don't want nar' thing but meal and water mixed together and baked in the fire. I don't want salt in the bread. I was raised on that bread and it is the best in the world.' " From her position as outsider, Morley commented archly, "Imagine a condition where one's physical wants are reduced to corn-meal and water." Similarly, Amelie Rives Troubetzkoy's 1893 novel, *Tanis, the Sang-Digger*, told the melodramatic story of a mountain woman who made a living digging ginseng root in Virginia until she met a Northern, middle-class family. In the novel, mountain resident Sam chose to eat corn pone and honey while waiting for his girlfriend to finish her domestic duties serving the wife of a railroad engineer. Even in Pettit and Stone's journals, we glimpse how pervasive cornbread was; they mentioned a "Mrs. Godsey, over seventy, [who] brought her turn of corn to the mill and then came here to learn to make bread." If we could ask her, Mrs. Godsey might have said that she was not ignorant of bread making, but that she first took care of her family staple and then learned a new luxury—wheat bread.

For turn-of-the-century mountain women, choosing whether to cook cornbread or biscuits was not simply a question of what a woman or her family preferred on any given day. Instead, the decision made a statement about class in the Appalachians. The biscuit, in other words, marked middle- and upper-class status in 1900. Pettit and Stone judged the households into which they were invited by the breads they were served for dinner. For instance, they reported that "the Cornets are all clean and thrifty"; yet, the only evidence of cleanliness and thriftiness that they give readers is: "They had a good dinner, beautiful honey and whole wheat biscuit from the wheat they had raised themselves." According to the Hindman teachers, the Cornets were a contrast to most of the mountain residents, who "live on fat bacon, cornbread and a few vegetables, all cooked in the most unwholesome way. Everything is fried in as much grease as they can get." Prioritizing their cooking plan, the Hindman teachers noted, "Our efforts in the line of cooking were to teach them to make good bread, to cook the vegetables in as many ways as possible, and the meat without so much grease." For Pettit and Stone, these domestic practices marked the achievements of superior social classes. Moral and intellectual lessons could follow once bread making was standardized.

John and Olive Campbell, acquaintances of the Hindman women, and author and editor, respectively, of the widely influential *The Southern Highlander and His Homeland*, proposed that class and bread could be charted on a continuum: "It is probably safe to say that the main sustenance of many a rural household a good share of the winter is fat pork, beans, potatoes, and cornbread, with the addition of sorghum or honey and strong cheap coffee. Soda biscuit of wheat flour, and 'grits' are also used extensively among families in better circumstances. 'Light bread' or raised white bread, is very unusual." In other words, cornbread was available to almost everyone; middle-class mountain residents added in wheat-based soda biscuits; but only the most financially and socially upper-class mountain people could choose to eat the yeast breads. In fiction, it is often passed as unremarkable that people of higher classes avoided cornbread. While Sam in Troubetzkoy's *Tanis, the Sang-Digger* ate corn pone in the servant's area, Alice Gilman, the middle-class railroad engineer's wife who was new to the mountains, offered her guests biscuits and milk. Although both corn pone and biscuits emerged from the same kitchen, Tanis was an Appalachian woman hired to serve biscuits but eat cornbread.

While Pool, Troubetzkoy, and even Pettit and Stone imply that all mountaineers were poor—eating cornbread, unaware of the modern world—memoirs of the time give support to the Campbells' implication that there was a range of class positions in the mountains. Breads can be traced through these varied positions. Joe Gray Taylor in his *Eating, Drinking, and Visiting in the South: An Informal History* argues that the richer you were, the more likely you were to eat wheat, or as he puts it, "everyone of substance that I knew ate them [biscuits] for breakfast." Tommie Bass reminisced, "Back in my days, biscuits made from wheat flour was special for the poor people." Alabama resident William Bradford Huie grew up in the southern tip of the Appalachians. In his semi-autobiographical novel, *Mud on the Stars*, he agreed with Bass and Taylor: "Biscuit for breakfast is a social and economic self-measurement among croppers and hands. Those who always have biscuit for breakfast regard themselves as successful persons of dignity. They pity and look down on the unfortunate who have to go back to corn pone during hard times." A friend of mine, who is a medical doctor, recalls her grandfather-in-law asking her upon her marriage whether she could make biscuits; when she said no, he said, "Well, can you at least make cornbread?"

Thus, we find a dividing line primarily between corn and wheat, with gradations on each side. Yeast bread and beaten biscuits occupy one end of this food-and-class continuum; the many varieties of cornbread occupy the other. Soda biscuits and quick breads stand in the middle ground. The logic of these divisions reveals much about gender and race in Appalachian culture around 1900 and can be seen when we examine the ingredients, equipment, leisure time, and national standards encoded in the recipes themselves.

The most obvious difference between biscuits and cornbread is their ingredients. Biscuits usually require wheat flour, but it was difficult for mountain residents to grow wheat. Significant annual rainfall and frequent shade around Appalachian fields meant that wheat was particularly susceptible to the growth of fungi. Joe Gray Taylor documents the effect of rust fungus on wheat and suggests that, compared to corn, wheat with rust yielded much less usable food. A mountain family needed large, cleared, unshaded fields and the economic security to afford less efficient planting if they were to grow wheat—or they needed the financial security to purchase imported food instead of food grown in their own gardens or farms. Although research is thin for early in the twentieth century, it suggests that African American Appalachian families in both rural and urban Appalachia tended to be in worse economic shape than their white counterparts—and thus even less likely to afford growing or using wheat regularly in their baking. Tommie Bass revealed another reason that mountain farmers favored corn when he remarked, "Corn is a wonderful plant, we didn't waste any of it." He then describes the medicinal value of cornsilk tea, recipes with hominy, corn as feed for both people and stock, and even corncob toilet paper. All of these factors were behind Pettit and Stone's comment that "very little wheat is raised in the mountains."

For women, the differences between wheat and corn were particularly significant. Unlike wheat, corn can be a garden plant; even a woman living in a rigid patriarchal system—which some parts of Appalachia surely were—could "handle" growing corn. Women in mill towns, women with children or other domestic responsibilities, black Appalachian women working in white women's homes (a common occupation throughout this time period), and women on their own could grow a patch of corn without too much physical or social difficulty. For mountain families without many resources, the return on the investment made planting corn by far the better decision.

Once grown, both corn and wheat were ground into flour. Yet, race, class, and gender differences in the choice between corn and wheat were not left behind at the mill. Visitors to and writers from Appalachia at the turn of the century often commented on the mountain residents' lack of proper cooking utensils. The Campbells noticed that, in one mountain household they visited, they "found the mother baking pies. She was rolling out the crust, not on a molding board but on a piece of cloth spread on the table, her rolling-pin being a round bottle." Tennessee native Emma Bell Miles, in her semi-autobiographical 1904 book, *The Spirit of the Mountains*, agreed with the Campbells: "I have seen a woman carry water, dress a fowl, mix bread, feed her cow and pick up chips all in the same big tin pan, simply because it was the only vessel she had; I have seen pies rolled out and potatoes mashed with a beer-bottle found in the road." But these were not isolated instances. Olive and John Campbell suggested that not even the country stores in Appalachia offered many cooking utensils to buy. Equipment for cooking targeted women's daily lives particularly; both Miles and the Campbells imply that even if mountain women wanted to move up the class scale from cornbread to biscuits, they might have had difficulty acquiring the additional equipment that biscuit making entailed.

Pettit and Stone, reflecting the philosophies of like-minded Progressive women, linked moral and mental strength to domestic science's emphasis on cleanliness, purity, and standardized cooking. Even if these mountain women were baking wheat-based pie crusts or bread, beer bottles would not have been acceptable equipment to do so. Thus, the class-bread continuum was not simply a matter of the end-product placed on one's family table. The equipment employed to cook was as important an element in the class-bread continuum as what was being cooked. Recalling her experiences as a teacher during the early Hindman years, Lucy Furman described the proper equipment and method of cooking in her 1923 novel *The Quare Women*: "[a] very pretty young woman, in a crisp gingham dress and large white apron, was kneading a batch of light-bread dough, and explaining the process of bread-making as she worked." Furman emphasized the clothes one needed to cook properly, the tables, ingredients, and recipes that would help in the kitchen. But the process, for Furman, did not stop when the kneading was over. She continued, "After the dough was moulded into loaves and placed in the oven of a shining new cook-stove," the crowd moved on to another tent to learn the proper way to set tables to receive the bread. This emphasis on process reminds us that the ultimate goal of these lessons extended beyond the recipe in question.

The Hindman teachers worried about their students, saying, "Add to bad air, dirt and bad cooking, the use of tobacco by men, women and even children as soon as they can walk and talk, and how can we expect good health? And without any regard to the laws of health, how can the people be strong, mentally or morally?" As their Reverend Mitchell suggested, moral and educational gains were supposed to follow from women teaching other women how to cook. But how were the activist teachers supposed to measure their moral successes? The visible signs of new cooking equipment became not only a way to judge material success—they also stood in for the mountain residents' spiritual accomplishments. Thus, rather than quizzing the Cornet family on their morals and beliefs, Pettit and Stone treated them as a successful mountain family on the evidence of the table their women presented.

Yet, few of these writers suggested how to make the biscuit's additional equipment available to all of the mountain women. Few questioned how the very class system into which they were placing biscuits contributed to the fact that some women had to use beer bottles while others got to judge the moral character of women without rolling pins. The difference between equipment for biscuits and cornbread was essentially, with the exception of the pan, a matter of local versus imported goods—and that was a question of barter and handicraft versus cash money. Biscuits work better with marble rolling boards, rolling pins, biscuit cutters, mallets or cleavers, and ovens with consistent and steady temperatures. Cornbread needs only a bowl, a spoon (although fingers will do), a skillet of some kind, and a heat source. Unlike many of the biscuit items, cornbread's bowls, spoons, and fires could be created out of resources readily available in the mountains. Wooden bowls, wooden spoons, and open fires or fires in hand-built hearths and chimneys work fine for cornbread; all could be made or traded for by the women themselves. National currency need not be involved. Even the poorest mountain woman could fashion the container, spoon, and heat source to produce cornbread for her family.

Another significant difference between the two recipes concerns the time necessary to produce each. In her journal May Stone related an incident in which "Miss Pettit went to make beaten biscuit for the sick boys while they all looked on." The boys then "asked if it was worth while to go to so much trouble." As I was writing this chapter, I tried out Bill Neal's recipe for beaten biscuits. Although I am sure Katherine Pettit was more practiced than I, she could not have significantly shortened the time and direct attention it took me to make them (and I just barely made it to the 300 strokes for family; much less the exemplary 500 strokes that were recommended).

Household economies encompass more than the labor of an individual. I had no help in beaten biscuit making, but some turn-of-the-century women did. The leisure time to put beaten biscuits on the table often suggested hired women's time and labor; in the South, that often implied black women's time and labor. Although many of Appalachia's corps of activist teachers were from the Northeast, Katherine Pettit and May Stone came from downstate Kentucky. While it is difficult to trace the origin of the first beaten biscuit recipe, some suggest that it began in the low-country South. As Joseph Dabney writes in his reflection on southern Appalachian cooking, *Smokehouse Ham, Spoon Bread, and Scuppernong Wine*, "My first inclination . . . was to omit any mention of 'beaten biscuits,' since they appeared to be more of an upper-class tidewater status symbol dish that depended on a lot of labor." He lists recipes for them from Philadelphia, Virginia, and Kentucky. In other words, the recipe that was so championed by activists in Appalachia seems to have developed in the race politics of the nineteenth-century South. Writing in the 1930s about south Georgia and Florida in *Their Eyes Were Watching God*, Zora Neale Hurston said her character Janie "went to see [her grandmother] Nanny in Mrs. Washburn's kitchen on the day for beaten biscuits," reminding readers of the time-consuming tasks the Mrs. Washburns of the world could ask of their black Nannies.

Teaching Appalachian women that they should find the time—their own or someone else's—to make beaten biscuits subtly supported the racial politics associated with other parts of the South (and existing throughout the United States). Indeed, in cooking and elsewhere, Pettit, Stone, and other white activists replicated these politics. Although Appalachia did not have so firmly entrenched a tradition of slavery and class division based on domestic workers, Pettit and Stone found African American Appalachian women servants to hire. These women, who were rarely named in Pettit and Stone's journals, primarily washed clothes; nevertheless, the teachers "made bread this morning and showed the washwoman how to make it." Cornbread, on the other hand, was something that could be easily prepared by anyone after other paid or unpaid work was completed.

This issue of available leisure time to prepare breads other than cornbread belies one of the tensions across women's activism throughout the nineteenth century: where and how a woman should spend that leisure time. Upper- or middle-class white women activists worked *outside* their homes—to improve society for other women and to spread the values of "feminine" virtue—but the ideal they presented to working women defined success as having the leisure to spend more time *inside* the home. Activists came to Appalachia to escape domestic life; they enjoyed the outdoors, hiked, sketched, and rode horses unaccompanied by fathers, husbands, or brothers. But these activists taught Appalachian women how to bake biscuits—and in so doing pushed the local women to stay inside domestic spheres. Had everyone the ability to bake biscuits, their own presence in the mountains would become unnecessary—so rarely do we find these activists questioning the economic and social reasons

ELIZABETH ENGELHARDT

behind Appalachians' seeming preference for cornbreads. Staying in Appalachia meant prolonging their own freedom and mobility; staying was an escape from domestic duties awaiting them at home. Ironically, this took away from some Appalachian women freedoms they had previously enjoyed. Emma Bell Miles suggested of the mountain woman that "at an age when the mothers of any but a wolf-race become lace-capped and felt-shod pets of the household, relegated to the safety of cushioned nooks in favorite rooms, she is yet able to toil almost as severely as ever." Miles found in this a "strength and endurance . . . beyond imagination to women of the sheltered life," and she was generally critical of making women stay indoors. Although not everyone would have agreed with Miles, many Appalachian women might well have questioned the double standard proposed by activist women.

Finally, biscuits and cornbreads differed in their participation in national, as opposed to regional or local, standards; definitions of race, class, and gender in Appalachia were nationalized as a result. Stone and Pettit returned after their first summer to find one mountain woman who "told us that she had tried to cook everything like we had taught her and that she had learned from the cookbook we sent her. She had a rice pudding with blackberries around it, just as we had served it the day she was with us. She said she had taught her friends our way of cooking and that she had made beaten biscuit for many weddings." Not only did this woman follow the educational lessons of the Hindman women, but she also followed a cookbook that was standard for all of the United States. This practice implied standard ingredients, equipment, and expectations, as well as definitions of proper white womanhood that could be generalized across the nation.

Imported wheat, marble slabs and rolling pins, technologically advanced and consistent cook stoves, and cookbooks were all parts of a national distribution system fueled by the buying decisions of women. The era's women's magazines especially promoted the new "homemaker," a newly coined term. In this rhetoric about women's important role in consuming wisely for one's family, female homemakers with more money (often a combination of class and race privilege during this era) were more valued. As Martha McCulloch-Williams suggested, "happy ever after" could come from the proper kitchen equipment in a turn-of-the-century home. In the burgeoning consumer culture in 1900, things moved in to supply satisfaction to women across the United States. More tools, more equipment, and mass market sources for both meant that Appalachians were participating in the nation's consumerist culture and that the Progressive activists who were helping them do so could claim success in their goals of "civilizing" the Appalachians. This new homemaker and her buying power had to decide between biscuits and cornbread in many mountain families.

Despite the general adoption of biscuits as a marker of higher class by mountain residents and newcomers, there was resistance to this hierarchy. Based on the erosion of women's precious free time, controversies over health effects, and, in at least one case, an overarching social critique regarding local values, cornbread did have its defenders.

Olive Campbell recorded in her travel journal from her research trip around Appalachia with her husband John, which resulted in *The Southern Highlander and His Homeland*, that she found "quite a prejudice against domestic science"—which would have included biscuits and cooking lessons—"as being merely 'dish washing' of which [the mountain women] say they have plenty at home." Such a sentiment was also expressed by the boys watching Pettit make biscuits; whether a food is worth the trouble to make is in fact a trenchant question. Time-saving devices for women, especially ones that target housework and food preparation, have, in fact, rarely decreased the amount of time that women spend on household chores. Resisting a new recipe such as the beaten biscuit that has the effect of eroding one's quality of life seems a reasonable tactic. Or, as an anonymous mountain woman told Pettit and Stone after watching their extensive preparations for bed, "Ye all must be a lot of trouble to yerselves."

The varied resistance to the soda biscuit in the mountains reached opposite conclusions but was united in the belief that soda biscuits were not a healthy food for long-term consumption. Independently, Maria Louise Pool and Margaret Morley used the assumed unhealthiness of soda biscuits to justify the superiority of yeast breads on the continuum of class and bread. Emma Bell Miles used the same assumed unhealthiness to argue for a return to corn-based breads, therein inverting the hierarchy.

Pool's narrator noted, "I had apple-butter and saleratus biscuit for my repast. I know they were saleratus biscuit because frequent yellow lumps appealed both to the eye and the palate. But I am not complaining. I knew that the apple-butter would not hurt me, and I was just as sure that, at one meal, I could not eat enough sal-soda to destroy the coats of my stomach." Morley made a similar comment when she reported, "The most frequent disorder among them is dyspepsia, for which the pale-green, or saffron-yellow, brown-spotted, ring-streaked and speckled luxury known as 'soda biscuits' undoubtedly bears a heavy burden of blame. These wonders of the culinary art are freely eaten by all who can afford to buy white flour, and their odorous presence is often discernible from afar as you approach a house at mealtime." Pool, Morley, and others like them (in other words, upper-class, white women travelers) felt that the leavening used in biscuits—in particular in the newer commercial baking powders—was quite dangerous to the digestive system. Beaten biscuits, made

ELIZABETH ENGELHARDT

with little or no leavening, would have an advantage over the risen biscuits that Pool's character encountered near Asheville, North Carolina, but was not offered. Behind this brief comment in Pool's novel lay national concerns about cuisine, health food, and nutrition.

Emma Bell Miles, who grew up in and lived most of her life in Appalachia, agreed with Pool and Morley about the dangers of risen soda biscuits, even as she reached a different conclusion about what to do with this knowledge. Miles worried that "Civilization is not likely soon to remedy this evil" of unhealthy food in Appalachia. But she blamed industrialization outside of Appalachia for "introduc[ing] cheap baking powders and the salicylic acid which is so dangerously convenient in canning fruit." She wanted mountain residents to avoid all of the store-bought food (including flour), and thus she supported the continued use of corn-based bread. Later in the twentieth century, this conversation about various breads in Appalachia moved into controversies over pellagra and the relative healthiness of any store-bought and commercially ground flours and meals. Today health food experts advocate for locally produced organic food, arguing that it provides protection against allergies, as well as more vitamins and minerals. Miles would have agreed.

Emma Bell Miles did not stop at insisting imported ingredients could be dangerous to individual women and families. She extended her argument to make a social critique that overarched the individual women involved. She suggested that, while it was "easier, far, to buy city tools with city money," they came with a high long-term cost. She argued, "the old-time mountaineer never knew the taste of ice-cream in summer, he was, on the other hand, never without corn-pones and side-meat in cold weather." She mourned to "see them buy meal by the half-peck to eat with the invariable white gravy" and concluded that the newcomers who had initiated this market economy in her community "would not think the pay so well proportioned to the sacrifice, after all," if they stayed to see the effects of their changes. She found local ingredients, indigenous traditions, and a barter economy to be more ecologically, socially, and individually sustainable. Cornbread, grown at home, using handmade equipment, as a part of a self-sufficient community, was a centerpiece of her argument. And while Miles used the third-person pronoun to write, we know from her biography that she was speaking out of her own individual experience of running a household of six in extreme poverty. Cooking nonlocal, more expensive, and time-consuming food was hardly an option for this social critic.

Like the cornbreads before it, the various forms of the biscuit, too, were eventually discredited and displaced. Creating standardized housewives across the country helped fuel the market for and influence of media targeted to those women, all of which resulted in the promotion of mass-produced, commercial, sliced bread. It may be that this ascension of toast into Appalachian and American kitchens helped move both biscuits and cornbread into their present-day category as Southern home food, into both being sources of nostalgia. Both foods continue to be gendered—women are responsible for preparing them and are identified closely with them in our nostalgia about their symbolic meanings. It is a rare man (with the exception of professional male chefs and cookbook authors) who is nostalgic for the process of *making* the biscuits or cornbread for a family's table. Many of us, male and female, have strong memories and emotions associated with *eating* these foods.

When I moved from western North Carolina to Atlanta, two restaurants teased me with the possibilities of biscuits and cornbread. One had people lined up for a three-hour wait each weekend to receive their order of huge, fluffy, but disappointingly (to my mind) sweet, risen biscuits. The other served cornbread with its three-vegetable plate during lunchtime only; that cornbread, although still a bit sweet to my taste, was much closer to my childhood memories. Although the evidence is only anecdotal, I have begun to wonder why the first restaurant attracted so many of Atlanta's white yuppies, transplants, and recently arrived residents. And why did the other draw working-class folk of diverse races, local and longtime Atlantans? Now I live in Texas and am frequently asked to choose between flour and corn tortillas. Gender, race, class, and bread may still be entangled if only we look for the web. For myself, I decided that I could enjoy the first restaurant's pastries as long as I did not call them "biscuits"; I continued to eat my lunch plate with cornbread; and I am happy to be able to pick between tortillas—while enjoying the rich social history behind the choices. My grandmother, I suspect, would have approved.

ELIZABETH ENGELHARDT

A Theory of Pole Beans

NIKKI GIOVANNI

(for Ethel and Rice)

that must have been the tail end of the Depression
as well as the depression of coming war
there certainly was segregation and hatred and fear

these small towns and small minded people
trying to bend taller spirits down
were unable to succeed

there couldn't have been too much fun
assuming fun equates with irresponsibility

there was always food to be put on the table
clothes to be washed and ironed
hair to be pressed
gardens to be weeded

and children to talk to and teach
each other to love
and tend to

pole beans are not everyone's favorite
they make you think of pieces of fat back
cornbread
and maybe a piece of fried chicken

they are the staples of things unquestioned
they are broken and boiled

no one would say life handed you
a silver spoon or golden parachute
but you still
met   married
bought a home   reared a family
supported a church   and kept a mighty faith
in your God   and each other

they say love/is a many splendored thing
but maybe that's because we recognize
you loved no matter what the burden
you laughed no matter for the tears
you persevered in your love

and your garden remains in full bloom

raising consciousness

Where I'm From

GEORGE ELLA LYON

I am from clothespins,
from Clorox and carbon-tetrachloride.
I am from the dirt under the black porch.
(Black, glistening
it tasted like beets.)
I am from the forsythia bush,
the Dutch elm
whose long gone limbs I remember
as if they were my own.

I'm from fudge and eyeglasses,
from Imogene and Alafair.
I'm from the know-it-alls
and the pass-it-ons,
from perk up and pipe down.
I'm from He restoreth my soul
with a cottonball lamb
and ten verses I can say myself.

I'm from Artemus and Billie's Branch,
fried corn and strong coffee.
From the finger my grandfather lost
to the auger
the eye my father shut to keep his sight.
Under my bed was a dress box
spilling old pictures,
a sift of lost faces
to drift beneath my dreams.
I am from those moments—snapped before I budded—
leaf-fall from the family tree.

Raised by Women

KELLY NORMAN ELLIS

I was raised by
Chitterling eating
Vegetarian cooking
Cornbread so good you want to lay
down and die baking
"Go on baby, get yo'self a plate"
Kind of Women.

Some thick haired
Angela Davis afro styling
"Girl, lay back
and let me scratch yo head"
Sorta Women.

Some big legged
High yellow, mocha brown
Hip shaking
Miniskirt wearing
Hip huggers hugging
Daring debutantes
Groovin
"I know I look good"
Type of Women.

Some tea sipping
White glove wearing
Got married too soon

Divorced
in just the nick of time
"Better say yes ma'am to me"
Type of sisters.

Some fingerpopping
Boogaloo dancing
Say it loud
I'm black and I'm proud
James Brown listening
"Go on girl shake that thing"
Kind of Sisters.

Some face slapping
Hands on hips
Don't mess with me
"Pack your bags and
get the hell out of my house"
Sort of women.

Some Ph.D. toten
Poetry writing
Portrait painting
"I'll see you in court"
World traveling
Stand back, I'm creating
Type of Queens.

I was raised by
Women.

Taking Stock of Being Appalachian

JAMES B. GOODE

There are those who grow up in America who are acutely aware of who they are culturally. They are usually products of tightly knit social, political, economic, and religious units that are usually formed in segregated enclaves. The Jewish, Amish, American Indian, Hispanic, and Cajun communities are examples of easily defined cultures. But not everyone in the United States possesses a distinct cultural identity, although many strive to "belong."

From my earliest recollection until now I have heard people in Appalachia say that they were "part Indian" or "part French" or "part Scotch Irish." My family's claim to fame is that we were "part Irish, Scotch, French, Indian, and Black Dutch." I often joked that all that meant was that we were hopelessly romantic, wandering alcoholics who didn't want to pay for any of our habits. I was never sure whether any part of this lineage was actual fact, although there was that picture of my great-great-grandfather Parsons who peered from the bowed glass, oval frame holding a Bible in one hand, a pistol in the other, and looking very much like Geronimo.

I was born August 8, 1948, in the back bedroom of the house at 342 Poplar Street in the International Harvester coal camp at Benham, Kentucky. My mother still has that very four-poster bed, complete with mattress and springs, upon which my grandmother delivered me. The first time I remember seeing my grandmother Goode was in that bedroom as I lay on a small cot, very sick with influenza and running an extremely high temperature. She brought a straw basket filled with fruit and comforted me with her very pale, blue-veined hand. The year was 1950, and she had been a widow for almost ten years. My paternal grandfather, Larkin Andrew, had experienced a horrible death from pneumo-coniosis on February 10, 1940. Just a few years after meeting her for the first time I began asking questions about the absence of my grandfather, which led to my realization that I had been born from an environment that had the potential to both sustain and destroy.

From the onset of hearing the words "coal mining," I developed a voracious appetite for learning all I could about this mysterious and dangerous profession. I was a member of a coal camp before I ever realized I was an Appalachian. My grandfather had died as a result of working as a miner, and because my daddy was a miner I feared for his life. Deaths and injuries from rock falls, electrocution, explosions, and other freak accidents were commonplace.

Being a member of a coal camp was a unique blend of urban and rural sociology. Because the very life of the camp depended on the work schedules of the mining company, we heard the work whistle blow every evening to signal whether the miners would report to work at 6 A.M. the next morning. If the whistle blew, my mother would put the battered aluminum dinner bucket into the porcelain-enameled, double drain board sink to scrub away the rock and coal dust, grease, and muck from the previous shift. A few nonperishable items were placed in the bucket the night before—an apple, homemade cookies, a dill pickle, and cold biscuits. The next morning at 4 A.M. she would finish with some sandwiches made from plain white bread and "coal miner's steak"—thick slices of King Cole bologna. The bucket was designed to hold about a quart of cold water in the bottom, and inserts of pans above the water held all the other food items. My job was to build fires in the two freestanding stoves—one in the kitchen and one in the living room. Daddy would call me once, and my feet would hit the floor before his voice quit ringing in the room.

Growing up in a coal camp meant having a company doctor who visited your home when you were sick. It meant attending a company school, buying 'most everything from a company commissary, seeing cowboy movies in a company theater, having your phone calls monitored by a company operator, celebrating the Fourth of July at company outings, watching baseball played by company teams, hearing the thunderous roar of the largest steam engines in the world pulling company coal gons, taking showers in the company bathhouse, waiting on the company crews to repair or paint the company house in which you lived, and being a true blue union believer.

I learned to mold the rhythm of my life to the corporate clock at an early age. We knew what it meant to be at the mercy of the company and the economy. The rise and fall of the steel market dictated whether Daddy worked five days a week with some overtime or only two days a week at straight time. This of course also impacted what appeared on the tables as food or on our backs as clothes. When times were good we ate hamburgers, chicken-fried steak, spaghetti, or pizza. When times were bad, we ate food provided from our garden or livestock. Fresh-killed chickens, lettuce and onions wilted with hot bacon grease, fried potatoes, green beans, pickled beets, poke sallet, and wild morels, called dry land fish, were among the many items on our menu.

The broad ethnic diversity also created an interesting plethora of additions to our meals. Almost everyone liked hot pickled Hungarian peppers stuffed with cabbage; chow-chow was always a garnish for soup beans and cornbread; Louisiana hot sauce found its way on everything from fried eggs to hot dogs; Polish sausage was served with potatoes and bell peppers; Deep South black-eyed peas and lean pork bits were frequently accompanied by the German-inspired pickled corn on the cob. My first realization that our eating habits were unique came when I moved to Lexington, Kentucky, to attend college. I couldn't find good salt bacon, souse meat, chitlins, collard greens, wild grape jelly, or any corn squeezins. When I lived in South Wales, I couldn't find a single sack of cornmeal in the whole damn country! One gracious clerk tried to sell me a one-pound bag of corn flour as a substitute. Obviously, he had never seen a hot pone of brown-crusted cornbread pop out of a dark iron skillet. Sometimes that cultural diversity wasn't totally comprehensive—my daddy told a story about his mother's seeing grapefruit for the first time. She loaded several of them in a canner and attempted to boil them for supper!

Because of the large number of Eastern European ethnics, a large Catholic population practiced their religion in three local churches. Greek Orthodox, Methodist, AME Zion, Jehovah's Witness, Mormon, Nazarene, Free Pentecostal, Apostolic Holiness, First Baptist, Holy Baptist, Southern Baptist, Old Regular Baptist, Missionary Baptist, Free Will Baptist, Church of God of Prophecy, the Church of God Gospel Assembly, Church of God Union Assembly, the Church of Christ, the Disciples of Christ, the First Christian Church, the Church of Christ in Jesus Name, Full Gospel Church of Jesus Christ, Presbyterian, and Episcopal churches also thrived and added to my religious cultural experience. I knew about every obscure Bible verse on which a church might be based. Serpent handling, all-day meetings with dinners on the ground, brush arbor revivals, Irish wakes, praying over, singing down, lining hymns, singing shape notes, laying on of hands, foot washing, and being given the holy sacrament were all part of my reference.

I soon became aware that because we lived in a "suburban-like" community, many rural people perceived us to be wealthy wage earners. All during the 1950s beggars from the rural countryside appeared at our door with burlap sacks extended for a handout. My mother always bought extra canned goods to give to these unfortunate people. Many were dirty and unkempt. Several extended tattered notes scribbled on notebook paper that explained that they were deaf/mute or had some other handicap that prevented them from working. We were living in the midst of a continuing transition from a rural, agrarian society where only the more prosperous landowners would survive. The rest would either work for the coal company or be cast into a vicious cycle of poverty, which was later recognized by John F. Kennedy and Lyndon B. Johnson and led to the social programs of Johnson's "Great Society."

What became of the stereotypical image of the Appalachian was of curiosity. The only log cabin left in our community had been the kitchen of the homestead pioneer Creech family, who had sold out to International Harvester shortly before the turn of the century. The coal company used it as a police station. Later, coal sludge covered it during one of the high spring "tides." The people who lived in the Linefork area of Letcher County played dulcimers, sang songs from the British Isles, danced the Kentucky Set Running, plowed with mules, planted huge fields of corn, had sorghum molasses stir-offs, told Jack Tales, wore bibbed-overalls, and made the best moonshine money could buy. Their culture was another important part of my education about the complexity of my place in this world.

I was educated into becoming Appalachian from the first time I realized my grandfather had died of black lung, through all the experiences of growing up in a coal camp, and with all the rich experiences with a diminishing mountain community. I have discovered that people belong to specific cultures once they have aged with its people and customs—it's almost a graduation process. Being a native is only one of many criteria. The rest is up to those who reside there. Becoming aware of who one is and why is the kind of stock one should take early in life. This is the base through which roots proliferate, prosper, and are found.

Steep

ROBERT MORGAN

Driven out from the centers of population,
displaced from villages and crossroads and too poor
to acquire the alluvial bottomlands
the carbon-dark fields along the creek,

forced back on the rocky slopes above branches,
to the flanks near the headwaters,
pushed to the final mountain wall, I brace
my faculties against the falling out of labor

and prop up or stake down every stalk, dig
terraces and drive fences to save what little
topsoil there is from the gullywashers
hitting almost every afternoon up here in summer.

Cow trails babel the steepest knobs, make
by spiral and switchback the sheer peaks
and outcroppings accessible, I plant only root
vegetables, turnips, potatoes, and prehensile creepers.

Too far to carry whole or raw things
into town, I take the trouble only with something
boiled down, distilled, and clear new
ground every three or four years.

I live high on the hogback near
dividing water, I disaffiliate and secede.
I grow ginseng in hollows unlit as the dark
side of the moon, and confederate with moisture and

insular height to bring summit orchards
to bear. I husband the scartissue of erosion.

From Oats to Grits, Mutton to Pork
North British Foodways
in Southern Appalachia

JIM WAYNE MILLER

Until I started leafing through the text, I had not realized how often in my autobiographical novel *Newfound* I was concerned with *food*—the gathering, preparation, preservation, and consumption of food; with attitudes toward food; even with superstitions relating to food. When I was writing the novel I was not concerned with food, as such, in the least. Yet since food, along with clothing and shelter, is the basic necessity, it should not be surprising that so much of the story touches on food in some way. Although I did not intend the novel to do so, I see now that *Newfound* provides a quite accurate account of foodways among people of modest background in the southern Appalachians in the 1930s and 1940s, when the economy had shifted from an almost exclusively agrarian base to a mix of subsistence farming and mill, mine, and factory work.

In the opening section the narrator's father, James Wells, has quit his job at a mine and undertaken a dubious venture in cement block making. Nora, the mother, is concerned about providing food for her children—the narrator, Robert, and his younger brother and sister, Eugene and Jeanette. The father has made a lot of cement blocks but hasn't sold any; his old Studebaker has locked up in reverse gear; and his block-making machine keeps breaking. The mother needs cash to buy some more jars and lids to can blackberries and to make blackberry jelly and jam.

June was as good as over and Dad hadn't sold the first block.

Mom threw it up to him that now we had no car, and she couldn't go where the best blackberries were. The ones near the house, where she'd been picking with Jeanette and Eugene, weren't very good. But on Cook's Mountain, where her brother Clinton lived, the briers were thick and the berries were big as your thumb. We'd always gone to Uncle Clinton's toward the end of June to pick blackberries. But now we couldn't go, Mom said, and we'd have very little jelly and jam come winter, and very few canned berries for pies. And if Dad thought the store bill we'd already run up was something, she went on, then wait and see what it would be come winter. Peaches. That was another thing. She always bought peaches from peddlers who came around. But there'd be no money this time, so we'd have no peaches either. And Dad had fiddle-faddled around in the spring when Ed Reeves had had three litters of pigs—three litters—and we hadn't bought one, and so come fall we'd have no hog to slaughter, no ham, no shoulder meat, no sausage.

"Will you ever wind down?" Dad asked, wild-eyed. He buttered a piece of hot cornbread and looked around the table at us children.

Mom said she wouldn't wind down. She reminded Dad that we were eating new potatoes and green beans and tomatoes and peas and squash and okra from Grandma and Grandpa Smith's garden. Grandpa Smith came every day with a basket of this, a bucket of that. And other things we needed we were buying out of Grandpa Wells's store—on credit. Mom threw that up to him. It was the farmer who was secure, she said. The farmer always had work and food to put on the table.

"I have work!" Dad said.

"Um-hummmmm!" Mom said disdainfully. She recollected aloud that years ago Grandpa Wells had tried to get Dad to take over the job of running the farm, but, no, Dad had to traipse off to the mines, drive a truck, then try to go into business for himself, then go back to driving a truck for the mines. If we had stayed on the farm, we'd be well off now. It broke her heart, Mom said, after all these years, still to be living off her mama and papa—and his.

Dad said he hadn't been cut out for a farmer, and Mom had never understood that, either. Oh, he loved the smoked ham and garden greens, he admitted, but that didn't make him a farmer.

And it was true: green growing things seemed to wither at his touch. Once Mom had kept after him until he ordered some seedling trees to set along the edge of the yard. Not one lived. . . .

No, Dad could stand oil and grease and coal dust, but he couldn't stand fresh-plowed dirt in his shoe-tops. I'd seen him plow a row or two of corn at Grandpa Wells's, and once or twice he'd helped out at tobacco setting time. He never lasted long, though, and he looked little and lost standing in plowed ground.

The father's block-making venture finally succeeds in a qualified way: he barters cement blocks for a supply of jams, jellies, and peach preserves, for a Poland

China pig and corn to feed it. He trades blocks to a local bootlegger for half-gallon jars of whiskey, which he converts to cash. But the mother's insecurity in a jerry-built economy, abetted by her husband's ongoing quixotic ventures, only increases and finally becomes intolerable. They separate, and the following spring the mother, taking the children with her, goes to live with her tenant-farmer parents, the narrator Robert's Grandma and Grandpa Smith.

Except for missing Dad [Robert narrates], I didn't feel I'd left home for I had always gone back and forth between our house and Grandma and Grandpa Smith's. Bertie, Grandpa's mule; Sarah, the brindled milk cow, and Betsy, the black-and-white one; his foxhounds, Luke and Leader, Jamup and Honey; the chickens that walked poles to roost at night; the snake-headed guinea hens that screeched and pottericked when they are excited—all this was familiar to me. And Grandma Smith made us apple turnovers, let me drink coffee, and treated me more like I was a grown-up than Mom did.

Food and food preparation loom large in Robert's recollection of the first summer he lives with his grandparents:

That summer we had tender new potatoes from the patch we'd planted, and okra and cucumbers, onions, peppers, and tomatoes from the garden. When we went with Grandma Smith to pick sweet corn Jeanette said, "Mind your tongue in the cornfield, because there are lots of ears listening! Right, Grandma?" Grandma Smith said that was right.

She made rhubarb pies for us. On weekends she and Mom [who has taken a job at Blue Ridge Manufacturing] canned corn and beans and tomatoes and little pint jars of chopped pickles called chow-chow. "What's green when they're red, and ripe only when they're black?" Grandma Smith asked. "Blackberries, of course!" Jeanette said. Grandma Smith said the blackberries were ripe, and she sent us out on the ridges and into the pasture field to pick them. She and Mom made blackberry jam and jelly.

In July peddlers came by with a truckload of peaches. Grandma and Mom bought several bushels and canned them. Eugene and Jeanette and I washed mason jars all summer, it seemed. After the jars came out of the pressure cooker, and before we carried them to the cool can house, they stood on shelves in the kitchen overnight. Before I went to sleep, I'd sometimes hear a jar lid go *plink*. The lids made that sound when they sealed, Mom said.

Robert's Grandpa Smith is a beekeeper. Robert describes how the old man "robs" his bees:

He stood over the bee gums wearing gloves, a long-sleeved shirt, and a wire cage over his head. He puffed smoke from his bee smoker on the bees to stun them and frighten them away. Eugene ate some of the honey while it was still warm, although Grandma Smith warned him not to, and the honey made him sick. I got too close to the gums and an angry bee buzzed my head, got tangled in my hair, and when I tried to slap it away, it stung me right on top of my head.

Mom, Jeanette, and Grandma Smith stayed in the house with the doors closed until Grandpa had finished taking the racks of honey from the gums. Then they cut the golden honey out of the racks and stored it in jars. Grandma Smith said she probably should have come outside and allowed herself to get stung on the hand, because a bee sting was good for arthritis. The jars of honey were a smoky blond color next to the yellow peaches on the shelves in the can house. We had honey with buttered biscuits for breakfast, and that August Mom and Jeanette used some honey in a birthday cake for Grandma Smith.

Grandma Smith's notion that a bee sting was good for her arthritis is but one of her many beliefs and superstitions. She has a saying for conjuring warts, one for "drawing" fire from a burn, another for making butter, and she knows that to do when a swarm of Grandpa Smith's bees threaten to fly away:

Grandma Smith knew spells to make butter come, and when she had Eugene and me take turns working the dasher up and down in the wooden churn, she taught us rhymes to say that would make the flecks of butter appear in the buttermilk.

She knew things about honeybees. Grandpa Smith had five beehives—he called them "bee gums"—and one day when we were working in the garden and Grandpa Smith was off helping Coy Marler, Grandma Smith dropped her hoe and ran toward the house as fast as she could. I looked in the direction she had looked, and saw that a great dark cloud of bees was rising from one of the bee gums. Grandma Smith came back out of the house with a pie pan and a big spoon, and she ran along under the slow moving cloud of bees, beating the pie pan with a spoon. She followed them far down into the pasture below the garden, still beating the pie pan, where the swarm settled on the limb of a jack pine. The bees were so heavy they made the limb droop toward the ground, like a branch weighted down with snow in winter. Then she sent me to find Grandpa. When he came he brought another bee gum from the barn, cut the whole limb off the tree with his pocket knife, and carried the swarm of bees to the new gum. Reaching into the clump of bees with his bare hand, he found the queen, coaxed her into the new gum, and finally the whole swarm followed her into their new home.

Grandma Smith, as Robert tells it, is also particular about the way she gathers guinea eggs:

I went to the woods with Grandma Smith to hunt for guinea nests. (Guineas were bad about stealing their nests away, she said.) On hot afternoons we'd stand by fence rows and cow trails listening for half-wild guineas screeching after they laid eggs in nests they'd find hidden in thickets, scrub pines, and chinquapins. And when we'd find a nest, Grandma Smith wouldn't take the eggs from it with her bare hand; she carried her little garden hoe, and she'd reach out into the nest with the hoe and carefully roll the eggs out, one at a time, always leaving one, so the guinea would continue to lay eggs there.

The picture that emerges from Robert's descriptions of life with his maternal grandparents is that of a subsistence farm in a particular time and place, which is also typical of many parts of rural America before and after:

We didn't buy many groceries out of the store after we moved to Grandma and Grandpa Smith's. They raised almost all their food. There were potatoes stored in a big cone-shaped mound, beneath straw. We had dried apples, ham and sausage from the smokehouse, and vegetables fresh from the garden or canned. Grandma Smith had a can house that was dug back into the side of the hill. It was always cool in summer and warm in winter. She raised two rows of popcorn in the garden, and Eugene, Jeanette, and I popped popcorn on the woodstove in the living room.

In early spring, when pussy willows were budding along the branch bank, Mom went with us to gather cresses. She said she had gathered cresses on that same branch bank when she was a little girl. She made a salad from the cresses that tasted better than the lettuce we used to get from the store.

Grandma Smith wanted to plant potatoes on Good Friday, but Grandpa Smith didn't have the ground quite ready, so we planted potatoes the next day. Grandma Smith said Good Friday was the best time to plant. Good Saturday was close enough, Grandpa Smith said. Eugene, Jeanette, and I helped. Mom stayed in the house and typed things she'd brought home from work. Grandma Smith showed us how to recognize the seed potatoes' "eyes," and how to cut them up so that each piece had an eye. The piece of potato wouldn't sprout and make a plant, she said, unless it had an eye.

"If they have eyes, can they see?" Jeanette said.

Grandma Smith said potatoes had eyes but they couldn't see. Neither could a needle, and a needle had an eye.

"A shoe's got a tongue, but it can't talk," Eugene said. He drew eyebrows over two eyes of a potato, and a mouth and a nose, and held it up for us to see. Jeanette had to draw a potato face, too.

After Grandpa Smith had the potato patch laid off in rows, we each took a row, carrying a pail of cut-up seed potatoes, and walked along dropping the pieces into the furrow about a foot apart. We stepped on each piece, pressing it down into the loose soil. Then Grandpa came along with Bertie hitched to a plow and covered the potatoes in the furrow.

Robert describes how, that fall, they harvest the potatoes and how they are "holed" in a cone-shaped mound (mentioned above). In this section Jeanette is preoccupied with plans for a birthday party, and more careless than usual:

Grandpa Smith had plowed up the whole potato patch. You could see down the rows and see the potatoes turned up in the warm afternoon sun. Grandma and Grandpa Smith and Mom were out in the patch gathering potatoes. Mom got us each a basket and set us to helping.

Working in the row beside me, Jeanette started to worry that Grandma Wells might not have any cake or muffins when we went down there on Wednesday for the birthday party. Maybe we ought to make a cake and take it down there with us, just to make sure we had one. We could hide it in the rosebushes and go in first, and *then* go out a few minutes later in bring it in.

"You're missin' a lot of 'em," Eugene told Jeanette. "You can't always see 'em. You have to stir the dirt around." He reached over into Jeanette's row, raked through the loose dirt with his hand, and turned up a big, fat potato. "Look!" he said. Then he uncovered another. "Look!"

But Jeanette was preoccupied with Grandpa Wells's birthday party. When she tried to get Grandma Smith to help her bake a cake, Grandma Smith said, "Why there's half a cake right there in the pie safe."

Mom heard them talking about cake, thought Jeanette was wanting to eat cake before supper, and said Jeanette couldn't have any.

Jeanette said she meant a cake for Wednesday.

"She's not finding nearly all of 'em!" Eugene said. Exasperated with Jeanette, he uncovered another potato she had missed. "Somebody might as well just do her row over!"

Grandma Smith said she didn't know what Jeanette was talking about— a cake for Wednesday? So Jeanette explained the whole thing how next

Wednesday was Grandpa Wells's birthday and we had already got him some gifts and hidden them in the house and we were going to go over there and surprise him.

Grandma Smith's right hand went up to the side of her weathered face, the way it always did when she was surprised.

Mom looked dubious at first. But it turned out she thought Jeanette was talking about a birthday cake for Grandma Wells. [Robert's mother never got along with her mother-in-law.] When she understood Jeanette wanted to bake a cake for Grandpa Wells, not Grandma Wells, she said that would be all right.

Mom, Jeanette, and Grandma Smith went to the house to stay for supper, leaving Eugene, Grandpa Smith, and me to hole up the potatoes for winter. We knew how to do it, for we'd helped do it last fall, too. Grandpa Smith said we had so many potatoes, this year, we'd have to dig two potato holes, so we dug two shallow depressions, piling them up until there were two cone-shaped mounds. We covered the mounds with straw from the barn loft, then, working with shovels, tossed dirt on the straw mounds. At the bottom of each mound Grandpa Smith placed a short length of stovepipe that extended beyond the dirt, but back through the straw to the potatoes. Finishing up, we stuffed the stovepipes tight with straw. Now when the cold weather came and we needed potatoes, we could remove the straw, reach into the pipe, and pull the potatoes out, one or two at a time. And as we used them up, others would roll down into their place.

There were no chestnuts to be gathered in the fall. The great chestnut trees had been killed by a blight earlier in the century. Robert heard stories from his grandparents about how abundant the chestnuts had been when they were growing up, but now the chestnut trees stood, gray skeletons, in the woods. But a chestnut-like nut called the chinquapin that grows on shrubbery bushes could be gathered when the prickly burs burst open: "Fall came, and we started to school again. . . . In the afternoon when we came home from school, and before we did chores, Eugene, Jeanette, and I picked chinquapins on the ridges above Grandma and Grandpa Smith's. We ate chinquapins, cracking the soft black hulls with our teeth, then turning the nut out of the hull with our tongues, until the tips of our tongues were sore. Jeanette made a necklace by stringing the shiny black chinquapins on fishing line with a big needle."

In autumn they also gathered walnuts and helped make molasses:

Fall came. Leaves turned yellow and blazing red and began to rattle in the wind. The air turned crisp. . . . We gathered walnuts and got our hands stained yellow from the walnut hulls.

We also helped Grandpa Smith and Coy Marler and Jess Woody make molasses. Grandpa Smith hitched Bertie to a long pole on the molasses mill, and Bertie walked around and around, turning the mill, pressing the sweet juice from the cane. Eugene tasted the dark syrup that remained after the juice had been boiled; it didn't make him sick the way the honey had.

Late autumn was also the time for hog slaughtering: "Just before Thanksgiving Grandpa Smith slaughtered the largest of the three hogs in the big pen out by the barn. Coy Marler came to help. They hung the hog on a gambrel stick with a rope that worked on a pulley suspended from a tree limb. They lowered the hog into a big barrel of steaming water, raised it again, and scraped off the loose hair. Soon the hog was hams and shoulders and sausage in the smokehouse, and Eugene had the hog's bladder for a balloon."

The Newfound grade school, which they had always attended, closes, and Robert and his brother and sister, Eugene and Jeanette, begin attending West Madison Consolidated. Robert misses the old school: "West Madison was very modern, bright and colorful. There were skylights in the rooms and halls; smooth tiled floors, which the janitors swept with green sawdust; pink, yellow, and green rooms; desks arranged in a semi-circle around the teacher's; green writing boards and yellow chalk. But I longed for Newfound School, with its old desks bolted to the oil-soaked floor, and the huge oak tree in the yard, scarred with everyone's initials."

Miss Hudspeth, a nurse at the new school, makes Robert, an eighth grader now, self-conscious about who he is, where he lives, and even about the food he eats:

Miss Hudspeth was relentless. The students from Newfound became her pet project. She had been a missionary in Central America, and I suppose we reminded her of the diseased, undernourished children she had known there. We shocked her with our ignorance, our backwardness, and our poverty in the midst of the splendor of West Madison. She disapproved of our sack lunches. "For only pennies a day you can have a hot, nourishing meal," she would say. "Be sure to tell your fathers and mothers."

When Miss Hudspeth brought just us students from Newfound together for a lecture, we at least enjoyed a kind of privacy in which to feel ashamed of ourselves. But usually we were scattered among the others, especially when she showed films in the darkened gym. One of these films was called "The Wheel of Good Health" and showed healthy, happy children eating fresh fruits, green leafy vegetables, yellow vegetables, cheese, milk, fish, poultry, and all the rest, maintaining all the while, in spite of the constant chewing, expressions of pure delight. A recurring wheel showed the basic seven daily requirements for good nutrition.

When the film ended, Miss Hudspeth motioned for the lights to be turned on, stood out on the gym floor with her hands clasped together and talked to us about our personal diets. She asked several students what they had for breakfast that morning, and they recited: bacon, eggs, toast, milk, cereal—all the lovely, approved things.

"What about you little Newfound folk?" she asked, pointing to my brother Eugene, who was sitting on the front row of bleachers looking up at her. Eugene always listened as if his life depended on it, but he never realized how backward he was. "You little brown-eyes," Miss Hudspeth said, "What did you eat for breakfast?"

Eugene started rocking back and forth nervously, and gripping his jeans at the knees. "Biscuits," he said, his voice sounding unusually high and thin in the gym; " . . . and sawmill gravy," he continued, in the singsong recitation. I could see Miss Hudspeth was shocked, as no doubt she knew she would be, for she smiled ever more fiercely, and pointed to another child. But Eugene was not through reciting. " . . . and molasses," he intoned, "*new* molasses!"

A half-mad, hysterical laugh rose to the high ceiling of the gym and bounced back before I realized that it was I who had laughed. I cringed down . . . and looked to see whether anyone on either side of me knew that Eugene was my brother.

The references to food in this growing-up novel, *Newfound*, are by no means exhaustive. In addition to those fruits and vegetables mentioned, our gardens also produced pumpkins, squash, turnips, parsnips, radishes, okra, cucumbers, asparagus, peppers (sweet and hot), and in addition to ordinary tomatoes, the small cherry tomatoes we called tommytoes. I mentioned corn in the novel, but not the golden ears of young garden corn, or sweet corn, which, boiled and served and eaten with butter and salt, are of course roasting ears, which we pronounced something like "roasenears." And with respect to wild things, in addition to picking blackberries, cresses, and chinquapins, we gathered hickory nuts, wild grapes (called fox grapes), and poke (for poke sallet, as my grandmother called it). In the spring, for the stout of heart, there were ramps, something like wild onions but with a more powerful, garlic-like odor. My grandfather taught me to eat ramps chopped up in scrambled eggs.

We also ate wild game: rabbits caught in deadfalls or rabbit "gums" (called Hoover boxes in the depression) or shot on rabbit hunts; squirrels, partridges, and mountain grouse, which we called pheasants, though they were not the ring-necked variety. Occasionally we had venison and bear, and some folks ate possums and coons. From the French Broad River we had black bass catfish, and from North and South Turkey and Big and Little Sandy Mush Creeks, suckers, which we caught not with hook and line but by "grabbling," which was done by wading the creeks and feeling back under banks and catching the fish with our hands. (I recollect that when my grandmother would remove one or two tender, young potatoes from beneath each potato plant in the garden row, digging them out with a clawlike utensil, then pushing the dirt back, leaving the other potatoes to grow to maturity, she also called this "grabbling" potatoes.) Grabbling in the creeks was usually a communal activity: a dozen or more men and older boys would wade upstream, tossing their catch up onto the bank to younger boys who carried wet burlap sacks to hold the fish. In early spring white suckers ran up the creeks in schools, much like salmon, and were so numerous that it was not unusual for a group of men and boys to catch dozens of them within a few hours. These fish, averaging a foot long, were cleaned and served up at fish fries, usually conducted by the fishermen themselves. These fish fries were often outdoor affairs where the whiskey was an obligatory accompaniment.

The only domestic animals slaughtered in *Newfound* are hogs. There is mention of hams, shoulders, and sausage in connection with the slaughter. But hog killing also provided us with a prepared food we called liver mush, which could be fried and served like pork sausage. And what remained after fat was "rendered" for lard were crisp bits not unlike pieces of pork rind, called "cracklins," which were added to a mixture of cornmeal, eggs, and milk (or buttermilk) to make "cracklin bread."

Though it is not mentioned in the novel, some people in the Newfound community slaughtered cattle. Typically, a farmer would slaughter a "beef," keep part of it for his family's needs, and give the rest to relatives and neighbors, or peddle the remainder, door-to-door. I know of no one in the southern Appalachian mountains, the setting of *Newfound*, who raised sheep. Consequently, no one ate mutton. But during World War II, when there was rationing of many foodstuffs, my father, the model for James Wells, the father in *Newfound*, raised goats (one of his many enterprises) and occasionally slaughtered one for our table—always after we children (and our mother, too, for that matter) had come to think of the goat as a pet.

Just like James Wells and Nora in *Newfound*, my father and mother were very different people, almost opposite in their views, tastes, and preferences. My mother was conservative and traditional, reluctant to try new things, new foods among them. (Her brother, home from World War II, where he served in Italy as an army cook, introduced her with some difficulty to Worcestershire sauce.) She did not approve of goats as a source of food for the table—because no one else she knew ate goats! She held a number of superstitious beliefs about foods and combinations of foods, her authority for these beliefs based vaguely on some Old Testament food law, or a confused, handed-down version of one of those restrictions. For example, she believed eating fish and drinking sweet milk at the same meal could prove fatal. My father delighted in demonstrating to her, by eating fried fish, drinking milk, and suffering no ill consequences, that her notion was just foolish. But she held firm to her belief in the face of the evidence. (My mother had also learned from her mother to refer to milk that had spoiled as "blinked." The term is said to derive from the belief that a mischievous supernatural creature from the realm of fairies, gnomes, and leprechauns could spoil milk by giving it a version of the "evil eye.")

My father was always affronting my mother with some new food he'd bring unexpectedly from Asheville—usually some variety of seafood. He brought home the first oysters we ever ate, the first shrimp, clams, and lobster. My mother would shrink back from such exotica, professing she wouldn't touch them. Besides, she didn't have the slightest idea how to prepare them. No matter. My father would swing into action and become chef, frying up oysters or shrimp or whatever with supreme confidence and great exuberance—and making a huge mess in the kitchen.

I have naturally inherited the foodways of my parents and grandparents, of the community in which I grew up. My tastes, attitudes, and preferences with regard to food are in some ways like my mother's, conservative and traditional. I like green beans heavily seasoned in the old-fashioned country manner and surely overcooked, like the roasts. Like my mother, I don't automatically gravitate to every trendy thing that comes down the pike. Like her, I am perfectly happy even without a Crock-Pot, a wok, or a microwave oven. (A wok, though, has much to recommend it!)

But I am also my father's son and not afraid to try something different. And my grandfather's grandson. I can whip up a passable scrambled eggs and ramps. I love every sort of seafood, but prefer fried to baked, broiled, or boiled. This is a regional preference, not just a family heritage. Early travelers in southern Appalachia remarked on the tendency of the people to fry everything. David Hackett Fischer, in his book *Albion's Seed*, says Southern highland cooking reflects its north British origins. Foodways in the Southern highlands, according to Fischer, are to some degree a product of frontier traditions, but "mainly they are an expression of the folk customs that had been carried from the borders of north Britain. Strong continuities appeared in favored foodstuffs, in methods of cooking and also in the manner of eating." The presence or absence in the

Southern highlands of certain foods and foodways is explained, Fischer maintains, by the blend of frontier conditions and cultural continuity with north Britain. In some respects, Southern highland foodways necessarily departed from the customs of north Britain. Oats yielded to maize, which was pounded into cornmeal and cooked by boiling. But this was merely a change from oatmeal mush to cornmeal mush, or "grits" as it was called in the Southern highlands. The ingredients changed, but the texture of the dish remained the same.

Another change occurred in the consumption of meat. The people of north Britain had rarely eaten pork at home. Pigs' flesh was as loathsome to the borderers as it had been to the children of Abraham and Allah. But that taboo did not survive in the New World, where sheep were difficult to maintain and swine multiplied even more rapidly than the humans who fed on them. Pork rapidly replaced mutton on backcountry tables, but it continued to be boiled and fried in traditional border ways.

New American vegetables also appeared on backcountry tables. Most families kept a "truck-patch," in which they raised squashes, cushaws (a relative of squash), pumpkins, gourds, beans, and sweet roasting ears of Indian corn. Many families also raised "sallet" greens, cress, poke, and bear's lettuce. Here again, the ingredients were new, but the consumption of "sallet" and "greens" was much the same as in the old country.

Everything Fischer describes comports well with the foodways of my Southern highland community, which I call Newfound. His mention of the change from the oatmeal mush of north Britain to the cornmeal mush of the New World reminds me that Big and Little Sandy Mush Creeks in my community were so named because settlers, taking water from the creek to prepare a meal, got sand in their cornmeal mush.

I may be typical of my time and place in that I learned my few culinary skills not from my mother, or grandmother, but from my father and grandfather and from hunting and fishing cronies. Like wilted (or "killed") cabbage and sausage. This dish, like the few other things I can prepare, is surely not something you'd invite people to, but it suits my taste, and the taste of people who would be present when I prepare it. The same goes for fried fish and hush puppies, which can be as tasty as hot dogs at a picnic or baseball game.

The way I learned to prepare fish (certainly nothing out of the ordinary) I learned creekside, or camped by the French Broad River, where we caught catfish on trotlines. You need a brown paper bag, some cornmeal, milk, eggs, cooking oil, and a frying pan. Dredge filets of fish through a bowl of milk into which you have beaten a couple of eggs. Toss a couple of cups of cornmeal into the paper bag, and on top of the meal place three or four filets. Shake the filets inside the bag until they are covered with cornmeal. Then place them in a frying pan in which you have already heated the oil. (You can heat the frying pan over a camp stove, small woodfire between two rocks, over charcoal—whatever.) When you have fried all the filets, mix the cornmeal you have dusted them with into the bowl of milk-and-egg mixture. Make hush puppies out of this mixture, adding chopped peppers, onions, anything you think would be good or that is available. If the cooking oil is deep enough, make the hush puppies round; if not, then flat.

This kind of food and its preparation will strike many people as laughably crude and primitive, which reminds me that an important ingredient in this food, its preparation and consumption, is an attitude—a combination of my father's confidence (despite experience or skill!) and willingness to improvise. A part of this attitude, too, is the notion that you eat the food because it is good, not because it is good for you. Food is not medicine, a class marker, or a badge of discrimination (though food may be all these things to some people). I certainly no longer feel apologetic about or ashamed of any food, as Robert does in *Newfound* when his little brother recites what he ate for breakfast. I do not assume, as Robert did, that the humble fare carried from home to school was automatically inferior to "store-bought" foods or food served in the school cafeteria. And I notice that in recent years such simple fare—ham, sausage, and steak biscuits, sometimes served with milk gravy—has become popular in fast-food franchises. At the same time we are surrounded by food fads that I can only understand as the result of some mass hysteria. I am reminded of Jack Sharkey's reworking of the nursery rhyme: "Jack Sprat could eat no fat, / His wife could eat no lean. A real pair of neurotics." Food should not be a religion, either, though it may be the culmination of a ritual, such as a hunting or fishing trip. A part of my mostly inherited attitude toward food is also qualified agreement with the notion that you are what you eat: no, you're not exactly what you eat, but still there is a resemblance. And not just what you eat, but how you eat, and even how you cook tells a lot about you.

Plenty

MICHAEL MCFEE

The battered pickup's bed
is a cornucopia
overflowing with sweet potatoes,
long tapered tubers
irregular and glorious as clouds
backlit by an orange sunset,
headed for roadside stand or market
or maybe back to Europe
where Spanish explorers, just home
from the New World, introduced them
half a millennium ago
as *batatas*, possessed (they insisted)
of aphrodisiacal powers,
which later inspired son-hungry Henry VIII
to import huge quantities
and gorge himself on sweet potatoes
baked into pie after pie
the way my father's mother cooked them,
with light brown sugar
and cinnamon and nutmeg and cloves,
those spices teasing the warmth
out of the smooth meat
that had banked its glowing coal
underground all summer long,
waiting to feed the family
and every famished ancestor
with elemental sweetness,
filling our mouths
with temporary plenty
bite after bite.

On the Appalachian Trail

. . . .

MATT LEE & TED LEE

Eighty-four-year-old Hazel Miracle sat in her armchair, chatting with us as she expertly cored, peeled, and quartered enough Black Ben Davis apples to fill a five-gallon bucket. "They aren't much to look at," she said in her deep eastern Kentucky drawl, and she was right; they were as tiny as golf balls, with olive-green skin darkened by powdery black patches. But when she offered us a handful of last year's harvest, the leathery chunks were the richest apples we had ever tasted—tart, sweet, and bursting with concentrated flavor. Once the bucket was full of apples, she would dehydrate them, and they would supply the filling for a year's worth of the dried-apple pies she had been turning out for most of her life. (This was her last batch, it turned out; she died a few months later.)

Let those dried Black Ben Davises stand as a warning to anyone who would write off this lean, mountainous corner of eastern Kentucky. Everything Hazel Miracle grew on her fourteen acres near the Cumberland Gap National Forest found its way into her kitchen or into the workshop of her son James, who chisels bowls from yellow poplars and sycamores felled just a few yards from his workbench. Wildflower honey flows from a hive behind the house, and a plot between apple trees is polka-dotted with teardrop tomatoes. In the Miracles' hands, such humble raw materials become objects of elegance and endurance.

We'd traveled from New York to Appalachian Kentucky against the advice of travelers who knew the place and assured us that this far eastern, mountainous end of the state, just over the western lines of Virginia and West Virginia, was strictly for backpackers. Mint-julep Kentucky, they said, with its immaculate, post-fenced Thoroughbred farms and its bluegrass, was more our speed. But we had a hunch, bred of years tasting great food in places where resources are slim and hard-won, that we might unearth a few culinary treasures here, and the possibility that they might be both unsung and served without fanfare only made the quest more alluring.

And there was a further quest: the elusive pawpaw. America's largest native fruit, the "custard apple" that had kept Lewis and Clark's ragged band from perishing and that every toddler learns occupies the patch "way down yonder," thrives in eastern Kentucky—but who's ever *seen* a pawpaw? Researching the eggplant-shaped fruit on the Internet before we left, we had turned up a lone photo. So we downloaded this mug shot and, after landing in Cincinnati, pasted it on the dashboard of the pickup truck we were renting. Then we set off, heading southeast on Route 8, the leafy, narrow road that traces the Ohio River through dusty gypsum mines and tobacco fields.

At our first stop, in Maysville, just forty miles downriver from Cincinnati, Judy Dixon gave us a taste of the shortbread-crusted "transparent pie" she's been making from scratch at Magee's bakery every morning since the 1950s, and we knew we were on the right track. She calls the pie transparent because compared to its close cousin the chess pie, it nearly is. The pie has so little yolk in it (and no corn syrup) that it appears just slightly cloudy, opalescent gray buttery gel with perfect sweetness. Dixon volunteered that her pies are "made of everything that's good for you—butter, sugar, eggs, milk," but when our praise began she'd have none of it and abruptly changed the subject: Had we seen Maysville's flood wall? On our way out of town, we noted the impressive three-story cement bulwark that keeps the town's tidy brick row houses dry when the Ohio floods its banks. Dixon's buttery 35-cent mini transparent pies seemed to us the greater achievement.

The road curved south with the state line, and we followed Highway 23 into the fog-shrouded mountains of the central Appalachian coalfields. Dubbed the Country Music Highway for all the big-time honky-tonk stars who grew up along its path (and some small-time ones, too, if the shiny vintage tour bus belonging to the Hayes Family Singers was any indication), to us the road seemed less a testament to the hard-luck days and lonesome nights of country ballads than to the mastery of that unyielding mountain range. Where turn-of-the-century travelers had had to clamber over Peach Orchard Mountain to get from Paintsville to Pikeville, we were speeding *through* it at 75 miles per hour, on a superhighway at the bottom of a manmade canyon whose rock walls were streaked with glossy veins of coal. These mountains have been fully wired, and when the indigo haze that shrouds their summits fades into the night sky, the lights of shopping-mall parking lots set the hills ablaze, a ghostly orange.

But take a few strategic turns and you can find yourself in a tangle of red-clay roads with only wild hare and penned hogs for company, or surrounded by the steel chutes and boreholes of a long-defunct mining operation graced with a daisy-strewn memorial to dead coal miners. The next afternoon as we drove along Route 160 (the Kingdom Come Parkway)—a steep, sinewy blacktop whose shoulders shimmer with purple, yellow, and orange wildflowers—to the top of Black Mountain, we didn't encounter a soul.

The following morning, on a tip from a friend, we set out for Whitesburg, a snug mountain hamlet twenty-five miles back up Route 119 that gives the impression of being held aloft by clouds. Our goal was Ramey's Diner, a quiet, dimly lit place that's been around since anyone in town can remember (though the posters of NASCAR racers speeding across the walls were strictly up to date). Aggie Hatton, the bun on the top of her head barely visible through the pass-thru window from the kitchen, has spent the last fifteen of her seventy-odd years in the kitchen at Ramey's, serving up authentic mountain cuisine and shrugging off the townfolks' raves. Her skillet-fried chicken and her wilted greens with spring onions have made Ramey's the de facto company cafeteria for another Whitesburg institution, Appalshop, an arts center that since 1969 has been sending reporters, filmmakers, and other volunteers into the mountains to document craftspeople and storytellers, to record dulcimer jam sessions, and to teach cutting-edge media technology to Kentucky teenagers.

When we arrived at Ramey's for lunch (the Monday special: soup beans and salmon cakes), the Appalshop gang was crumbling warm skillet-baked cornbread and diced raw onion into bowls of pinto beans that had been slow-cooked with a hunk of country ham—a mountain ritual older than radio.

Distances on a map are deceiving in this craggy terrain. What looks like a short jaunt on paper can easily meander into a whole afternoon of climbing, twisting, descending, and climbing again. As we pressed on toward Corbin, we kept our eyes peeled for the great white pawpaw among the lush roadside foliage, but all we saw was plenty of pokeweed, a tasty treat in the early spring but a powerful emetic in the late summer once it puts out seeds.

We had to stop in Corbin to visit Harland Sanders Café and Museum, a.k.a. the world's first Kentucky Fried Chicken, built in the 1930s. Though the motor court's long been demolished, there's a Colonel Sanders museum of sorts in the café, whose kitchen and dining room have been lovingly preserved. Adjoining the café is a spanking-new KFC franchise with some of the Colonel's original recipe cards on display not far from the cash register. His scalloped tomatoes, chess pie, and buckwheat cakes seemed far more ambitious, appetizing even, than the Triple Crunch Zinger sandwiches we got.

Just south of Berea, on I-75, we tuned in to a country station and heard Don Williams croon, "I don't care for superstars, organic foods, or foreign cars. . . ." A great lyric, maybe, but not an accurate expression of the mountain attitude—the people here care deeply about their vegetables and hold fast to their preferences. At the Lexington farmer's market, we eavesdropped on a man bagging handfuls of "greasy" beans (so called for their waxy appearance), who was musing, "You can't beat these long greasies for flavor." A woman hefting tomatoes shot back: "I've always been a half-runner girl myself."

Eastern Kentucky's bean pride has made it command central for the effort to preserve native bean varieties. Bill Best, a Berea farmer who, with his son Michael, founded a seed bank to preserve heirloom beans (they share them with other enthusiasts and sell them at the Lexington market), estimates there are more than a thousand varieties growing in the region. Since bean plants mutate more readily than other vegetables, many of the beans they collect are so distinctive in color, flavor, and texture that they're named for the family who grew them.

After we'd talked for a while, Best invited us out to his farm. The sun was low in the sky when we rolled onto his slim twelve-acre plot, which is tucked into the side of a small mountain. He ushered us down the bean rows at a rapid clip, stopping every few yards to show off features of the eighty varieties he grows. Some pods were longer than a pencil, others quite short; some appeared swollen and others gaunt, revealing the contours of the seeds within. Best split open bean pods with his thumb to reveal further differences—a purple-spotted hull here, a "speckled" bean there, or the squarish ends of a "cut-short" variety.

"I grew up on a hardscrabble, subsistence farm, and we didn't have much," he told us as we walked between trellises of head-high heirloom beans. "But back then I always thought we ate the best food available. Now I *know* we did." We didn't have to imagine what he meant for long since he invited us to a summer supper with his wife, Irmgaard, and their two granddaughters.

Back at the house, the two girls bounced around the room while we helped ourselves to roasted new potatoes dug up that afternoon, a pot of beans so fresh they had a green-pea-like sparkle, and onion-garnished tomato slices as big as pancakes, with flavors as intense and vibrant as their colors—from the persimmon orange of a Carolina Gold to the burgundy shot through with blood red of a Cherokee Purple.

When we marveled over the crowds we'd seen at Best's stand in Lexington, he chuckled and said, "Beans won't get you a whole lot at market. What they will get you is a reputation for being eccentric." It turns out he has a second full-time job, as a professor of English at Berea College. After the meal, he walked us back to our truck and spied our pawpaw photo on the dashboard. He didn't know of any trees nearby, but he gave us directions to a pawpaw orchard just an hour up the highway, in Frankfort.

If bean lovers were eccentrics, what would pawpaw people be like? "Fanatics!" according to the stout, bespectacled Dr. Kirk Pomper, who, as director of Kentucky State University's Atwood Research Facility, the only pawpaw experiment station in the country, has about him something of the air of the nutty professor. We'd put some distance between us and the mountains on our drive northwest to Frankfort and were now strolling through hilly, impossibly gorgeous farmland, toward a neat grid of 1,700 pawpaw trees of varying sizes, their branches heavy with fruit.

A pawpaw's greenish-white skin covers yellow flesh as soft and as dense as an avocado's. Under a blazing sun, we picked fist-sized fruits, sliced off their tops, and sampled. Pawpaws are exotic and delicious—as rich and creamy as custard, which is why they're also known as custard apples. Some tasted like mango crossed with apple, others like banana crossed with strawberry; their flavor, it seems, varies according to small degrees of ripeness. Slightly overripe ones had a richly caramelized, Madeira-like note that we loved.

Pomper's ambition is to create a new agricultural industry for the Appalachians. But the fruit presents some serious obstacles: Pawpaws ripen very quickly; the harvest lasts only a few days; and once the fruit is picked, it bruises easily. When we asked Pomper how long the pawpaws we were taking with us would last in the air-conditioned cab of our truck, he looked at his watch. We got the picture.

We had higher hopes for the seeds they would yield, and once we'd returned home we planted a few in our garden plot. If all goes as planned, in about eight years we'll have our own fruit-bearing trees. Until then, we'll just look forward to frequent trips back into the mountains.

Homesick

DIANE GILLIAM FISHER

What is the thing inside
that follows the earthy smell of morning
out into the day, carries me down the road
in my car to the fabric store, to hover
over remnant tables, finger folds
of blue and green calico—little Dutch
girls and shamrocks, linger over cards
of brightly colored bias tape and silvery
snaps? The thing inside that pulls
me further down the road to wander
through nurseries, yearning
for yardfuls of lilac and peony bushes,
tugs me toward antique stores,
something about a pitcher, clear
glass, and milk so cold it hurts?
The thing inside brings me home,
knows what it is
I am trying to remember.

At home, my girls are needful, weary,
too much wear and tear
in their days. I spoon mellow,
peppery chicken pie into creamy dishes set
on October-blue mats, watch them lift the crust
with their forks to see what's inside, suspecting
vegetables in there with the chicken. "You know
what my mamaw used to say
to me?" I tell them, "Eat every carrot
and pea on your plate."

I tell them about a salt-and-pepper
woman, round faced like me,
in a hairnet and blue cotton duster,
her yard full of cousins, hiding
in flowering bushes
and twilight from parents
already in their cars.

Oh I yearn to live
for the things I love, for the thing I put
inside the food and girls
who eat, for the road
and the thing inside the road that follows
after me and calls me back, to the pitcher
Mamaw trusted me to lift from the refrigerator
and pour, not because I was big enough,
but because I was
so in love with the pitcher
and with her.

The Dollmaker

HARRIETTE SIMPSON ARNOW

Editor's note: If we are what we eat, who do we become when life takes us away from our gardens, our families, and the mountains that have sustained us? Harriette Simpson Arnow's Gertie Nevels confronts the question in this excerpt from Arnow's classic novel set in the hillbilly diaspora of World War II Detroit.

Four mornings gone now, and this, the fifth. As usual, the alarm had gone off at six o'clock so that Clovis could be at work by seven. Six o'clock, she understood now, was four back home; too early for getting up in winter. Clovis, never eating enough at breakfast, seemed like, to keep a working man alive, went away in the dark with a bottle of coffee, sandwiches, a piece of pie, and beans in his lunch box. Six-thirty to seven-thirty was pure dark still, like the middle of the night. It was a lonesome in-between time when her hands remembered the warm feel of a cow's teats or the hardness of a churn handle, or better beyond all things, the early-morning trip in starlight, moonlight, rain or snow, to the spring—the taste of spring water, the smell of good air, clean air, earth under her feet. Her feet remembered the soft earth when they took the few steps over the ice and cement for a bucket of coal. She never lingered searching for the stars. Unless it were quite windy, there were no stars, and even in winds so bitter they brought tears, the alley smelled still of smoke and fumes.

Two mornings now, after searching for some quiet work that would not waken the children, sleeping so close behind the flimsy walls, she had sat in the kitchen whittling on a piece of scrap wood Clovis had bought for kindling. This, like the borrowed kindling, was a maple, harder and finer-grained than any she had known. It came in curious little chunks and squares that Clovis had said was scrap from that kind of war plant.

One little piece had seemed familiar in all strangeness, and she had begun whittling on it. Slowly and aimlessly at first, she had worked, not able to forget the knife, herself, everything except the thing growing out of the wood, as she had used to be in stray moments of time back home.

The hard white light overhead hurt her eyes and made a shadow on her work. The night sounds of Detroit came between her and the thing in the wood, but worse than any noise, even the quivering of the house after a train had passed, were the spaces of silence when all sounds were shut away by the double windows and the cardboard walls, and she heard the ticking of the clock, louder it seemed than any clock could ever be. She had never lived with a clock since leaving her mother's house, and even there the cuckoo clock had seemed more ornament than a god measuring time; for in her mother's house, as in her own, time had been shaped by the needs of the land and the animals swinging through the season. She would sit, the knife forgotten in her hands, and listen to the seconds ticking by, and the clock would become the voice of the thing that had jerked Henley from the land, put Clovis in Detroit, and now pushed her through days where all her work, her meals, and her sleep were bossed by the ticking voice.

Now, between strokes of the knife, she would glance at the clock to make certain that it was not time to waken the children; and the thing in the wood would seem wood only, and not her big-behinded hen that had eaten corn from her lap. But little by little, the hen mastered the clock, and by Friday morning was there waiting in the wood for the knife to free her, a good hen, ready to lay many eggs.

Gertie was working on a feather of the up-curving tail when a passing train brought back the world of the clock. She glanced at it, then sprang up, and hurried to awaken the children.

Cassie, though the many strange sounds at night often caused her to cry out with fright, awakened of mornings more slowly than the others. Twice, in her half-sleep, she had run to the door in her nightgown, crying she had to go outdoors; then, awakening quickly to Enoch's jeering laughter, she had gone silent and ashamed to the bathroom. Quiet, forever quiet, was Cassie. She showed no sign of loving school and feeling at home there as did Clytie and Enoch, or of half hating it like Reuben. More lost and lonesome than afraid, she always seemed like a child away from home.

This morning's breakfast was like her others in Detroit. Meekly she sat and put bites of egg and biscuit into her mouth, chewed, swallowed, then took a sip of milk, gagged, set the glass down hastily; then came the trembling, guilty whimper: "I'm full, Mom. I cain't eat no more."

"Aw, Cassie," Gertie began, and stopped. Scolding her for taking food on her plate and not eating it was no good. She'd have to find something the child would eat. She looked at the half-eaten egg, flat-yolked, gray, rubbery, and white, the biscuit burned on the bottom, too pale on the top, smeared with margarine instead of butter. She wasn't any good at coloring the stuff, but butter cost so. None of them ate the way they had back home. Enoch was gone from the table, his egg unfinished. But he could snack off and on all morning, for Enoch, like the other third graders, went only half a day, his shift in the afternoon.

Gertie remembered the clock, looked, and quickly started the job of getting them off to school. Cassie, as always, was tangled up in her snow pants. Clytie was complaining that she could find no clean handkerchiefs. Enoch was reminding her that it was the day for Cassie's milk money. This made Clytie recollect that soon the mother's club would have their Christmas bake sale, and couldn't her mother come and bring something for the sale; and wasn't there anything she could take for the Christmas basket drive; and how much money could they have for TB seals? Couldn't they each have at least a dime?

Gertie took change from the high shelf. She gave milk money, TB money, a can of pork and beans to Clytie, a can of tomatoes to Reuben for the food drive. Each child kissed her with a quick dabbing as it went out the door, hurriedly, for in the alley children were passing. Mike Turbovitch was begging Enoch to come play on the hockey pond, and behind him a girl in a bright red coat was calling Clytie. Even Cassie ran down the steps. Cassie had never told her, but Clytie had said that in the kindergarten room, right up on the wall where everybody could look at it, was a big picture Cassie had painted—a green hill with a black tree.

Gertie closed both doors on Reuben, the last as always. She looked down at her hand. One nickel was left over the 15 cents for Enoch this afternoon. Last night at the big store there'd been all that silver left. She had watched the machine and thought a twenty-dollar bill would do it. Then the girl had punched on the 60-cent tax, and Clovis had reached in his pocket again, brought out a one, and paid it all without a word.

She had been silent, shaking her head in weariness and wonder, as they drove homeward through the ugly, dimly lighted streets. "I wouldn't mind so much," she had complained at last, "if'n all that money ud buy a egg that was real fresh er some good fresh meal."

"Aw, Gert," Clovis had said, "they's millions an millions a people never tastes nothen but what they get outa stores. They've never tasted real good cornbread with butter an fresh eggs, so's they don't mind eggs that ain't never fresh, an store-bought bread with oleo. If'n," he had gone on, half teasing, "spenden a nickel's goen to be like losen a drop a blood fer you, why you'll be bled dry in no time atall."

She remembered now, looking down at the nickel, that she had forgotten potatoes. The buying of potatoes was a part of the never-ending strangeness. Back home no matter what the season, she had always raised enough to carry her from one potato-digging time to the next. Now she would either have to go to one of the small stores near the project, where, Clytie had said, there were strange-talking clerks that a body couldn't understand at all, or buy from the man she had seen in the alley, selling stuff from a truck. He was maybe cheaper.

It was almost school letting out time in the afternoon before she heard the calling like a crying in the alley, and remembered with a sigh that she needed onions and cabbage as well as potatoes. She waited in the snowy alley, standing somewhat apart from the other women, many with babies in their arms, and all seemed like with young children who came crowding round the truck crying: "Mom, I wanta apple. Gimme grapes, Mom, gimme. Buy um, Mom, buy oranges."

"Buy, um, Mom. Buy um." Amos, loud and brash almost as the Dalys, was yelling for some great greenish-blue grapes, the like of which she had never seen. So much foolishness. Youngens didn't need grapes in December, or did they? Shoestrings or bubble gum? She stared at the grapes, conscious of the quick, mildly interested glances of some of the women, more conscious that most noticed her not at all. All were buying, crowding round the truck, and she felt foolish and stingy hanging back with Amos pulling at her coat, begging, "Git grapes, Mom, please."

She felt more stingy still when a little redheaded Daly came, grapes spilling from his cupped-up hands, holding the grape-heaped hands in front of Amos, commanding: "Yu want grapes? Here."

Amos helped himself if they had been free from his grandmother's vines. Money enough to buy her youngens a mess of grapes would buy a vine. . . .

"Some a th potatoes," Gertie said into Joe's asking eyes. "About a peck."

She bought, or tried to buy, the things she might have had this time of year at home—cabbage, onions, and a few apples. She only looked longingly at the sweet potatoes. At two pounds for 25 cents, a mess of baked sweet potatoes would cost almost a dollar. Back home she'd sold near twenty bushels for 50 cents a bushel. She wished the molasses, somewhere on the way like the block of wood, would come. It seemed a year since she had seen the wood.

Mrs. Anderson hurried toward the through street after suddenly remembering that she had not seen her young son George for the past five minutes. Gertie realized the others were all gone. Joe had shut the doors in the back of his truck, and was now looking under it for stray children and dogs. Still Gertie lingered, the heaped Josiah basket on her arm. She stepped up to the dark surly man just as he was getting into the cab. "They's something I want to ask you."

"Cigarettes all gone," he said with a swift impatient glance at her, his hand on the door handle.

She shook her head. "I mean—I wondered—I jist got here. Did it take you long to—well, to kinda learn to like it, this country. I figger it's so diff'ernt frum mine—it must ha been worse fer you."

He had listened, his thick black brows drawn somewhat together with his efforts to understand. At last he smiled, shrugged one shoulder. "I did not come to like."

Cooked Food

ROBERTA BONDI

When Benjamin was five, he looked down at his plate one morning at breakfast. Then he looked up at me and asked, "Mama, when you were a little girl, did they have cooked food?" "Are you kidding?" I answered, sympathetically, knocked breathless by the question. Who did he think his mama was? How many aeons of life does he think mine has spanned?

When my own mama, in Louisville, Kentucky, moved from her big house on Willow Avenue into her tiny two-bedroom condo on Village Drive, my two aunts came to help. My mother's sisters, Kas and Suzie, had awakened early to leave their farms outside Sturgis in Union County. They arrived after their four-hour trip shortly after I'd gotten up. It was late in the move, and most of the work of dismantling my mother's household and reassembling it in a very small space was already done.

Immediately, they started in on wrapping the jelly glasses in newspaper. I tried to stay quiet and absorb caffeine as quickly as I could. I knew I was in for it when they started to talk about how hard life used to be, and how my great-aunt Becky, who was eighty at the time, still works, and how people just don't work like they used to. Of course, they were right on all points.

Life on a farm is no picnic right now, but it is nothing like my memories of visiting my grandmother when I was a city child. Until I was eleven I grew up in Bayside, New York, within striking distance of my other grandparents, who lived in Manhattan. Our home in Queens was a small complex called "garden apartments." To go from playing in the yard with a flock of assorted children in New York to a farm in western Kentucky for three weeks each summer was to enter a world that was at the same time intensely boring and amazingly terrifying.

My grandparents' house was old, built around the time of the Civil War. It was one fairly dilapidated story, white frame, with four huge, high-ceilinged, long-windowed rooms and two little rooms. The fixed rooms were the living room on the front and the kitchen on the back. The other two shifted in use. Sometimes the dining room would be on the front of the house next to the living

85

room, while my grandparents' room connected the kitchen and the living room. Sometimes it was the dining room that lay between the front and the back. My uncle Quentin and my aunt Suzie were not married yet. The two small rooms were theirs.

The central focus of the house, however, was the kitchen, and this is where I remember most of the household work being done. It had three windows. Two of them on the side almost overlooked a neighbor's house, which was partially hidden by a rickety and overgrown trellis covered with sweet peas. Through the window on the back, over the sink, you could see my grandmother's grapes, also overgrown, a barbed wire fence against which blackberry bushes grew, the smokehouse (if you stood on tiptoe and strained to look to the right), and the chicken yard, containing the terrible outhouse beyond it. Straight out the window were open fields, and at a great distance beyond the fields lay the low ridge of Dyer Hills that enclosed the landscape.

My grandmother, indeed, did work hard in that kitchen. There was an enormous black coal stove she cooked on, with its kettles and skillets and dented-up enameled pan. When she opened that stove, the red light of the fire looked like hell itself and scared me twice as badly. Under the back window was a sink with a hand pump for cold well water at its edge. I still remember the metallic taste of that water that was too cold to wash in. A great square table with a tablecloth that always seemed mostly worn out stood in the middle. Off to one side of the kitchen was a cold room for storing canned and preserved foods, and in the floor of that room, a cold cellar you got to by lifting a trapdoor in the floor and descending into the earth.

This wasn't the farm my mother had grown up on. My grandparents had lost that one in the Depression. That former farm, however, was close enough to the farm of my childhood to make me wonder. How did my grandmother rear six children and feed all the farm workers? Nothing anybody ate ever seemed to come easily or cleanly out of that kitchen.

Every meal was a hot meal, including biscuits or rolls or cornbread. I remember taking turns with my little brother Freddie churning sour butter that I couldn't eat in a tall tapered wooden churn from unpasteurized milk. My grandmother made wonderful fruit pies, but the apple pies were made of tiny wormy apples she had us pick up off the ground behind the house in the long wet grass where the dog played and the chickens ran. The peach pies had an unspeakable origin: the half-rotten freckled peaches had fallen from their trees into the dusty, bare dirt right inside the gate to the chicken yard. Her fried chicken was heaven, but I think I was nearly forty before the memory of the smell of boiling water poured over chicken feathers and the feel of those feathers coming off in my hands began to fade. Vegetables grown in the garden, eggs from the henhouse, canning and preserving, the smoking of hams and the making of sausage all boggle my mind and memory.

Though they most certainly took place, I don't remember large family gatherings of cousins, aunts and uncles, and great-aunts and uncles before the big kitchen was redone as another bedroom and one of the small rooms was turned into a modern kitchen. The new kitchen was very long and narrow, and even when it was brand-new I remember it as dingy and rickety, an old woman's kitchen—though my grandmother wasn't old when it was added—without the solidity and significance of the old kitchen. Nevertheless, it had hot and cold water with a real sink, a refrigerator, a gas stove, a washing machine, and a chrome and formica dinette set with the table still covered by a worn-out table-cloth. I remember very well the family dinners that came out of the new kitchen when we visited in the summers as I grew older.

These dinners were complex affairs. Orchestrated by my aunts and my mother, they took place on Sundays after church. The assembled family included not only Panny and Papa Charles, my grandparents, my aunts and uncles, and my first cousins. They usually also included at least a great-aunt or two and occasionally some second cousins as well.

These gatherings occurred in three movements. The first movement, of moderately quick tempo, was in three parts. Providing one part, the menfolk sat on the wide front porch staring toward the road and talking about the crops and other uninteresting subjects. The next was played by the children, who were almost all male. In the backyard, the side yard, and the front yard the little ones ran around and whined, while the older ones teased each other, scuffled, and tussled. The third and central part came out of my grandmother's kitchen, and the players were my mother, my aunts, and my grandmother, with an occasional female first cousin to set the table, pour the iced tea, and so forth.

The second movement was much slower and was in two parts. All the men and the younger children performed first, coming in off the porch to eat by themselves without the women. Men at one end, children at the other, they would assemble in the darkened dining room at the long white dining room table, while the overhead fan would stir the hot summer air.

Sometimes the meal would be pot roast, new potatoes, and beans boiled forever with a piece of salt pork. Sometimes it would be ham or the infamous fried chicken and fried corn. Never were we without tomatoes from the garden, slaw, and little onions, and usually a white cake with caramel icing, falling apart in the middle with the icing running into the crack, and a fruit pie or two. Even the children drank gallons of the sweetened iced tea, which was served in big stemmed glasses with little dents in the sides. But most of all, there were wonderful rolls or biscuits, which would be provided by hovering aunts who kept them coming steadily, always hot, always crisp on the outside and soft on the inside. Only after the men and children had eaten and the table was cleared did the women gather together their own meal and go to the dining room for the "second sitting."

For the women, the major portion of the much more rapid third movement was again the kitchen and cleanup. Unlike the time before dinner, when conversation was fairly well restricted to discussion of food and gossip about the present, during cleanup time my good-natured, joking aunts, great-aunts, and grandmother would tell stories of their own aunts, great-aunts, grandmothers, cousins, and great-grandmothers. All the while, the men smoked smelly cigars on the porch, continuing to talk about crops, deals, and the weather, and the children played and napped around the house and yard.

How to understand these dinners from this distance? One key is in the breads. I'm not sure how old I was when I began to realize the special importance that hot homemade breads held for me as a female family member. How I came to know that everything a woman is or is not is wrapped up in her rolls and biscuits. I know I learned late about chicken. I remember as a fourteen-year-old being mortified at my own gaping lack of womanly abilities when I heard my aunt Suzie exile a neighbor from the entire race of women by saying of her, "She's a good woman, but she can't pluck a chicken!" But there never seems to have been a time when I didn't know that, whatever else my grandmother, my mother, my aunts, and my great-aunts were able to do, their power, their honor, and their mysterious authority lay in their ability to make those perfect biscuits, like the women in the family before them, and bring them to the table throughout the meal, forever golden, full of buttermilk, and always hot.

I may not know how old I was when I began to understand the significance of biscuits for a real woman, but I do know that it is only recently that I have come to begin to understand the real power structure of my family, which was revealed in those Sunday dinners.

Although I was loved in New York City as a child, and although I was the daughter of Kentucky on my mother's side, the law of my father's Yankee family prevailed in our household. A dazzlingly intelligent and entertaining sophisticated Manhattanite, my father ruled our home with the same grace and power as any other absolute monarch. Obedience without argument or questioning was demanded and received from wife and children equally, and speeches detailing the moral, psychological, and physical weakness of women provided the justification for the law.

ROBERTA BONDI

Naturally, therefore, on my grandmother's farm all I could see were the men on the porch rocking while the women worked, men sitting to eat while the women stood up to wait on them. I was afraid of my big uncles. I knew they believed women should work while men played. Even on Sunday in their good clothes their hands were huge and rough and cracked, and the smell and feel of large animals, as well as of intricate and spiked farm equipment, enveloped them.

When I would come onto the porch, Uncle Bob Wesley and Uncle Bo especially would tease me. "You talk like an Eye-talian!" "Say 'Pie in the sky when I die!'" And most humiliating of all, "Well, well, little lady, you ain't nothing but a horse's titty!" I thought they despised me and wanted to make me cry. Uncle A. D., my aunt Kas's husband, was kinder and sweeter, and Uncle Bob, married to my aunt Suzie. was the quietest of all. I don't remember much from then of Quentin, my then college-aged uncle who is now a lawyer. I did not know how grindingly hard my farming uncles worked. I could not see that their relationships with my aunts, though I know now as an adult that the marriages in my family were remarkably happy, were based on a kind of equality and respect that was invisible to me.

The truth is, as I have been able to work it out over the intervening years, the position of the men in the family is somewhat ambiguous. I know now, as I did not then, that my family is an intricately structured matriarchy. Living as I had with only a mother, an authoritarian father, and younger brothers in New York, the patterns of the larger family had escaped me, and so I could not see the smaller ones within the larger family, either.

Yet even then, if I had been asked to diagram the Wynns and the Wesleys, I would have known that my great-grandmother Grammar, a Withers before she was married to Bob Wynn, was the center and source of power in the family. Only incidentally, it seemed to me as a child, was Pap married to my great-grandmother. When I thought about it, I knew that all Grammar's children lived on farms close by; that when her daughters married, her sons-in-law came to live with her daughters close to their mother; and that her son John Bundy didn't marry at all but continued to live with his mother. I knew that among my grandmother Roberta's children, the same was true. They all settled around their mother. Only the oldest, my own mother, had broken that pattern.

I knew, even as a child, that within the hierarchy of the family, one's status depended on whether one was male or female first and, only after, whether one was born into the family or had married into it. In the Wesley family, the aunts ranked first, followed by their husbands, then came the aunts-in-law, trailed by their husbands, the natural-born uncles. Among the cousins, the children of daughters were closer to the sources of power than the children of sons, and the daughters of daughters were both most favored and had the most expected of them.

Once when I was about ten, when it was the turn of the front room to be the dining room, I watched my mother ironing. I saw a little white piqué skirt on the ironing board. "Whose little tiny skirt is that?" I asked. Immediately, I received a shock. For the moment I asked the question I knew the answer. "Why it's yours, silly! Whose did you think it was?" "I knew that," I said pitifully. I had thought I was almost grown up.

When I see those childhood dinners now, I find the players in them have changed size and shape as radically as I changed myself when I saw the real nature of that white skirt on my grandmother's ironing board. From this distance the men in the family appear dull, living in a clumsy world of language made entirely of plodding ideas badly expressed. Although I was afraid of them, I saw even as a child that to them, being a man depended on showing no softness, accepting no ambiguity, rejecting men who enjoyed the company of women. They ate first with the children because they were like the children. They were too simple for the company of women, and their memories were too short. They did not carry in their bodies and their minds the skills, jokes, and history of the family.

Now I remember the plates of fried chicken with some of the best pieces saved back for the women. Though my mother was my father's weak woman at home, I recognize now how articulate, self-confident, and strong even my mother, as well as my aunts, were in that place. Their skills at sewing, quilting, gardening, laughing, and storytelling were enormous. Now I know how little and confused I felt about what I needed to be myself in the face of their competence. I had been raised to be obedient, but my aunts were not obedient, and neither was my mother in this place. They were in charge. My aunts and my great-aunts summoned me to take my place of authority as the eldest granddaughter in a matriarchy that went back as far as I could see; but how could I even let myself know it? If I took a place of competence, I would betray my father. If I did not take it, I would turn my back on my own strength. As it happened, I wanted my father too much. I chose the second option long ago, and only many years later did I begin seriously to undo that choice.

It is true that on me fall the expectations and responsibilities of the oldest daughter from all those generations of women whose memories I inherit. I suppose this is why sometimes I feel myself to be a failure in the family in some important respects. Though the biscuits I bake are as good as they come, and I can bake rolls from my great-grandmother's roll recipe that any woman in the family would be proud of, I don't live in Union County. I am not a matriarch. I feel myself to be a branch, still green but fallen off the family tree—the feeling Eve had, perhaps, as she made a life for herself and her family outside Eden. Though I hang on to the memories of my great-aunts' and grandmother's generation, I don't keep track of my cousins as I should. I'm a city woman. I can't can. I don't quilt. I certainly don't know how to work like my aunts and my mother.

Even in that far-off time, however, when I was twelve, I began to cast my lot with Kentucky women. I had a second cousin my own age named Sam. Sam was my great-aunt Blacky's son. He was mean and didn't like my Yankee mouth and cringing shyness. One day, out in the yard behind his house on the hill he grabbed my two pinky fingers, and he started bending, outward. "I'm gonna bend your fingers till you yell uncle," he taunted. I didn't say a word. "Say uncle!" he said. While I felt a fire in my joints, I gritted my teeth and said nothing. "Say uncle, say uncle!" he yelled, and he kept on bending. By the time he was finished, my fingers were bent so out of shape they never recovered. They hurt all through high school, and they are still misshapen.

After my aunts and Mama and I finished our morning packing to get her out of the big house and into the little condo, we had a lunch unthinkable from my childhood—fancy chicken salad, a green salad with an intricate dressing, and croissants. While we scraped the plates into the garbage disposal and put them into the new dishwasher, I mentioned my memories of Aunt Suzie's biscuits. "Oh, no," she laughed. "I never make biscuits anymore. They're not so good for you, you know. They have too much cholesterol, and we're all too fat, anyway."

Astounded, I mull over the meaning of what Aunt Suzie has said. Earlier, and inexplicably, she has told me how proud of me my aunts are because of the work I do. For years within my own family, I have felt embarrassed by my university work. I have avoided talking about it, as though it were a not very good substitute for the practice of the real skills of the women of the family. What does it mean that she doesn't make biscuits because they're not good for you? Has she just taken away from me the power of my womanhood, or has she set me free? Feeling a bit betrayed by the aunts I thought I had myself betrayed, I wonder over the mystery of time passing, and of cooked food.

Grandma's Table

STEVE YARBROUGH

At one time my grandmother was a legendary cook. She excelled at a kind of country cooking that you will no longer find much of in the Mississippi Delta, where I grew up. You will no longer find much of it because these days, more often than not, Deltans cook out of boxes. They make cakes the way everybody else does, from Duncan Hines containers, and they make their cornbread from prepackaged mixes. If they remain resistant to canned biscuits, they have come to terms with Bisquick. Frozen vegetables, they have learned, cook nicely in microwave ovens. So does bacon. Soup does, too.

But when I was growing up, in the late 1950s and early 1960s, country people made their cakes and breads and biscuits from scratch. They created their own sauces and gravies, seasoning them to taste, and the vegetables they ate came from their gardens. They made their own sausage. The chickens they fried had, until lately, been their neighbors.

Grandma scrambled eggs for me for breakfast, then she tore a couple of fluffy biscuits into bite-sized bits and mixed them in with the eggs. If I asked her to, she would fry me up three of four slices of bacon—and the bacon, by the way, had come from our hogs. Sometimes for a change she gave me biscuits with a jar of her homemade molasses. The molasses was dark brown, and it was so thick that when you stuck a spoon into it you had a hard time getting the spoon back out, almost as if it were trapped in a pool of quicksand.

Grandma was, at that time, an energetic, hardworking woman. Though blind in one eye from a childhood accident, she was the one who jumped in the pickup truck in the middle of the night to pull cotton trailers to the gin. When the farmhands chopped cotton in June and July, she was out in the field with them, leading the way. She worked her own garden, cleaned the house, and cooked, and for a few years, in the late 1950s, she took care of her bedridden mother.

If Grandma was troubled by the harshness of the life she'd known, she seldom let on. Yet she had raised my mother during the Great Depression, and I knew from my grandfather, who talked about such things, that the family had almost starved. The WPA saved them. He got a job helping to build the Yazoo County Courthouse. Between the small amount he made there and Grandma's ability to create meals out of vegetables and fatback, the family survived.

By the time I came along Grandma and Grandpa were living in a house on sixteenth-section land. They owned a television, an old car, and a truck. The house was equipped with running water. There was always plenty to eat— neighbors liked to joke that, at mealtime, the table sagged from all the good food Grandma laid on it. Considering where they had been, she and Grandpa must have felt like they had come a long way. I don't think it's an exaggeration to say that they were both fairly proud of themselves.

At least both of them were until Nick Miller came to stay at their place, at which time Grandma's feelings about food and family, house and hearth, underwent certain changes.

Nick Miller was from Texas. He was from Texarkana, Texas, but if you pointed out that the city of Texarkana was only half-Texan, he would puff himself up and tell you, "A little bit of Texas is still a hell of a lot." He pronounced the word Texas just like Ernest Tubb did. *Tex-Us.*

Nick had married my second cousin Lynn, who I always thought was the most beautiful girl I'd ever seen. I remember going down to Gulfport when I was two or three to watch her being crowned homecoming queen at her high school. She wore a long white gown that night, with sequins on it that sparkled under the stadium lights. Her blonde hair seemed to sparkle as well. On the way home that evening I told Grandma that I hoped to marry Lynn.

Naturally enough, I was pissed when I found out about Nick. She'd met him at a dance in Texarkana, where she had moved with her mother—my aunt Lena, who was Grandma's sister—and her father and two younger brothers.

She and Nick came to stay at Grandma's house one weekend in the summer of 1963. Lynn wanted to show him off to all her relatives, so they planned several stops. Because she lived so close to Highway 82, Grandma was first.

It's been more than thirty years since the afternoon I stood on the porch of my grandparents' house and watched, with the special kind of eagerness that I'm convinced only country kids feel, as Nick and Lynn drove into the yard. They were riding in a long, silver Cadillac. The Cadillac sported Texas license plates. A sticker on the front bumper announced Nick's allegiance to the Dallas Cowboys. He'd played football in college, Grandma had told me, but she was uncertain exactly where.

Chickens scattered, squawking, when the Cadillac pulled in. Nick parked beneath the chinaberry tree, next to the rusty pitcher pump where, for many years, Grandma and Grandpa had drawn their drinking water.

Nick did not cut the engine right away. For a minute or more the Cadillac idled. Through the windshield I could see my new cousin. He had wavy black hair that looked like he'd applied Brylcreem to it, and his chin was big and square. He stared at me, at the porch I was standing on, and at Grandma, who had just walked out the screen door. Then he looked around the yard—at the chickens; at the old section harrow that stood near the road, overgrown by Johnson grass; at the tractor tire in which Grandma had planted a bed of azaleas.

Then he looked at Lynn. He said something to her, and her face, which seconds before had worn a big smile as she waved at me and mouthed the word "hi," suddenly went slack. It was as if she'd suffered some massive muscle failure.

"Y'all get out and come in," Grandma hollered. "I just about got supper on the table."

It would help to say a few things about the house Grandma lived in.

The house had a tin roof and tar-paper siding. Because it was very close to Beaverdam Creek, it flooded from time to time. Grandpa had killed a water moccasin in their bedroom once, and they were always finding snake skins in the chest of drawers and the closet.

It wasn't that the house wasn't clean; it was as clean as any house could be, given the fact that it occasionally flooded, that it had the kind of roof that was bound to leak. It was clean, given the fact that it was built two feet off the ground, so that chickens could walk around beneath it and do their business there, as could Grandpa's dog Buster, who was beset by ticks and fleas. But if you lived in a modern ranch-style house in the suburbs, and if you had a maid who came twice a week to clean, Grandma's house left something to be desired.

The room Grandma put Nick and Lynn in was next to the kitchen—between it and Grandma's own bedroom. You had to walk through that room to get from one end of the house to the other. It was the room I slept in when I spent the night with my grandparents—and most nights in the summer I stayed at their house. I remember the room now as the place in which I spent many of my happiest times. I recall the shape of the water stains on the ceiling—one of the stains, Grandpa told me, was shaped exactly like Lake Michigan, and he showed me a map of the Great Lakes to prove it. I remember the way the floor creaked when you put your foot on one particular floorboard in the middle of the room, and I remember how you could hear Buster whimpering beneath you at night when he had a bad dream.

I also remember the conversation that took place between Nick and Lynn in that room the day they arrived. Grandma had led them in there and closed the door so they could get out of their traveling clothes before supper.

Nick's voice was resonant. He was trying to whisper, but he didn't succeed. "I can't do this," he said.

I was in the kitchen helping Grandma. She'd fried up a huge mess of catfish that Grandpa and my father had caught that morning in the Sunflower River. There were homemade hush puppies and a tangy slaw she'd made of shredded cabbage, chopped celery, sweet pickles, and mayonnaise, with a dab of French's mustard thrown in to enhance the flavor.

The kitchen was full of good food, and getting it all on the table, along with the plates and knives and forks and the big Mason jars we drank tea from, was going to take a while. But Grandma had stopped moving. She stood there next to the sink, listening, and so did I.

"I can't sleep on this bed," Nick said. "I can't shit in that toilet, I can't eat at that table. Hell, I'd be scared of the food."

We couldn't hear what Lynn said, but in some form or fashion she must have asked him why.

"Because," he said, "I haven't ever done it before."

I did not, at that time, understand that a fair amount of what is wrong with the world on any particular day, in any particular century, is apt to be the result of somebody's unwillingness to experience something he's never experienced before. I did not, at that time, even understand what a person like Nick would find wrong with the bed I'd so often slept in or the toilet I'd relieved myself in almost every day of my life.

But there was one thing I knew for sure: If he sat down at Grandma's table and ate this meal, he might very well want to spend the remainder of his life in this house.

Of that there could be no doubt.

Many years later, after I had moved to California to teach at a university, my cousin Lynn came to visit my wife and my daughters and me. She still lived in Texarkana, but she and Nick had been divorced for almost ten years. She was in her mid-fifties, a tall silver-haired woman with a deeply tanned face. She came to Fresno in a new Mercedes. It was one of the V-12s, a car that cost more than our house.

She said the Mercedes belonged to the man she was seeing. He lived in Orange County. He was a developer, she said. She'd met him the previous summer on the beach in Key West.

In the backyard, while I cooked burgers on my gas grill, I asked her if things between her and the developer were serious.

"When you're my age," she said, "everything's serious."

She had called me a few days earlier and said she was on the West Coast and would like to visit. She had read both my books, she said, and she was proud to have an author in the family.

"And you're a college professor, too," she said. "That's wonderful."

I believed she meant it, but as I stood there flipping burgers, it crossed my mind that maybe she'd learned her lesson. Our English Tudor might have looked as lowly to her Orange County magnate as Grandma's house had looked to Nick. Maybe that's why she'd come to see us by herself.

At dinner that night she asked my daughters lots of questions about their school and their hobbies, and she asked my wife, Eva, who is Polish, lots of questions about Poland. Lynn said she and the developer had talked about visiting Eastern Europe next spring. They were mostly interested in seeing Prague and Budapest, but she said they might put Krakow on their list, too.

Then she leaned back, surveyed the four of us, and said, "It's nice to see two people from such different backgrounds make such a wonderful family."

That seemed as good a time as any to raise the specter of Nick. Where was he now, I asked her; what was he doing?

She said he managed a factory in Bryan, Texas. She never saw him anymore, and neither did her sons. The last few years they were all together, she said, had been pretty awful.

"But you know what?" she said, brightening. "He never did quit talking about that meal your grandma cooked him. You remember the night we stayed there?"

I said I did.

"He always wanted me to cook catfish that way and hush puppies, too, but I never could do it to satisfy him. He said that meal your grandma cooked him was the best he ever ate in his life."

"Do you remember the pictures?" I asked.

"What pictures?"

"The ones Grandma sent you after y'all had been to see us."

Lynn frowned. "I'd forgotten those," she said. "Hey, what was all that about, anyway?"

All of us sat at the table in the dining room. Nick and Lynn, Mother and Dad and I, Grandma and Grandpa. Nick was accorded a place of honor at the end of the table.

He had changed clothes. He was wearing white pants and a short-sleeved Hawaiian shirt. It looked like he'd rubbed another layer of Brylcreem on his hair. It was stiff now and shiny.

He sat there with his arms crossed, staring at his plate, steeling himself for the worst. *The Beverly Hillbillies* had entered the American consciousness the year before, and you could tell he was preparing himself for the kinds of concoctions Granny Clampett might serve. Possum fried in lard, owl cutlets, stewed ground-hog—that sort of thing.

Earlier, when Grandma and I were still in the kitchen and they were in the bedroom, Grandma and I had heard Lynn pleading with him. "She's my favorite aunt. She helped Momma raise me. Please, just bear it tonight, and we'll leave in the morning. They can't help it if they're poor."

"I knew they were poor," we heard him say. "I was ready for that. It's unsanitary here. That's what worries me. Who knows whether or not the food's safe to eat?"

"It's safe. They've been eating it all their lives. I used to eat it, too."

"If I get sick," he grumbled, "you better haul me to a hospital quick."

Now, the catfish and hush puppies had been dumped into a huge green platter, which rested in the middle of the table. The coleslaw was in a big brown bowl. A bottle of Hunt's ketchup stood near the catfish. The plates that we would eat from were three different varieties. There were four heavy brown plates, a couple of white plates with Christmas designs around the rims, and one off-white plate that had no design at all on it, though if you turned it upside down you would find an inscription on the bottom. The inscription read: "property of south sunflower county hospital."

"Nick," Grandpa said, "you want to say grace?"

It was customary to ask the guest to say the blessing. No one had ever refused. But Nick Miller did. "I'm not the churchgoing type," he said.

"We got married in church," Lynn blurted out.

"Yeah, we did," Nick said. "But it was mostly just a social occasion."

For the last half-hour, ever since we'd overheard the argument between Nick and Lynn, Grandma had been silent. She had replied to every question I'd asked her about setting the table with a shake of her head. Now she said, "Ain't this a social occasion?"

As I've said, we didn't know much about Nick except that he played football in college. We also knew that he worked for some company of sorts, that he was an executive, a man who wore a suit to work and gave orders and fired people. He didn't own the company, though, so he must have taken orders, too. He must, at some times, have found himself in a position in which his word was questioned. Knowing what I know about people like Nick Miller, I will risk a guess and say that when his word was questioned by a superior, he behaved in a very obliging, perhaps apologetic manner.

But Grandma was not his superior. He uncrossed his arms laid his arms flat on the table, and spread his fingers out as if he were getting ready for action.

"Well, now," he said, "ain't this a social occasion? Yes, by doggie, it sure enough is."

While the rest of us sat there stunned, Nick Miller bowed his head and shut his eyes. "Jesus," he said, doing his best to sound like Billy Graham. "Yes, *Jeez Us.* Bless these fish. Bless these hush puppies. Bless this house and them that's in it. Bless the dogs and the cows and the chickens and the pigs. Bless all their leavings in the yard outside. Bless the hay and the cotton and the soybeans and John Deere. Bless this cole, coleslaw as you bless our hard, hard hearts."

And then Nick Miller raised his head and opened his eyes and picked up his fork. "Let's eat," he said.

He stabbed a piece of fish and laid it on his plate, then he picked up a hush puppy and popped it in his mouth, and when he started to chew, I swear you could see a light enter his eyes. Slowly, while he and he alone ate, while the rest of us sat there and watched as he swallowed one hush puppy after another, as he ate piece after piece of catfish, and pile upon pile of coleslaw, as stains appeared on his Hawaiian shirt, and his hands became so greasy he wiped them on his thighs, the snobbery drained out of his face.

I didn't know that day what it was that had left him, and I didn't know that it would leave for only a little while and then come surging back, but I knew in my heart that his heart had softened. And I knew what had brought on the change: not the prayer he had spoken, but the meal he had eaten.

At Grandma's table, the food was a blessing in itself.

But having said that, I am saddened to have to say this.

Just as the blessing wore off Nick Miller, so that a few years down the road, after *Deliverance* hit the screens, he would disrupt cocktail parties by suggesting certain familial links between Lynn and the men who raped Ned Beatty, the blessing wore off the food on Grandma's table.

The change, unlike the change that had overcome Nick that night in 1963, was not sudden. It came about gradually. It came with many other changes that, at first glance, would seem to have little or nothing to do with food. Grandma began to look at new cars. You would sometimes see her walking around the lot at the Pontiac dealership or, at other times, down the road at the Ford dealership. Finally, she found the one she wanted, a new cream-colored Tempest. I remember the day she drove it home. She parked it in the front yard, near the chinaberry tree, in almost exactly the same spot where Nick Miller had parked his silver Cadillac. Grandpa's pickup truck had never looked strange there, but the Tempest, so shiny and new, seemed out of place. And so, a few years later, Grandma told Grandpa she wanted him to build a carport.

She bought a new refrigerator with an ice maker in it, and she bought a color TV. She visited Lott's Furniture Company and bought linoleum rugs for each room in the house. She bought a stereo, though she almost never turned it on, and she bought several standing lamps and a new bathtub and toilet. She re-papered the walls in every room.

She quit raising chickens. When Grandpa's dog Buster showed the first signs of illness, she insisted Grandpa shoot him, and they never had a dog again. She made Grandpa nail tin siding around the bottom of the house so that animals could not get under it.

She began to buy canned or frozen vegetables, and these were what we ate for supper. She discovered Swanson frozen roast beef and gravy. It came in a pouch, and all you had to do was drop the pouch in boiling water for three or four minutes, and you had yourself a main dish. She bought apple pies frozen. She bought pecan pies that came in a box with a clear layer of plastic on top, so you could see the pie, which had been baked in Cincinnati or St. Louis within the last two weeks. She developed a preference for Wonder bread. Any suggestion that it was made of Styrofoam would turn her livid. "I've got better things to do," she would say, "than stand in the kitchen half the day making pies and cornbread. This ain't the days of covered wagons. This is the modern world, and I for one refuse to regret it."

One night, two or three years after Nick and Lynn came to visit, she brought a Polaroid camera into the dining room where Grandpa and I sat, resigned to a supper of Oscar Mayer weenies chopped into links and buried in a casserole dish full of Kraft macaroni and cheese. Alongside that, on one of Grandma's new plates from the set of chinaware she'd bought at United Dollar Store, was half a loaf of Wonder bread, all the slices stacked neatly on top of one another. A blueberry pie, still in the box, was next to the bread.

"What are you doing?" Grandpa said.

He thought she had planned to take a picture of him and me. I thought so, too. But when she aimed the camera, she aimed at the food. The flash clicked once, then twice, and she was gone.

Roadside Table

MICHAEL MCFEE

It was an ugly slab of rough concrete
or warped green boards carved and stained
by greasy sticky previous picnickers

but still we'd pack the creaking station wagon
with hungry relatives and cardboard boxes
full of deviled-egg luster under wax paper

and fried chicken's golden warm aroma
and the moist strata of granny's coconut cake
then drive for what felt like forever, starving,

till dad saw a blue sign for one just ahead
and pulled off into a shady dirt turnout
between the busy highway and some river

where we all waited while meticulous aunts
brushed off the crumby weathered surfaces
then unfolded a tablecloth of newspapers

which we held down with the now-cooled feast
before suffering through interminable grace
and loading our flimsy plates with layers

of food as if we never ate at home,
as if we didn't have our own picnic table
around which, anytime, we all could gather.

Tourists driving by us might have laughed
at this simple mountain clan that had to eat
at a borrowed wayside table, too dirt-poor

to afford an inside dining room of their own,
just as shoulder-walkers were to be pitied
for not having enough money to own a car,

but they'd have been wrong: it was pure holiday
to linger in that place, in public privacy
between the currents of road and water,

cooled by the luxurious breezes of both
as cousins skipped flat rocks to the far bank
or waded on shivering legs into the river

and cigarette smoke rose toward the understory
and the ripening barrels hummed electric with bees
and watermelon seeds shone blackly under the laurels.

Affrilachia

. . . .

FRANK X WALKER

(for gurney & anne)

thoroughbred racing
and hee haw
are burdensome images
for kentucky sons
venturing beyond the mason-dixon

anywhere in Appalachia
is about as far
as you could get
from our house
in the projects
yet
a mutual appreciation
for fresh greens
and cornbread
an almost heroic notion
of family
and porches
makes us kinfolk
somehow
but having never ridden
bareback
or sidesaddle
and being inexperienced
at cutting
hanging
or chewing tobacco
yet still feeling

complete and proud to say
that some of the bluegrass
is black
enough to know
that being "colored" and all
is generally lost
somewhere between
the dukes of hazard
and the Beverly hillbillies
but
if you think
makin' 'shine from corn
is as hard as kentucky coal
imagine being
an Affrilachian
poet

cultivating community

Holy Manna

ROBERT S. RICHMOND

Sol sol-la do do re re-do mi-re-do-la, sol sol-la do do mi re do

The people who come down from D.C. and Boston
and sing the old shapes on their home ground
east of Knoxville, up in Boogertown, and Cades Cove in the Park,
have notions of raised sixths and almost-Dorian scales,
and never quite get it about Dinner on the Grounds.
They never get that exquisite green bean consciousness,
have no trepidations about poke sallet,
miss the acres of cakes, the sweet potato pie,
the abounding noonday fuel for the singing square,
that none too heavenly choir, unbroken circle.
Mostly they bother the Sacred Harp people
down in Alabama, around Sand Mountain,
about the Denson alto parts, and lead too fast,
and arrive too late for Dinner on the Grounds.

Brethren, pray, and holy manna
Will be shower'd all around.

Ramp Suppers, Biodiversity, and the Integrity of the Mountains

MARY HUFFORD

It is mid-April and throughout the tributaries of West Virginia's Big Coal River, peepers are announcing spring. High in the hills, coves drained by chortling creeks are alight with the whites of trillium, the yellows of spice bush, the reds of wake robins, and the bright greens of ramps. From the valleys the bare woods appear spangled with the russet blooms of hard maples, the green-tinged yellows of soft maples, the white bursts of service and dogwoods, and the deep pinks of Judas trees. Soon, they say, the bass will be leaving the river and swimming up into the creeks to spawn.

I am sitting fairly high in the hills myself, paring knife in hand, in a modest rectangular building officially known as "The Ramp House." Perched as far up the hollow of Drew's Creek as a person can drive in a two-wheel-drive car, the Ramp House faces the Delbert Free Will Baptist Church across a small parking lot. For more than forty years the Ramp House has functioned as a community center, where women of the church hold weekly quilting bees and families assemble for reunions. But its name registers its most public and celebrated purpose: sheltering friends, neighbors, and kin who come together each spring to feast upon ramps.

Ramps, *Allium tricoccum*, are wild leeks. Thriving throughout the Appalachian range in rich, dark woodlands near mountain streams, ramps are among the first edible foods to appear in the early spring, when they pierce the gray and brown leaf mold with a spire of tightly furled, onion-scented leaves. In June the lance-shaped leaves wither, and the plant sends up a stalk with an umbel of white flowers. Underground the stems swell into white bulbs connected by a mass of fibrous rootlets. These diminutive leeks reek of garlic, only stronger.

Throughout the Appalachian South, ramps are hailed with feasting at ramp suppers and festivals. The most famous of these community fund-raisers include the Ramp Festival at Cosby, Tennessee, and the Feast of the Ramson at Richwood, West Virginia. Richwood, in fact, is home to the NRA—the National

Ramp Association. But many smaller events proliferate throughout April and well into the month of May. From noon until 8 P.M., the women who organize this particular event at the Ramp House will serve nearly 500 plates piled high with potatoes, fried apples, pinto beans, cornbread, and ramps.

The week before the ramp supper is one of the year's busiest, and members of the Delbert Free Will Baptist Church divide the labor of production. Each evening the women meet in the Ramp House to clean and refrigerate the ramps brought in by the men from the upper-elevation hollows wrinkling the ridge-lines. The female camaraderie on these evenings, pungent with the aroma of ramps, coffee, and sassafras tea and punctuated with laughter, makes this an event in its own right. "We sit in a circle and clean ramps and talk," Delores Workman told me at last year's ramp supper. "It's a lot of fun. I love my ramp circle."

"You should hear the tales Jenny tells," laughed Judy Griffy. Hoping to, this year I am in the Ramp House the night before Ramp Day, chopping ramps and tape-recording the talk of a dozen women, worn out from a week of preparation, but excited about the day ahead. Only one man is present, Laffon Pettry's husband, Bob. Bob tolerates the women's razzing with good humor. "You put down that cigarette and get your knife and get busy," Mabel Brown warns him as he tries to take a break. "You'll be the first one we fire, Bob!"

"He's slightly outnumbered, isn't he," murmurs Theresa Elkins.

"He'd better watch it here with this gang of females!" Mabel teases, brandishing her knife.

Dusk gathers outside, and in the wake of the setting sun the stars are brightening into the sign of the ram, for which it is said that ramps were long ago named "ramsons" by the Swedes. Inside, the air is thick with the smell and the talk of ramps. Jenny Bonds tells about a ramp-themed basket her granddaughter gave her for Christmas, containing ramp vinegar, ramp seeds, dried ramps, ramp jelly, pickled ramps, even ramp wine. "I had some of the jelly," said Jenny. "It stunk." Other possibilities are advanced: ramp pizza or Jenny's ramp casserole, with sausage, potatoes, and cheese.

Historically, in these mountains, female sociality has flourished around the gathering and processing of greens and other wild produce. On the heels of ramps a host of other greens start popping up: dandelions, poke, shawnee lettuce, woolen britches, creasies, and lamb's tongue. And around these, women have fashioned women's worlds. "That was the big deal when everybody used to go green picking," said Carrie Lou Jarrell, of Sylvester, West Virginia, on another occasion. "That was the event of the week. Mrs. Karen Thomas would come up and she always brought Jessie Graybill with her, and then Miss Haddad would come, and most of the time Maggie Wriston came with her. And usually Sylvia Williams was always there to do green picking with them. I knew from the time I came into the world that she was just a good friend. But that was the thrill of my life to get to go with all of these women, because they talked about good stuff."

Such talk is one means of crafting locality. It catches people up into a dense fabric of kinship and community and fastens that fabric to places and events in the mountains. Through such talk the women enunciate their place in the hills, a place remarkable not only for its biodiversity but for the interweaving of bio-diversity and community life. In the Ramp House the women laugh over how Violet Dickens once mistook sassafras tea for bacon grease and poured it over the frying ramps: "We need you to come season the ramps," Mabel kidded her the other day. They compare the aromas of poke and collard greens and marvel at how window screens get black with flies when you're cooking them. They wonder where the creasies (dry land cress) are growing this year, and Jenny points out that creasies won't grow unless you till the soil.

In southern West Virginia a mixed mesophytic forest (known among ecolo-gists as the world's most biologically diverse temperate-zone hardwood system) is not just a product of nature. It is integral to a cultural landscape that has taken shape over many generations. On Coal River, I have heard people say the best place to look for red mulberry trees, now in serious decline, is on farms; that the cows that grazed throughout the mountains well into the twentieth century kept the snake population down; and that Peach Tree Creek was named for peach trees encountered there by the first white settlers entering the region in the early 1800s. In the Ramp House they say you can start your own ramp patch from the bit of root they're chopping off at the ends. "Mabel has a few ramps growing in her yard," said Jenny. "I do, Edna does, and Sadie does. You don't, do you Theresa? You're going to have to plant you a patch of ramps and some molly moochers."

This week the molly moochers are coming in. Molly moochers are morel mushrooms. They say you can hear them popping up through the dried leaves when it rains. Old apple orchards, scattered throughout the woods where people used to live, make good places to go molly mooching. A neighbor found fifty-six today in an old apple orchard behind Laffon's house. "He found thirty-seven yesterday," said Laffon.

"Gladys was finding them out there," says another woman.

"Oh Gladys," Laffon chuckles. "She's the queen of the molly moochers!"

The salient feature of ramps is the smell. The Menominee Indians called it "*pikwute sikakushia*": the skunk. "*Shikako,*" their name for a large ramp patch that once flourished in northern Illinois, has been anglicized to Chicago: "the skunk place." Our chopping of leaves is filling the air with aromatic organo-sulphur compounds, characteristic of members of the *Allium* family but carried to extremes in ramps and their consumers. Some have seen in this practice of restoring the body while emitting a sulphurous odor a rite of death and resurrection, serendipitously coinciding with Easter. Actually with ramps the motif appears to be breath and insurrection. Liberating organosulfides seems to comprise, if not a rite of inversion, at least a delicious form of back talk: the country back-talking the city, the improper back-talking propriety. The efforts of official institutions to quell this annual olfactory uprising have been rehearsed at every ramp supper I've attended.

"Let me get this down so I can move on," said John Flynn at the 1995 ramp supper. "We did not eat ramps. There were very strong women in my family who did not like the odor. Also, if you ate ramps and went to school, they sent you home because of the odor. There were a lot of authoritarians in the school, so you didn't do a lot of ramp eating. Someone might get up the guts to do it once, but they didn't do it twice. The odor was the issue." Ways of annulling the odor creep into ramp talk.

"I like them raw," said Jess Duncan of Sylvester, "like you'd eat a hot pepper or something with a sandwich."

"Fried potatoes, pinto beans," added Pat Canterbury.

"You can't beat them," said Jess, "and they don't stink if you don't eat very many of them."

"They do too," said Pat.

"If you eat them with a sandwich, they don't," Jess insisted. "My wife's never complained."

"Now, if you're confined close," cautioned Bob Daniel, of Dry Creek, one morning in Syble's Bed and Barn, "say in an office with people, I'm sure it would offend people like that, but in my line of work I don't think I bother anybody with them."

"If you don't like the smell," laughed Mae Bongalis, "go the other way. Stay at your house!"

The most famous official censure of ramps was brought on by the late Jim Comstock, editor of the *West Virginia Hillbilly*. Comstock, inspired by scratch-and-sniff advertising for perfume and coffee in several local papers, announced the Richwood ramp supper one year by lacing the printer's ink for his spring issue with ramp juice. "We got a reprimand from the postmaster general," Comstock recalled. "And we are probably the only paper in the United States that's under oath to the federal government not to smell bad."

Behind the powerful aroma it appears there really is something good for what ails you. Ramps have long been recommended for their germicidal and toning effects. The beliefs that ramps are good for the heart, that they thin and purify the blood, and that they relieve the common cold are widespread. Scientific research suggests that such faith in ramps is well placed. The allicin (diallyl-sulfide oxide) in ramps, which has antibiotic properties, has been linked with reduced rates of cancer. Ramps are higher in vitamin C than oranges. They contain cepaenes, which function as antithrombotic agents. Ramps also contain flavonoids and other antioxidants that are free-radical scavengers.

As the first of the wild foods to appear, ramps satisfy the body's craving for living food at the end of a winter filled with produce that's been dried, canned, frozen, or shipped from faraway places. "They used to say," said Jenny Bonds, "that people that lived out like we did didn't live near grocery stores, so they said in the springtime you always need green things, like vegetables. So they said in the springtime the country people got ramps, that was our spring tonic."

"What does a spring tonic do?" I asked.

"Cure for spring fever, I guess," said Jenny.

"Strawberry rhubarb pie is my spring tonic," said Laffon Pettry.

Spring fever is twice cured by ramps, which lure people into the higher reaches of the mountains. "Ramps are fun to hunt," said John Flynn. "You can go out in the yard and get all the poke you want, but you have to go into the forest to look for ramps."

"The higher you go," said Woody Boggs on another occasion, "the more ramps and the bigger."

Ramp patches in the mountains have long functioned as a common resource. Most of the ramps served at the ramp supper, some fifteen bushels, do not come from people's personal patches. They come from the upper-elevation coves rising high above the Ramp House. "I've got a few planted up the holler here," said Dennis Dickens, of Peach Tree Creek, a beloved octogenarian who passed away this year. "They just grow at an elevation of about, I'd say, 2,000 to 2,500 feet. Real rich soil."

For many, eating ramps in the mountains is as much a rite of spring as attending the ramp supper. "I love them," said Bob Daniel, over breakfast at Syble's one spring morning. "I like to dig them and eat them right there. Sit down in the woods with a piece of cornbread and eat them."

"That's the fun part," said Mary Jarrell, speaking in Lloyd's Convenient, which she operates with her husband at the mouth of Rock Creek. "Getting them and cooking them out. We'd go to several places, like Hazy, where they've closed it off. We would always go and take a skillet and make cornbread and take some potatoes and get the ramps and clean them and fix them on top of the mountains."

"We'd take our cornbread and pinto beans," said Mae Bongalis, of Naoma, during the 1995 ramp supper. "And go to the mountain, up Board Tree Hollow, dig ramps all afternoon. Then we'd clean them in a little stream coming through the patch, wash them and cook them and then have dinner. They taste better that way, too."

The higher elevations, known simply as "the mountains," have long functioned as what anthropologist Beverly Brown terms a "de facto commons," an open-access area where people go to hunt, picnic, and party, gather a variety of roots, herbs, nuts, and fruit, or to enjoy some solitude. Ramps inaugurate an annual round of small-scale subsistence harvesting of woodland bounty, and they afford the first opportunity to get back into the mountains. But they are fortifying throughout the growing season. "Ramps are sweet this time of year," said Tony Dickens of Pettry Bottom, one late September evening. "You'll come across a ramp patch when you're out ginsenging. Last week I dug more ramps than ginseng!"

Supporting an unusually diverse seasonal round, central Appalachia's mixed mesophytic forest distinguishes these mountains among America's de facto commons. Telltale signs of this diversity abound in the hollows and coal camps, and in yards and homes on the river: the handful of butternuts curing on a step, the coal bucket of black walnuts ready for shelling, the hellgrammites seine at the ready on the porch, the ginseng drying in the rear window of a car, the squirrel meat marinating in a bowl, the gallon of blackberries ready for canning, the plastic bag full of homemade "deer jerky," the jar full of "lin" (white basswood) honey, the pawpaws in the freezer, the molly moochers soaking in salt water, the pickled ramps in the pantry.

The traditional knowledge that sustains this annual round of harvesting is anchored in a people's landscape inscribed all over the mountains, a literary work writ large.

The hills rising away from the Ramp House are rich in family and community history. Names bestowed on every wrinkle in the ridgeline commemorate people, events, and moments in the seasonal round. What appears to be a jumble of coves, ridges, creeks, knobs, branches, gaps, and forks is as legible to some residents as a metropolitan grid is to an urbanite. "These different little hollows," said Howard Miller, "they had a name for each one, so when a neighbor talked to another neighbor about a certain thing that happened at this holler, they knew exactly where it was at, they knew even from Beckley down to Racine down to Madison."

The names for the coves anchor local history and knowledge in the land: Mill Holler, Peach Orchard Holler, School House Holler, and Bee Light Holler, where they baited bees in order to "line" them to wild hives, filled with honey from mixed mesophytic flowering trees like basswood ("lin"), tulip tree ("yellow poplar"), and yellow locust ("mountain locust"). Thus indexed, the landscape is a dynamic repository of rural life, knowledge, and history, which elderly raconteurs render into narrative. "Quill Holler's below the ramp house," Howard went on. "They used to get a hollow straw and drink sugar water where they notched a sugar tree. Something like these straws at a restaurant, but it's a plant."

The cultural landscape is rife with landmarks. Over generations of working the seasonal round, a language for navigating the mountains discriminates them into a wide array of landmarks: not only the high walls, mine breaks, auger holes, and other traces of industry, but into "knobs," "drains," "coves," "swags," "ridges," "crossings," "gaps," "flats," "bear wallows," "orchards," "home places," "sink holes," "walk paths," "hill climbs," "camp rocks," "bottoms," "brakes," "graveyards," "bee trees," "den trees," and "benches."

This landscape supports the common world celebrated in the Ramp House. Cultural practices like ramp suppers, ramp talk, and roaming the mountains have co-evolved with an industrial landscape as ways of holding together a world chronically visited with environmental, social, and economic crisis. Only by bracketing out the civic commons is it possible to reduce a mountain to "a worthless piece of dirt," as one industry spokesman put it, "good for nothing, save for snakes and scrub pine." An alternative view—of biodiversity flourishing in the context of community life—is rehearsed in stories and jaunts that map the commons back onto the land.

Many of the ramps for this year's ramp supper came from Hazy Creek, a long, lush, meandering hollow that hooks around Shumate's Branch like a sheltering arm. Hundreds of people lived at the mouth of Hazy in the 1940s when the coal town of Edwight was the bustling hub of the river between Whitesville and Glen Daniel. Though Hazy Creek and Shumate's Branch were evacuated of dwellings in the 1980s, people continue to comb the hollows of Hazy Creek for ramps, ginseng, molly moochers, yellow root, mayapple, bloodroot, berries, and signs of history.

According to Dennis Dickens, Hazy got its name before the Civil War. "Some hunters came through there," said Dickens, "and they camped over along Drew's Creek. And they decided to go over in Hazy to hunt one day. They got to the top of the mountain, they looked down in there, it was foggy and hazy. They said, 'No use to go down in here, it's too hazy. We'll not do any good.' And called it 'Hazy Creek.'" Though the coal industry has closed Hazy Creek to the public (Cherry Pond Mountain is slated for mountaintop removal), people still enter with permission to gather plants and hunt, or to visit historic sites and cemeteries.

On a trek up Hazy for ramps in 1996, Dave Bailey and Woody Boggs distilled sights on the overgrown landscape into signs of former communities everywhere: the rusting incline hidden on the hillside; the sludge pond, its banks "reclaimed" in thorny field locust; a stand of Indian corn near Charlie Rock, named for Charles Wiley; the remains of a "splash dam" once used as a skidway for easing timber out of the mountains; red dog from the slate dump that burned for years and was haunted by an old woman's ghost; a big rock that Woody says Hobart Clay could have cleared in his Hazy machine, and campsites marked by the presence of ramps. "People have camped there for years," commented Dave. "They set them out so they'd have some."

As access is increasingly curtailed, people vividly reconstitute Hazy Creek through stories. In a conversation that Woody Boggs videotaped in Andrew, Dave Bailey and Cuba Wiley conjure and reoccupy Hazy as a capacious and generous landscape where they both lived for many years. Cuba, who hasn't been up in Hazy lately, wonders what it's like since the people moved out in the late 1980s. "People tell me I wouldn't know it up that hollow now," he says.

Dave imaginatively takes him up there, and Hazy Creek floods into the room through their words and gestures. "You go up there, Cuba, where the mines is, you go across that creek, go over to the left, go right on up that road to the mines. You can stop the car where the road's washed out, you walk maybe to the top of the hill, and the side of the mountain is covered with ramps."

"Well," picks up Cuba, invoking another space where ramps grew, "what about the Straight Fork of Hazy, where Three Forks used to come in together, and I used to go in the Straight Fork of Hazy, and just go up there a little piece on up that hollow and walk in on the right, and that scoundrel mountain was lined with them."

"That's right," says Dave. "Just as far as you could see."

They go on to the Everett Fork, Hiram Fork, and Bradley Mountain (where Lige Bradley fled from marauding Yankee and Confederate troops during the Civil War, and where people returned to tend and harvest apples in the Wayne Bradley Field long after Bradley was evacuated for strip-mining). On the way out, Dave and Cuba pause for moment at Road Fork and Sugar Camp.

"You know what?" says Cuba, "I'm gonna tell you something. I was in Sugar

Camp, way up in there, I could look down over there at the Coffee Pot Restaurant and all that, and that walk path that goes right on up through there takes you to Bradley."

"Yup," says Dave. "I know where it's at."

"I believe I could find it yet," Cuba resumes. "That walk path, I'd turn left and go up just a little ridge, about fifty or seventy-five yards and that scoundrel ridge was lined with ramps, and I'll tell you who else went in there and found them before he died: Calvin Clay. Calvin Clay and them found that patch."

"I didn't know they were in there," Dave marveled.

"Sugar Camp," says Cuba. "Good patch, buddy."

Reconstituting Hazy, Dave and Cuba walk its paths, populate it with fellow gatherers, and savor its views, routes, and destinations. Stories of plying the seasonal round, of gathering ramps, molly moochers, fishing bait, and ginseng, are like beacons lighting up Hazy's coves, benches, walk paths, historic ruins, and camp rocks. In fact, such stories and inscriptions constitute a rural industrial landscape as coherent, as saturated with "traditional cultural properties," as representative of America's rural-industrial history as any landscape recorded on the National Register.

Like other productions of the commons, ramps, ramp patches, and ramp talk are resources for holding together a way of life that is continually being dismantled by plans for progress. The civic commons of the Ramp House and the commons of the cultural landscape are mutually sustaining and cannot be reclaimed by covering a stream with spoil and putting a pond on top of a highland complex, moving a smokehouse from a home place to a pioneer village, or relocating a family cemetery from its ancestral grounds to a commercial cemetery many miles away.

The commons on Coal River models an alternative, integrated, community-based approach to the conservation of natural and cultural resources. The seasonal round, itself a cultural production, outlines a roster of "services" we might expect from central Appalachia's post-mining landscapes. Common pool resources like the ramp patches of the named systems of coves might qualify for protection not as endangered species but as vital resources for mountain life— "traditional cultural properties." Such sites, scattered throughout the mountains, define the social collective, serving both as touchstones to a shared past and as thresholds to a future in which a historic, mixed mesophytic landscape continues to form a hedge against chronic social, environmental, and economic crises.

MARY HUFFORD

April in Helvetia

1995

. . . .

SALLY SCHNEIDER

The first house you see as you come into Helvetia, West Virginia, from the Mill Creek road is a log cabin with a weathered sign above the door that reads "*Zeit und Raum ist Alles*" (Time and Space is All). I had been coming here for ten years before I met the woman who built the cabin with the extraordinary sign— and before I entered the life of this town, deep in the Appalachian Mountains.

My first trip to Helvetia was with college friends. We were in pursuit of the wild leeks called ramps, or rather, the ramps were our excuse to run wild down breathtaking country roads, to funky roadhouses like the LuLu Belle Inn and the Rebel Lounge, through tiny towns with mysterious names like Junior and Czar. I was not a cook then and never imagined that a lark to the Helvetia ramp supper would be the catalyst for twenty years of returns each spring and eventually to a kind of adoption, to my finding roots that had nothing to do with my own. The people of Helvetia captured my heart with their generosity and spirit, and they have taught me more about food than anything in my life.

From my first breakfast at the town's only inn of thick slices of toasted homemade bread, tomato jam, and the butter and cheese made by three old sisters on a remote mountain farm, I encountered a world where food is a language unto itself, welcoming the visitor and eloquently expressing Helvetia's culture. Perhaps that's because so much in Helvetia takes place around food: the growing and preparation of food draws family and friends together, and they are the primary ways that people who don't have much could give to each other.

"You know you'll never be hungry in Helvetia" I was told, and it's true. I've come away from people's houses with mason jars of ramps, venison, and spiced peaches, tomatoes from the garden, slices of pie, homemade wine. Even perfect strangers give away food as a kind of "hello." Lucky Farr's shy wife didn't say a word when we met but knocked plums off the tree in her yard and filled my pockets with them. There seems to be a great cook in every house: Margaret Koerner, her white hair in neat braids, standing barefoot in her spotless kitchen frying doughnuts; Bernadine Whooten, round and comforting in a flowered dress, plying me with her raspberry cobbler, still warm in a black iron skillet.

Food in Helvetia is generally simple rustic fare—Southern farm cooking with a strong Swiss pulse that traces back to the original settlers. From the Swiss side come the spicy sweet-and-sour flavors of sauerbraten and sauerkraut, rich quiche-like onion pies, noodle-like dumplings, and spicy cookies. From the South come cornbread and ham, messes of greens, and lard-crusted pies.

At first glance Helvetia, nestled in a lush valley near the state's eastern panhandle, appears to be a private, quiet little place that you can drive through in less than a minute: church, post office that doubles as a general store, museum, library, community hall, restaurant, twenty-five or so homes. It has a population of some 150 people, most of whom live on farms outside of town. After the ramp supper my friends and I would drive back over the mountains to stay in a seedy motel with an ice machine and a sign that advertised "colored TV." Then one year I heard there was an inn in Helvetia, and I stayed on after my friends had left.

The Beekeeper Inn, an old house at the confluence of two forks of the Buckhannon River, is owned by Eleanor Fahrner Mailloux. Eleanor grew up in Helvetia in the early 1920s, left to travel the world, and came back to nurture the fragile culture of her childhood. "Even as a small child, I could see how beautiful Helvetia was. I wanted it always to exist. That was my dream." Like many Appalachian towns, Helvetia had been losing ground over the years, a victim of the state's poor economy and changes wrought by an increasingly urbanized society. Eleanor set out to fight the decline.

After her return, Eleanor enlisted the support of Rudolph Zumbach, an old-timer and leader in the village. "Well, Eleanor," he said, "we're all in favor of progress as long as we don't make any changes." "It sounds funny but I understood what he meant and felt the same way," Eleanor explained. "We didn't want Helvetia's integrity—its heart—to change."

The proprietor of one of Randolph County's best restaurants, the Hutte, ("Little House" in Swiss-German), Eleanor has been a one-woman historical society, organizing the refurbishing of many of the town's buildings and the landscaping of public areas. Largely through her efforts, the Village of Helvetia was placed on the National Register of Historic Places in 1978.

Eleanor gave me my first glimpse into the complex history of the area, which was settled by Swiss immigrants in 1869. She told me stories of the early families with names like Merkli, Betler, Isch, Daetwyler, Burki, Fahrner, and Zumbach, many of whom were driven by crop failures in their native Bern to carve a thriving town out of the mountain wilderness that reminded them of their homeland. They named their settlement Helvetia, the Latin appellation by which their country has been known since antiquity.

Over the years, nothing earth-shattering happened in Helvetia, no great battles, inventions, or natural disasters. What is remarkable is the way of life the immigrants created—independent, courageous, mischievous, sometimes eccentric, completely original—which still exists here.

I've sought to understand that life and to record as much of it as possible. I've often roamed the area with a grizzled-looking Appalachia native named Rogers McAvoy, a psychology professor at West Virginia University and a Helvetia home owner. Rogers and I have spent hours driving around the mountains in his old jeep, stopping to talk to people we found sitting on porches and in bars or walking along the roads. He has been a guide and resource for tracing the convoluted lineages of families and exploring the complex mores of a community—part industrious Swiss, part American pioneer—that eludes definition.

Rogers debunks many common misconceptions about Appalachia, which he says, "to the rest of America, is like another civilization." He explains how the rugged mountains have acted as a barrier to the homogenizing influences of mass media and modern urban life, preserving the area's uniqueness and shaping its character. Rural mountain living fosters both fierce independence and self-sufficiency, as well as a strong sense of community and family, qualities that make Helvetia an anomaly today.

Irene Hartford and Mary Hicks epitomize what I love and find remarkable about Helvetia. The two sisters, now in their eighties, are half Irish and half Swiss, reflecting the gradual integration of other immigrant settlers in the area. They were born MacNeil on a neighboring farm, then moved to a big house in town where Mary still lives. Irene, who looks like Gertrude Stein, lives across the road in the log cabin with the "*Zeit und Raum ist Alles*" sign, which she put up in the 1930s as a joke with cosmic underpinnings.

Mary did much of the cooking on the family farm. She is one of the best cooks in town and acts as its memory (in lieu of written recipes) for the town's fund-raising suppers. She always appears at the community hall just as the preparations for these monumental undertakings hit a crisis point, when nobody can quite remember the proper way to cook the beans for the ramp supper or the gravy for the chicken supper.

Although the sisters' house is enormous, everything seems to take place in the kitchen, which is a study in benign chaos and immensely welcoming at the same time. The table is always a disarray of supermarket coupons, ripening tomatoes, shopping lists, jars of pickles and jams, coffee creamer, seedlings in paper cups, a glass of mismatched teaspoons for coffee. There is usually a half-finished project going on: cucumbers salting in a basin on the porch for pickles, wild grapes being picked over for pie.

Visitors always find something good to eat, and Irene and Mary feed a lot of people in the course of a week, as everyone seems to pass the house at some time or other. "Are you hungry?" Irene will ask. "Well, we've hardly a thing to eat!" Mary will say, shaking her head and then pulling out a ham, or delicious beans cooked with home-raised pork, or some hot yeast rolls from the oven. There is usually a pie around, always preserves with something to put them on, along with coffee and a gallon jar full of cookies.

I have sat at Irene and Mary's kitchen table for hours at a time, listening as they reminisce, embellishing and correcting each other's stories. Memories and recipes intertwine, one sparking the other. The recipe for buckwheat dumplings reminds them of the buckwheat mush with the sauce of creamed elderberries that they hated as girls, which leads to a story of when Irene ate with the men at threshing time, consuming huge potato dumplings stuffed with ham until she thought she would burst. The apples Mary is preparing for pie remind them of the cold cellar, built by a Swiss, that was so perfectly designed it would keep butter hard as a rock and never smell of mildew. At that table I heard the stories of Dora, the young black girl raised by the innkeeper after she had been abandoned in the town; the couple thought to be courting who were secretly making moonshine; Kopro, the brilliant eccentric who paraphrased the theory of relativity, who carried a chair on his back at night so he could sit and look at the stars, and who figured out how to bank the intersection of the river's two forks with stone.

Mary cooks by feel and by eye, as do most of the older cooks around. She knows innately what works and what doesn't, although she can't always explain why. When I ask her for quantities in her recipes she has to think hard to pin them down and sometimes can't quite resolve the amounts. "Well, I don't know. You just take whatever you have and go from there"—a logical approach for a cook accustomed to making do with whatever is on hand. "If you don't have it, you don't need it" is a philosophical principle in Helvetia, where stores are many miles away on winding mountain roads.

Everything in Irene and Mary's kitchen seems to have layers of associations. Take the salted trout. Mary still buries fresh trout in a bucket with salt to preserve them, the way her mother did. The trout are then soaked for days to remove the salt, dusted in cornmeal, and fried crisp in bacon fat, their bones tender. From that simple preparation, I garner my own memory of eating the delicious trout one night in Mary's kitchen with Rogers, Eleanor, and Irene. I also conjure the kitchen where Mary and her mother prepared huge meals for family and friends and gain an inkling of the ways an industrious people preserved their food with no refrigeration.

Just about everybody in Helvetia puts food by for the winter, meaning they preserve fresh foods in canning jars. They do it as a matter of course whenever there's a lot of something: everything from applesauce to venison, with all manner of pickles and butters in between.

The jars are always stored in the cellar on wooden shelves. Everybody's cellar looks and feels different and seems to reflect the personality of the keeper, what his or her interests and tastes are. Irene and Mary's cellar is rather unkempt-looking, dark and mysterious, with a plank set over a gully in the dirt floor. It houses Mary's endless projects, like sauerkraut and jugs of homemade wine. Margaret Koerner's cellar is the pinnacle of Swiss neatness, pristine, with not a thing out of place, the dustless jars glistening like jewels. The Balli sister's cellar has a mind-boggling array of canned goods, all manner of vegetables, fruits, pickles, meats, and poultry, along with curing cheeses they make from the cows' milk. Other cellars include bins of apples and root vegetables and baskets of eggs.

To a city kid like me, canning and pickling always seemed like a fearsome science, so Irene once gave me a lesson in making pickles. "I've made a study of pickles," she told me one day, and proceeded to tell me what she had found out and decided was best, from the salting of the baby cucumbers in a big basin on the porch, to the exact proportions of the pickling liquid and cooking time to produce a slightly crisp yet tender pickle with the perfect balance of sweet and sour. "Fill these jars," she told me, pointing to a sea of sterilized jars and cucumbers that had been sliced into spears. She let me fill all the jars before she told me that I had put the spears in the wrong way. Having taught school all her life, she knew that lesson would make me remember the right way. According to Irene, arranging the spears with their skins to the inside makes for a better presentation and helps them process better. Anyway, she gave the lesson, but Mary actually canned the pickles. I took home several jars of those pickles as well as an audiotape of the whole affair which, like all things in Helvetia, was about much more than pickles.

Beans and cornbread, one of the most common meals in these parts, offer another example of the way food is a window on Helvetia's way of life. The first time I had them was at the hilltop farm where Eleanor's sister Margie Daetwyler, age seventy-four, lives with her daughter Nancy Gain, son-in-law Leroy, and their kids. It is one of those perfect combinations of foods, comforting and nourishing, created from necessity by frugal people. When larders were spare, there were always cornmeal and beans and a little ham.

That day Margie had set her beautiful old kitchen table with woven red placemats and shallow soup bowls with fading flowers on them. There was a big old crockery bowl of beans cooked with bits of ham, a platter of fried ham, and a basket of corn muffins, along with several small glass bowls with Margie's pickled beets, homemade cottage cheese, and Leroy's spicy pickled cabbage, which was sublime on the beans. Dessert was canned homegrown peaches and pears. It was as well thought out and executed a meal as I have ever had.

Margie's memory is as acute as that of the MacNeil sisters. She talked that day about all the wild spring greens they used to collect and enjoy, many of which the young no longer know how to identify: wild mustard, poke, dandelion, nettle, sheep's sorrel, and lamb's tongue, along with blackberry and violet leaves. She described in detail the sausages her husband Norman made at hog-butchering time and his extraordinary recipe for mincemeat created from the hog's head.

Later, I visited Nancy and Leroy's house next door. I was astonished at the array of foods they harvest, can, freeze, or dry, a measure of Helvetian industry and self-sufficiency, as well as of the valley's plentitude: scores of fruits, vegetables, herbs, and nuts. They raise pigs, beef, chicken; make cheese, butter, and sausages; hunt wild turkey, deer, and grouse.

I also visit the Balli sisters, as they are known throughout Helvetia—three sisters well into their eighties who still work the farm on which they were born. Frieda and Gertrude are twins; Anna is the eldest. They speak with a strong German-Swiss accent. Their remote 200-acre farm nestles into the crest of a hill along the dirt road that leads from Pickens across the mountain into Webster County to Holly River State Park.

The sisters are famous for their cheese making, an Appalachian version of a Swiss mountain cheese that everyone used to make in Helvetia. People come from miles around to buy their cheese, huge double-size chicken eggs, and quilts, which they sew during the cold winter months. I suspect, too, that they just come to see the Balli sisters and witness their remarkable life.

The Balli kitchen is painted green with orange trim, with a worn linoleum floor. The big wooden kitchen table set against one wall is covered with many layers of oilcloth, the underneath ones worn from use. "That's where we butcher the hog" Anna told me one day, matter-of-factly. On the wall above the table are oil paintings of woodland scenes, painted by a friend, that they love to announce are for sale. A broom with a bright red handle stands in the corner. Clothes hangers hang from lines strung above the wood stove.

The fierce work of making cheese begins before dawn each morning, as Frieda and Anna put on layers of clothing in preparation for milking. In winter this means several pairs of old pants full of patches, sweaters, and jackets, home-made hoods of thick, checked cloth that tie under the chin, rubber boots over fleece-lined booties. The arms of Anna's quilted jacket are completely tattered from all her hard work and milking. But as tattered as it is, the jacket still has a purpose, so she wears it. The Ballis, being Swiss, are frugal and waste nothing.

Every morning and evening Anna and Frieda herd the five cows into the barn to be milked by hand. They make cheese with some new milk mixed with the previous day's milk, which they refrigerate overnight to allow the cream to separate. This they skim off to make into butter in an old electric churn.

After separating the cream, the sisters heat the milk slowly on top of the wood stove, until it reaches 86 degrees. Then they add rennet, a coagulant derived from the lining of a calf's stomach, mixed with some buttermilk, and leave the milk to cool.

Gertrude climbs onto a high stool by the stove. Frieda and Anna lift one of the heavy pots of cooled milk back onto a burner. As the milk begins to form curds, Gertrude stirs it with one hand, breaking apart the curds with her fingers until the milk reaches 106 degrees. Again they lift the heavy pots to strain the curds from the whey. They pour the curds into a wooden mold lined with cheesecloth, then fit the mold into a press.

Frieda turns a wheel that presses the curds into a block. The firm block of cheese will now be left to age in one of the wire cheese cages in their cool cellar. It will be turned and washed daily to prevent mold and rubbed weekly with salt for the first month. It generally takes at least five weeks to age properly and to develop a sufficient rind and complex flavor.

Once during the cheese making, Frieda said, "We earn our money." And indeed they do. It takes many hours and eight gallons of milk to make a single five-pound brick of cheese, for which they charge $2.50 a pound. They make about forty pounds a week.

Some of the younger people realize the threatened beauty of what they have in Helvetia and are actively trying to record the old ways. Nancy has been learning needlework like tatting and quilting, as well as the recipes. She is also beginning to create her own traditions, inspired by those she grew up with. She makes an astonishing jelly out of the wild violets that grow in the field behind her house, which she picks with her young sons in the spring. Eleanor's daughter Kathy has brought similar enthusiasm to the traditional Swiss food served in the Hutte restaurant where she is chef. Alvin Burky, age thirty-three, also a fourth-generation descendant of the original settlers, makes butter and cheese by hand on the family farm he manages himself.

Still, I worry sometimes that this way of life, so suffused with memory, will disappear when people like Eleanor and Irene and Mary are no longer around. Every year, I make the long trek from New York to this Appalachian town that I still find rare and mysterious and where I have always had the feeling of being home. I continue to record stories and recipes, as though trying to fix on paper what is so deeply imprinted on my heart.

A Talk with Adriana Trigiani

FRED SAUCEMAN

The late Anthony Trigiani was a great respecter of tradition. He loved to take in the old-time music performances at the Carter Fold at Maces Spring, Virginia, where he taught his guests the history of clogging, for instance. But once he reversed 300 years of his family's history while preparing for a supper at St. Anthony's Catholic Church in the coal-mining community of Norton, Virginia. Someone had burned the tomato sauce. Spaghetti was about to be served, and Anthony had no time to follow his mother's ancestral practice of browning the meatballs first. So he formed them and plopped them into an unburned batch of sauce. Now, all five of his daughters, both of his sons, and his widow, Ida Bonicelli Trigiani, prefer poached meatballs.

The technique is described in Cooking with My Sisters: One Hundred Years of Family Recipes, from Bari to Big Stone Gap, *written by novelist Adriana Trigiani and her sister Mary Yolanda Trigiani. The book traces this family's culinary heritage from the Italian Alps and the canals of Venice, to a community of Italian immigrants in Roseto, Pennsylvania. It then returns the reader to a mountain setting, in Big Stone Gap, Virginia, where those seven children were expected to gather around their parents' flower-laden table every evening. We spoke with Adriana about the experience of growing up both Italian and Appalachian.*

Fred Sauceman (FS): Relate the story of your first encounter with spaghetti as it was served at Big Stone Gap Elementary School in southwest Virginia.

Adriana Trigiani (AT): We were all excited because they said we were having spaghetti. So this meant we were going to have Eye-talian, which we were very thrilled about. So we go into the cafeteria, and the noodles were very short. That was the first thing. They were shaped like spaghetti, but they were so boiled. I mean, "al dente" was not in the lexicon. And they were so boiled you could see through them, and you could probably mash them into a clump in your hand, which we were not used to. And they were rinsed, which we never do. We strain them and get all the liquid off of them, but if you rinse the noodles after you boil them, it takes the flavor out and then they don't hold the sauce. You want them hot to hold the sauce. On top of them was basically chili. It had nothing to do with spaghetti, as we knew it. So we tried to tell the kids this isn't exactly what spaghetti should be, and then through the years when enough people came over to our house and ate, they got the gist of what real Italian food was.

FS: Another practice you encountered at Big Stone Gap Elementary was pouring peanuts into Cokes. Your mother was a very strict librarian who wouldn't let you turn down the pages of books. How did she react to the Coke and peanut combination?

AT: My mother was horrified by that. Of course we didn't know it at the time, but she was concerned about cavities. Because it was real Coca-Cola and peanuts that were caramelized, since you put them in the Coke and shake it up. You know the old Southern fizzy drink you do. My mother couldn't believe it.

FS: I think your father had to pay a visit to the school one time over what he thought was a violation of your Catholic upbringing.

AT: My father complained to the assistant principal of the school about his children being served hamburgers on Fridays during Lent. "Don't worry," the school official responded. "There's no meat in those hamburgers. They're all soy."

FS: What brought you all to Big Stone Gap in the first place?

AT: My father was in his early thirties with seven kids under the age of ten. My husband and I have one child. My mother had seven in nine years. The Lord sends you what you can handle. After I had a baby, I couldn't figure out why there were so many people in the world. Anyway, my father was looking to start his own mill. He had been working with his parents. It was the end of the War on Poverty, around 1968. Dad got a low-interest government loan, and the caveat of the loan was that you had to build this mill in "poverty-stricken" Appalachia. I remember hearing those words and not understanding what poverty meant. My father opened a blouse factory, providing jobs and a future for hundreds of people in the community.

He was enchanted by Big Stone Gap, for the very reasons that I was, and I ended up writing about it. There's something very haunting about it. It was a town that was supposed to become something. It was supposed to become the Pittsburgh of the South, and there were many famous people who came. They were going to try to make it an area for vacations and tourism for very wealthy people, on the backs of the coal industry. But what ended up happening when they went into the mountains, and this is documented, was that there was no iron ore, so they couldn't make steel. So it ended up not becoming the Pittsburgh of the South. It ended up being another in a series of coal camps. You can see the vestiges in the post office. The building is very ornate, and down the block from there was a big hotel that covered almost a city block. It was called the Monte Vista Hotel. Gone. The house we grew up in was like a haunted mansion when we moved in. The windows were shot out, and my mother had to get in there and scrub. Because it wasn't fashionable to have an old house. Everybody wanted new homes. But my mother's still living in that house.

FS: What brought the early Italian immigrants to Big Stone Gap?

AT: There is an area of Big Stone Gap called Italy Bottom. In the late teens and early twenties of the last century, Italian coal miners came over looking for work, as well as Czechs and Polish people. Some changed their names. Most of the Italians had moved on by the time we got there in the late 1960s. Some had moved to Kentucky and Tennessee. The Caruso family, grocers in Norton, were dear friends of ours and still are. What was interesting, the outsiders came together. There were Lebanese people and Syrians, too.

FS: Take us back to your childhood and describe what it was like late in the afternoon in that old house as your mother was preparing dinner for the family.

AT: Autumn was my favorite time in Big Stone Gap, always. People used to still be able to burn their leaves in the 1970s, and there was that smell. I'd hang out up on the hill with my best friend as the sun would go down. We could talk for hours. Then I would walk home, and the first thing I would see would be my mother in the kitchen window with the strainer and the steam coming up, and she would disappear behind the steam. And then you'd know you were having spaghetti, which was my favorite night.

My mother is a very elegant person, and we were robust kids. Our kitchen table always had a cloth on it. In autumn, it was orange. The table was set, and we all sat in the same seats, and the number one rule was you had to be home for dinner at six. And my father would come from the factory, and we'd have dinner. Sometimes he'd go back to work afterward. Not usually, though. And then we'd do our homework. She always had a salad, and everybody always had wine, even the littlest kid. Very, very little, sparing, and cut with water. Nobody in our family ever had a drinking problem because it was introduced as part of fine dining from the beginning. I never saw either of my parents drunk. One of our favorite side dishes was sliced oranges. You peel them and slice them very thin and place them on a plate with olive oil and cracked pepper.

FS: Describe your mother's method of making braciole.

AT: In really traditional Italian eating, when you go to Italy, meat is a side dish, never a main dish. You'd never go out and have a steak. It's always part of the whole. Braciole was a special occasion dish for us. It's a very, very expensive flank steak that's thin and pounded, and then we would fill it. Now my mother had different fillings from my father's side of the family. In our book, we show you how to do it almost pesto style, except it's heartier, and you kind of ice it and you roll it, tie it with string, brown it, and cook it. And then in the oven you can cover it with your traditional sauce. When you slice it, it's a pinwheel, almost like that candy they make down here with peanut butter in it. Readers have told me they stuff it with pine nuts and raisins, but, for us, it's always that fresh basil, which my mother used to grow.

FS: When you were growing up, how difficult was it to find Italian food products in southwest Virginia?

AT: Christmas Eve, seven fishes were hard to find in Big Stone Gap. My grandmother Viola would come down two or three times a year with coolers full of cheese and different things. The blouses from my father's mill were delivered to New York in a truck, and one of my clearest memories of him is waiting for that truck to come back with pastries from Ferrara's on Grand Street in Greenwich Village, and it's so funny because I live there now, and I used to think when those pastries arrived, "Can't they get better packages?" because it was cardboard with the string, and they were soaked, from the baba au rhum and the sauces and stuff. My grandmother, when she got out of the car for the first time in Big Stone Gap, said, "It's very pretty here, but I can't live in a place where they don't make cheese." We had to really improvise. Cheese was the big one. We froze grated cheese. And my grandmother canned enough tomatoes for her four children.

FS: How did your family adapt to mountain cookery?

AT: Our food was just very different from what people in southwest Virginia were eating, but we loved their food, too. When my mother cooked in the mountain style, she'd make desserts like chocolate Coca-Cola cake. Some of those church supper cakes, you can't beat them. Also, she would do fried chicken, which she was very good at, and she would do collard greens. We loved them. To this day I love them with vinegar on them. White vinegar or wine vinegar. My father appreciated churned butter and honey with the comb for our Easter bread.

FS: I would imagine that the buttermilk cake you write about in *Cooking with My Sisters* went over well in Big Stone Gap.

AT: When the buttermilk cake hit Big Stone Gap, that was pretty profound, because my grandmother made it. Now my grandmother was a farm girl, but they were from the Veneto in Italy, and that recipe in our book is over 200 years old. It's her great-grandmother's recipe. They've made it in the Perin family for generations. Sort of a version of a pound cake but not really because it's more moist than a pound cake, and it's less high than a pound cake and has this crumbly stuff on top. Some people want it at their wedding, they love it so much. That was great in Big Stone Gap because the women there, they make cakes like the best bakers in the world. Their pound cakes are phenomenal. I remember that cake, the Watergate Cake, that made the rounds. And the chocolate in the South, to me, I like it better because it's more caramelized. In the North it's very dark. But the buttermilk cake really fit right in. That's a great church supper cake because it's like the loaves and fishes. The thing's huge, and it just never goes away.

FS: Big Stone Gap is still known by many as the place where Elizabeth Taylor choked on a chicken bone back in 1979 while she was accompanying her husband, Senator John Warner, on a campaign stop, a scene you describe in your novel *Big Stone Gap*. What do you recall about that incident?

AT: My parents and my brothers were there; the girls didn't go. Everybody I've met since the book came out was in that kitchen when she choked because everybody's got a story to tell about it. The best was what Senator Warner told me himself, which I couldn't believe. I very much want him to be in the *Big Stone Gap* movie, and I hope when the time comes he'll step up and do it. He was familiar with the book, and he thought it was very funny. He said, "You got one thing wrong," and I said, "What did I get wrong?" and he said, "Well, the rescue squad didn't carry her out of there. I picked her up and carried her, and at that time it was no small feat."

FS: One of your grandmothers actually hid recipes so no one could match her cooking.

AT: I'm a product of a mixed marriage. My father was southern Italian and Venetian. Venice is its own planet. My father's mother was Venetian, very secretive and hot-tempered and could go without speaking to someone for years. She was highly competitive. My mother's side is from Bergamo-Schilpario. They're like mountain people, like you find here. My Venetian grandmother, Yolanda "Viola" Trigiani, wouldn't give her own sisters recipes. We had to videotape her to get recipes. And when she died, her oven wouldn't work, so my husband took it out of the wall, and all these bits of paper came flying out from a false drawer: poems, cocktail recipes like Santa's Helpers, which made me laugh, and all these recipes.

FS: How did the idea for a cookbook develop?

AT: We had gotten so much mail about the recipes that were in my novels. That led to the cookbook idea. We're not Jacques Pepin; we're cooks for our families. What's really great about it is you can make the stuff. Some of the things look fancy, but they're really not. The collaboration took three years, and we tested every recipe five or six times.

There's an element in all the recipes in Cooking with My Sisters *that comes through as brightly as the chopped basil leaves in the stuffed and rolled steak dish called braciole, as cleanly as the fresh lemon juice in the sauce of garlic and oil for capellini pasta, and as boldly as the pink-rimmed pickled eggs. That element is respect. Respect for the traditions of Italy, for the pound cake and beans-and-cornbread cuisine of Appalachia, and respect for the blessings of family.*

Two Americas, Two Restaurants, One Town

REBECCA SKLOOT

To call Baristas a restaurant would be a serious understatement. It is a restaurant, but it's also a barbershop. And a coffeehouse. And, of course, a massage parlor. Naturally, it's run by the same guy who turned the funeral home around the corner into a gym, with cardio machines in the viewing room and free weights in the old embalming chamber.

Baristas occupies a huge turn-of-the-century white house in New Martinsville, West Virginia, with steep, fire-engine red steps, a porch full of rainbow-colored tables, and pillars painted to look like cloudy skies and candy canes. You walk inside to high ceilings, oak floors, purple walls, and one of the owners, Jill Shade, making her famous mocha crushes or hopping around singing an old Cher song she has had stuck in her head for weeks. When I first walked in, Shade pointed to a huge wooden board behind her. "Menu's up there," she told me, "but if you're craving something you don't see, just holler and I'll try to make it."

Baristas's menu is not exactly an exercise in overwhelming choice—a couple of homemade soups, a salad, some appetizers, sandwiches, and one dinner special on Friday nights. But ambience is another story. You can eat in the basement pub, with its low oak ceiling and stone walls. You can eat on the patio overlooking the Ohio River, in the garden next to the hibiscus plants, or in the café surrounded by walls of local art. You can get a haircut or a bona fide Swedish massage while you wait, then sit at a table covered in quotes from Camus or Malcolm X. It's exactly the kind of place I love, and exactly the kind of place I would never expect to find in New Martinsville, where I live part of each year. It's a town of about 5,000 people and thirty-six churches, a town full of all-you-can-eat buffets, Confederate flags, "No Trespassing" signs, and folks who still feel the need to point out the local lesbian couple. But then again, I never expected to find Jeff Shade in New Martinsville either.

Shade is a local boy, a thirty-eight-year-old former high school football star who left West Virginia with dreams of becoming a minister. But he lost God somewhere in Texas and got kicked out of seminary, he says, for "asking too many questions." He studied philosophy and theology at Princeton, then went to massage school in Manhattan while serving as the pastor for a New Jersey church, where he preached from the *New York Times* instead of the Bible. A few years later, he headed back to New Martinsville with his wife, Jill, their two-year-old son, Soren Aabye Shade (as in Søren Aabye Kierkegaard), and degrees in Greek, theology, philosophy, and massage. With all that education, he and Jill decided they wanted to expand the minds of the folks back home. The tool they chose was the burger.

The Baristas burger is the creation of Tammy Wilson, a compact, pony-tailed whirlwind with tie-dyed flip-flops and a T-shirt that says, "Save the drama for your mama." Wilson is Baristas's main cook, and she works in a kitchen that looks more like a home than a restaurant. Teenaged girls run in and out asking her questions about prom dates and haircuts, Jill appears from the garden with a bag of peppers for roasting, and Jeff wanders around tasting soups and sauces while cracking jokes about politicians or saying things about Foucault that nobody understands. Wilson spends hours each week pressing fresh garlic and adding it to vats of ground beef for burgers; when she's done, she rolls up her sleeves and plunges her hands into the meat. "I learned to cook from my hillbilly grandma, and I'm proud of it," she told me. "And if there's one thing I know, it's that burgers only taste right when you mix the spices by hand."

Clearly, she's on to something. People drive sixty miles up and down the Ohio River for her burger: a juicy half-pound of ground beef with hints of ginger and garlic and soy, some spices, a touch of West Virginia honey, and enough sweet smokiness from the grill to make you think she cooked it over fresh mesquite. Mix that with a salad fresh from the garden and hand-cut fries, and you've got a room full of people who simply can't believe anyone wouldn't want to eat at Baristas.

But in fact, a lot of locals can't imagine even walking into Baristas, let alone eating there. The truth is, most of them would rather go to Bob Evans.

The first time I drove up to the New Martinsville Bob Evans, Billy Joel's "Just the Way You Are" was echoing through the parking lot from the speakers above the doors. Everything about the place said "national chain." I walked past a red, white, and blue banner into a world lined with plaid curtains and Old Fashioned things, like copper teakettles and washboards that looked so new they might as well have still had price tags on them. The eggnog- and pecan pie–scented candles by the cash register overwhelmed any smells from the kitchen. A short woman in black polyester slacks and a white button-up shirt with a Bob Evans logo stitched on it smiled at me, menu in hand, and said, "Hi, welcome to Bob Evans. One for dinner?"

Baristas and Bob Evans are less than a mile apart, but they might as well be in different cities. Baristas sits on Main, a quiet, tree-lined street with wide sidewalks and a historic courthouse. You're guaranteed to miss it if you don't know to turn toward the river at the BP station. But you can't miss Bob Evans. It has the tallest sign on this strip of Route 2, a highway lined with a Wal-Mart, a McDonald's, a Dairy Queen, and a Pizza Hut.

There is only one Baristas, but there are 576 Bob Evanses, in twenty-one states; in 2004 the company rang up $1.2 billion in sales. Bob Evans is part of a giant and fast-growing retail category known as "full-service family-style dining" (you know the kind: Cracker Barrel, Denny's, Friendly's); it's a sit-down restaurant that leans more toward down-home than fast food, with a serious emphasis on all-day breakfast. Like most Bob Evanses, the one in New Martinsville is a red and white "farmhouse" with a sprawling parking lot and a few benches out front.

The goal at every Bob Evans restaurant is to be the same as every other Bob Evans restaurant. "We want to make sure the experience someone has in New Martinsville is the same as the one they'd have in Orlando, St. Louis, or Baltimore," said Tammy Roberts Myers, the PR director at Bob Evans headquarters in Columbus, Ohio. The company's guiding principle is simple: consistency, in everything from ambience to the distance between tables to the arrangement of food on your plate.

"Going out to eat is risky," said Steve Govey, the Bob Evans regional manager for the Ohio Valley. "You never know what you're going to get. But at Bob Evans, that's not true. Our strategy is being completely predictable, something people know they can count on."

Bob Evans was packed when I arrived. It was full of customers of all ages and sizes, with lots of khakis, denim shorts, and camouflage hats with pictures of guns or slogans like "National Wild Turkey Federation." There were three women at three different tables wearing identical neon orange T-shirts. I'd just come from Baristas, where people danced at the counter to Ray Charles and talked across the room about how so-and-so woke up with a weird rash yesterday and what John Kerry said at the rally in Wheeling about helping mill workers. At Bob Evans I sat alone at the counter. The people around me stared at their plates and ate in silence; behind me, people spoke so quietly I could barely hear their murmurs over the clanking silverware.

I ate a raspberry grilled chicken salad with exactly four slices of strawberries, four chunks of pineapple, and a tough sliced chicken breast with raspberry vinaigrette. I followed that with a classic turkey dinner. The stuffing was great, but the rest was just barely edible—a little dry, too salty, with oily biscuits and mashed potatoes that tasted like fake movie popcorn butter. Honestly, I didn't get it.

But I went back to Bob Evans the next day, and I kept going back and kept trying things on the menu. I was determined to understand why so many people in town chose this place over Baristas. (The prices at the two restaurants, by the way, are about the same.) I ate a southwestern omelet smothered in jack cheese, and a pork chop dinner that took four people to make. None of the chefs spoke while they cooked; they just threw still-frozen vegetables and meat straight onto the griddle. (They let me watch.) They measured lettuce and arranged the food on my plate so it would look exactly like the instructional diagram hanging on the kitchen wall: pork chop over here, frozen vegetables over there, one sprig of parsley right there.

After a waitress put the whole package down in front of me, I took a bite and thought, "They're right, it is just like Grandma used to make." Thing is, my grandmothers couldn't cook. From my New York grandmother, I got burned matzo brei and gefilte fish from a jar. From my southern Illinois grandmother, I got food that tasted just like Bob Evans's: soggy vegetables, rubbery bread, and meat so overcooked it crumbled when you bit it.

I'd gone meat shopping a couple of days earlier with Tammy Wilson from Baristas, and I watched her handpick every pound of meat from the butcher's counter as he leaned through the window and told her it had just come in fresh. "He gets most of his meats local," she told me. I wanted to find out the same sort of thing about the Bob Evans pork chop, so I called the folks in Columbus. Tammy Roberts Myers said she would be happy to trace my dinner for me, all the way from the animal to the table. But a couple of weeks later, she called to say that someone at headquarters had a change of heart. "Sorry," she said. "We can't tell you that because it's proprietary information. What I can tell you is, it was on a farm somewhere at some point."

I didn't start to understand the appeal of Bob Evans (for other people, anyway) until I met Daisy and Wally Kendall. They eat at Bob Evans nearly every day, sometimes more than once. They sit in a maroon vinyl booth giggling and finishing each other's sentences. When I asked why they eat at Bob Evans all the time, Daisy said, "It's clean, and there are no surprises. I know what I'm going to get." Wally shrugged and said, "People say, 'Why do you only go to Myrtle Beach for vacation every year? Don't you want to see somewhere else?' We never know what to say—we tried it, we know we like it, why risk spoiling our vacation somewhere new when we might not like it?"

When I asked other people why they chose Bob Evans over Baristas, most folks just smiled and shook their heads. One young woman told me her father doesn't like her eating at Baristas because "it's like feeding your money to Satan." One regular said he didn't know why he ate at Bob Evans, but he thought it might have something to do with it being so consistent. "I'm not big on change," he told me. "That's why I'm voting for George W. It's just too dangerous to change stride now. It's best to leave well enough alone."

One woman lowered her voice and whispered, "Baristas's problem is, they try to make fancy food. We're simple people here. We don't like a lot of spices and stuff. A little salt and pepper is good enough for us. You have to develop a taste for that fancy stuff, and we don't really want to."

Another woman pointed to my pork chop dinner and said, "You've got to remember, this is what we were raised on. If people want to go into Baristas for a bean sprout sandwich, that's fine, but around here, we don't do that sort of thing."

In fact, Baristas's menu is full of traditional New Martinsville food (hamburgers, grilled cheese sandwiches, steaks, fried green tomatoes), and there isn't a bean sprout sandwich in sight. But there are a few things on the menu that give some locals the creeps: hummus, pesto, eggplant, feta. The way they see it, Jeff's a local boy, and New Martinsville loves him, but that doesn't mean they're about to eat weird food in a restaurant that sounds as if it might as well be a brothel, what with all the drinking and massaging going on there.

Daisy and Wally have known Jeff Shade since he was a kid. When I asked them why they'd never gone to Baristas, they looked at each other as if it had never occurred to them. "We love Jeff," Daisy said. "The only reason we haven't gone there is really just negligence."

"We were going to go there once," Daisy went on, "but a deer ran into the car." Then she paused. "We really should go sometime," she told Wally.

How about now, I asked. I'll go with you.

"Oh, no," they said in unison, then giggled. "We're expecting a call from Wally's doctor later."

Daisy and Wally have always been Bob Evans people, but they didn't start going daily until they came down with severe health problems—lymphoma for Wally and serious respiratory problems for Daisy—which they attribute to years of breathing in toxins while working at a local chemical plant. They got sick and weak, they couldn't cook, and Bob Evans became their life. Daisy looked at me and whispered, "You know, the food here is wonderful. We've never had a bad meal. But really, we don't come for the food. We come for the people." She gestured around the restaurant. "This is our social life."

When I walked back into Baristas after a few days of nothing but Bob Evans, I literally felt as if I had come home. The walls were the exact shade of purple that I painted my bedroom when I was a teenager, and these days my kitchen is maroon, just like Baristas's back dining area. One of my favorite Jayhawks songs was playing, and I sat down at the bar next to Gary, a former airplane-engine specialist who lives in an octagonal penthouse he built on top of an old hog barn.

I told him what I'd been doing, and he looked at me as if I were crazy. "I can't imagine hanging out at Bob Evans every day," he said. "I just find that place so . . . so . . . the same." I knew what he meant. I loved talking to Daisy and Wally and a few other regulars at Bob Evans, but I couldn't handle going in there every day. I'm a Baristas person to the bone—just as Daisy and Wally are pure Bob Evans. The question is: Why? What makes them Bob Evans people and me a Baristas person?

Some of it is simple aesthetics: I think fresh food tastes a lot better than frozen, and I want herbs instead of salt. Local art on colorful walls makes me happy, and fake old-fashioned teakettles make me sad. Mostly I love Baristas because of the buzz, the energy I feel when I'm in the midst of people who thrive on resisting predictability, like the Catholics who come to Baristas to hear Buddhist monks speak about reincarnation, or the Republicans who came in to meet the Kerry people who stopped one night to stump.

Maybe I had an idea that I could convert people—that I could persuade some Bob Evans folks that they should open to change, that the food really was better at Baristas; and maybe persuade some Baristas people that Bob Evans people are interesting and funny and friendly, too. But in all my time shuttling back and forth between the two restaurants, I didn't change a single person's mind. At some point, it hit me: it's not just New Martinsville. Bob Evans people and Baristas people live together all over the United States. They often go to the same stores and send their kids to the same schools, but try as they might, they simply can't understand why anyone in his right mind wouldn't eat the way they do, think the way they do, and vote the way they do. Unfortunately, I'm not sure a burger can change that, not even a really, really good one.

The Anthropology of Table Manners
from Geophagy Onward

GUY DAVENPORT

A businessman now risen to a vice presidency tells me that in his apprentice days he used to cross deepest Arkansas as a mere traveling salesman, and that there were certain farms at which men from his company put up overnight, meals being included in the deal. Once, on a new route, he appeared at breakfast after a refreshing sleep in a feather bed to face a hardy array of buttery eggs, biscuits, apple pie, coffee, and fatback.

This last item was unfamiliar to him, and from the looks of it he was damned if he would eat it. He knew his manners, however, and in passing over the fatback chatted with the lady of the house on how eating habits tend to be local, individual, and a matter of how one has been raised. He hoped she wouldn't take it wrong that he, unused to consuming fatback, left it untouched on his plate.

The genial Arkansas matron nodded to this politely, agreeing that food is different all over the world.

She then excused herself, flapped her copious apron, and retired from the kitchen. She returned with a double-barreled shotgun, which she trained on the traveling salesman with the grim remark, "Eat hit."

And eat hit he did.

Our traveler's offense was to reject what he had been served, an insult in practically every code of table manners. Snug in an igloo, the Eskimo scrapes gunk from between his toes and politely offers it as garnish for your blubber. Among the Penan of the upper Baram in Sarawak you eat your friend's snot as a sign of esteem. There are dinner parties in Africa where the butter for your stewed calabash will be milked from your hostess's hair. And you dare not refuse.

Eating is always at least two activities: consuming food and obeying a code of manners. And in the manners is concealed a program of taboos as rigid as Deuteronomy. We rational, advanced, and liberated Americans may not, as in the Amazon, serve the bride's mother as the wedding feast; we may not, as in Japan, burp our appreciation or, as in Arabia, eat with our fingers. Every child has suffered initiation into the mysteries of table manners: keep your elbows off the table, ask for things to be passed rather than reach, don't cut your bread with a knife, keep your mouth closed while chewing, don't talk with food in your mouth, and on and on, and all of it witchcraft and another notch upward in the rise of the middle class.

Our escapes from civilization are symptomatic: the first rule we break is that of table manners. Liberty wears her reddest cap; all is permitted. I remember a weekend away from paratrooper barracks when we dined on eggs scrambled in Jack Daniel's, potato chips, and peanut brittle, while the sergeant major, a family man of bankerish decorum in ordinary times, sang falsetto "There Will be Peace in the Valley" stark naked except for cowboy boots and hat.

But to children, hardest pressed by gentility at the table, a little bending of the rules is Cockayne itself. One of my great culinary moments was being taken as a tot to my black nurse's house to eat clay. "What this child needs," she muttered one day while we were out, "is a bait of clay." Not until I read Toynbee's *A Study of History* years later did I learn that eating clay, or geophagy, is a prehistoric habit (it fills the stomach until you can bring down another aurochs). I had the opportunity, when I met Toynbee at a scholarly do, to say that I had been in my day geophagous. He gave me a strange, British look.

The eating took place in a bedroom, for the galvanized bucket of clay was kept under the bed, for the cool. It was blue clay from the creek, the consistency of slightly gritty ice cream. It lay smooth and delicious-looking in its pail of clear water. You scooped it out and ate it from your hand. The taste was wholesome, mineral, and emphatic. I have since eaten many things in respectable restaurants with far more trepidation.

The technical names have yet to be invented for some of the submissions to courtly behavior laid upon me by table manners. At dinners cooked by brides in the early days of their apprenticeship I have forced down boiled potatoes as crunchy as water chestnuts, bleeding pork, gravy in which you could have pickled a kettle of herring, and a purée of raw chicken livers.

I have had reports of women with skimpy attention to labels who have made biscuits with plaster of paris and chicken feed that had to be downed by timid husbands and polite guests; and my venturesome Aunt Mae once prepared a salad with witch hazel and, once, in a moment of abandoned creativity, served a banana pudding that had hard-boiled eggs hidden in it here and there.

Raphael Pumpelly tells in his memoirs of the West in the good old days about a two-gunned, bearded type who rolled into a Colorado hotel with a viand wrapped in a bandanna. This he requested the cook to prepare and, seated at a table, napkined, wielding knife and fork with manners passably Eastern, consulting the salt and pepper shakers with a nicety, gave a fair imitation of a gentleman eating. And then, with a gleam in his eye and a great burp, he sang out at the end, "Thar, by God, I swore I'd eat that man's liver, and I've done it!"

The meaning of this account for those of us who are great scientists is that this hero of the West chose to eat his enemy's liver in the dining room of a hotel, with manners. Eating as mere consumption went out thousands of years ago; we have forgotten what it is. Chaplin boning the nails from his stewed shoe in *The Gold Rush* is thus an incomparable moment of satire, epitomizing all that we have heard of British gentlemen dressing for dinner in the Congo (like Livingstone, who made Stanley wait before the famous encounter until he could dig his formal wear out of his kit).

Ruskin and Turner never dined together, though an invitation was once sent. Turner knew that his manners weren't up to those of the refined Ruskins, and said so, explaining graphically that, being toothless, he sucked his meat. Propriety being propriety, there was nothing to be done, and the great painter and his great explicator and defender were damned to dine apart.

Nor could Wittgenstein eat with his fellow dons at a Cambridge high table. One wishes that the reason were more straightforward than it is. Wittgenstein, for one thing, wore a leather jacket, with zipper, and dons at high table must wear academic gowns and ties. For another, Wittgenstein thought it undemocratic to eat on a level fourteen inches higher than the students (at, does one say, low table?).

The code of Cambridge manners could not insist that the philosopher change his leather jacket for more formal gear, nor could it interfere with his conscience. At the same time it could in no wise permit him to dine at high table improperly dressed. The compromise was that the dons sat at high table, the students at their humbler tables, and Wittgenstein ate between, at a card table, separate but equal, and with English decorum unfractured.

Maxim's declined to serve a meal to Lyndon Baines Johnson, at the time president of the United States, on the grounds that its staff did not have a recipe for Texas barbecue, though what they meant was that they did not know how to serve it or how to criticize Monsieur le Président's manners in eating it.

The best display of manners on the part of a restaurant I have witnessed was at the Imperial Ramada Inn in Lexington, Kentucky, in the Middle Lawrence Welk Baroque dining room where I once went with the photographer Ralph Eugene Meatyard (disguised as a businessman), the Trappist Thomas Merton (in mufti, dressed as a tobacco farmer with a tonsure), and an editor of *Fortune* who had wrecked his Hertz car coming from the airport and was covered in spattered blood from head to toe. Hollywood is used to such things (Linda

Darnell having a milkshake with Frankenstein's monster between takes), and Rome and New York, but not Lexington, Kentucky. Our meal was served with no comment whatever from the waitresses, despite Merton's downing six martinis and the *Fortune* editor's stanching his wounds with all the napkins.

Posterity is always grateful for notes on the table manners of the famous, if only because this information is wholly gratuitous and unenlightening. What does it tell us that Montaigne gulped his food? I have eaten with Allen Tate, whose sole gesture toward the meal was to stub out his cigarette in an otherwise untouched chef's salad; with Isak Dinesen, when she toyed with but did not eat an oyster, with Louis Zukofsky, who was dining on a half piece of toast, crumb by crumb.

Manners survive the test of adversity. Gertrude Ely, the Philadelphia hostess and patron of the arts, was once inspired on the spur of the moment to invite home Leopold Stokowski and his orchestra, together with a few friends. Hailing her butler, she said breezily that here were some people for potluck.

"Madam," said the butler with considerable frost, "I was given to understand that you were dining alone this evening; please accept my resignation. Good night to you all."

"Quite," said Miss Ely, who then, with a graciousness unflummoxed and absolute, set every table in the house and distributed splinters of the one baked hen at her disposal, pinches of lettuce, and drops of mayonnaise, not quite with the success of the loaves and fishes of scripture, but at least a speck of something for everybody.

I, who live almost exclusively off fried baloney, Campbell's soup, and Snickers bars, would not find table manners of any particular interest if they had not, even in a life as reclusive and uneventful as mine, involved so many brushes with death. That great woman Katherine Gilbert, the philosopher and aesthetician, once insisted that I eat some Florentine butter that Benedetto Croce had given her. I had downed several portions of muffins smeared with this important butter before I gathered from her ongoing conversation that the butter had been given her months before, somewhere in the Tuscan hills in the month of August, and that it had crossed the Atlantic, by boat, packed with her books, Italian wildflowers, prosciutto, and other mementos of Italian culture.

Fever and double vision set in some hours later, together with a delirium in which I remembered Pico della Mirandola's last meal, served to him by Lucrezia and Cesare Borgia. I have been in extremis in Crete (octopus and what tasted like shellacked rice, with P. Adams Sitney), in Yugoslavia (a most innocent-looking melon), Genoa (calf's brains), England (a blackish stew that seemed to have been cooked in kerosene), France (an *andouillette*, Maigret's favorite feed, the point being, as I now understand, that you have to be born in Auvergne to stomach it).

Are there no counter-manners to save one's life in these unfair martyrdoms to politeness? I have heard that Edward Dahlberg had the madness to refuse dishes at table, but he lost friends thereby and became a misanthrope. Lord Byron once refused every course of a meal served him by Breakfast Rogers. Manet, who found Spanish food revolting but was determined to study the paintings in the Prado, spent two weeks in Madrid without eating anything at all. Some privatdozent with time on his hands should compile a eulogy to those culinary stoics who, like Marc Antony, drank from yellow pools men did die to look upon. Not the starving and destitute who in wars and sieges have eaten the glue in bookbindings and corn that had passed through horses, wallpaper, bark, and animals in the zoo; but prisoners of civilization who have swallowed gristle on the twentieth attempt while keeping up a brave chitchat with the author of a novel about three generations of a passionately alive family.

Who has manners anymore, anyhow? Nobody, to be sure; everybody, if you have the scientific eye. Even the most oafish teenager who mainly eats from the refrigerator at home and at the Burger King in society will eventually find himself at a table where he is under the eye of his father-in-law to be, or his coach, and will make the effort to wolf his roll in two bites rather than one, and even to leave some for the next person when he is passed a bowl of potatoes. He will, naturally, still charge his whole plate with six glops of catsup, knock over his water, and eat his cake from the palm of his hand; but a wife, the country club, and the Rotarians will get him, and before he's twenty-five he'll be eating fruit salad with extended pinky, tapping his lips with the napkin before sipping his sauterne Almaden, and talking woks and fondues with the boys at the office.

Archaeologists have recently decided that we can designate the beginning of civilization in the concept of sharing the same kill, in which simple idea we can see the inception of the family, the community, the state. Of disintegrating marriages we note that Jack and Jill are no longer sleeping together when the real break is when they are no longer eating together. The table is the last unassailed rite. No culture has worn the *bonnet rouge* there, always excepting the Germans, who have never had any manners at all, of any sort.

The tyranny of manners may therefore be the pressure placed on us of surviving in hostile territories. Eating is the most intimate and at the same time the most public of biological functions. Going from dinner table to dinner table is the equivalent of going from one culture to another, even within the same family. One of my grandmothers served butter and molasses with her biscuits; the other would have fainted to see molasses on any table. One gave you coffee with the meal, the other after. One cooked greens with fatback, the other with ham hock. One put ice cubes in your tea, the other ice from the ice house. My father used to complain that he hadn't had any cold tea since the invention of the refrigerator. He was right.

Could either of my grandmothers, the one with English country manners, the other with French, have eaten on an airplane? What would the *Roi Soleil* have done with that square foot of space? My family, always shy, did not venture into restaurants until well after the Second World War. Aunt Mae drank back the tiny juglet of milk that they used to give you with coffee and commented to Uncle Buzzie that the portions of these things in cafés were certainly stingy.

I was raised to believe that eating other people's cooking was a major accomplishment, like learning a language or how to pilot a plane. I thought for the longest time that Greeks lived exclusively off garlic and dandelions, and that Jews were so picky about their food that they seldom ate at all. Uncles who had been to France with the American Expeditionary Force reported that the French existed on roast rat and snails. The Chinese, I learned from a book, begin their meals with dessert. Happy people!

Manners, like any set of signals, constitute a language. It is possible to learn to speak Italian; to eat Italian, never. In times of good breeding, the rebel against custom always has table manners to violate. Diogenes assumed the polish of Daniel Boone, while Plato ate with a correctness Emily Post could have studied with profit. Thoreau, Tolstoy, and Gandhi all ate with pointed reservation, sparely, and in elemental simplicity. Calvin dined but once a day, on plain fare, and doubtless imagined the pope gorging himself on pheasant, nightingale, and minced boar in macaroni.

Honest John Adams, eating in France for the first time, found the food delicious if unidentifiable, but blushed at the conversation (a lady asked him if his family had invented sex); and Emerson once had to rap the water glass at his table when two guests, Thoreau and Agassiz, introduced the mating of turtles into the talk. Much Greek philosophy, Dr. Johnson's best one-liners, and the inauguration of the Christian religion happened at supper tables. Hitler's table talk was so boring that Eva Braun and a field marshal once fell asleep in his face. He was in a snit for a month. Generalissimo Franco fell asleep while Nixon was talking to him at dinner. It may be that conversation over a shared haunch of emu is indeed the beginning of civilization.

To eat in silence, like the Egyptians, seems peculiarly dreadful, and stiff. Sir Walter Scott ate with a bagpipe droning in his ear and all his animals around him and yards of babbling guests. Only the truly mad eat alone, like Howard Hughes or Stalin.

GUY DAVENPORT

Eccentricity in table manners—one has heard of rich uncles who wear oil-cloth aviator caps at table—lingers in the memory longer than other foibles. My spine tingles anew whenever I remember going into a Toddle House to find all the tables and the counter set; not only set, but served. One seat only was occupied, and that by a very eccentric man, easily a millionaire. He was, the waitress explained some days later, giving a dinner party there, but no one came. He waited and waited. He had done it several times before; no one had ever come. It was the waitress's opinion that he always forgot to send the invitations; it was mine that the guests could not bring themselves to believe them.

And there was the professor at Oxford who liked to sit under his tea table, hidden by the tablecloth, and hand cups of tea and slices of cake from beneath. He carried on a lively conversation all the while, and most of his friends were used to this. There was always the occasional student who came to tea unaware, sat goggling the whole time, and tended to break into cold sweats and fits of stammering.

I was telling about this professor one summer evening in South Carolina, to amuse my audience with English manners. A remote cousin, a girl in her teens, who hailed from the country and had rarely considered the ways of foreigners, listened to my anecdote in grave horror, went home, and had a fit.

"It took us half the night to quiet down Effie Mae," we were told sometime later. "She screamed for hours that all she could see was that buggerman under the table, with just his arm risin' up with a cup and saucer. She says she never expects to get over it."

Syrup Boiling

JANISSE RAY

Strangely, I feel as if I descend into the syrup boiling, although I park in the pasture like everybody else and walk up. It is the day after Thanksgiving, and I am here at the invitation of my cousin Sue. This is the scene if you could look down on it: steam leaks out of a long building that is open on one end, the light from inside casting an isosceles triangle onto the ground. Outside the building, in a circle inscribed by a yard light, a fire blazes in a metal drum and a couple of sawhorse tables sag with food. People mill in and out of the light. At the periphery children chase each other in the dark, harvested field.

Near the drum fire a knot of people, maybe nine or ten, have drawn together, their hair and shoulders silvery as moth-glitter in the night light. They face inward, intent.

They are singing! I can barely keep from running.

Once among the singers, I find my brother, and Sue, singing harmony with a strong, clear voice. Other faces are familiar, and some turn toward me, smiling, holding notes and singing hard, *When morning breaks eternal, bright and fair.* They edge together to make space in the circle. *The saved of earth shall gather, over on the other shore.*

When the song ends, Sue grins, says, "We're glad you made it," and introduces Uncle Mark, her daddy, and Uncle Tump and Walter and Linda. Minnilee, to my right, won't stop hugging me, and I don't mind. She knows me less than whom I came from—my grandmother—and it is a long, trusting history.

More arms get thrown around me, and I don't know whose they are—people who are kin or not kin or neighbor to kin or neighbor. Their names puddle up in my mind, and I don't even try to figure out the big tangle this community appears to be, having landed so abruptly in the middle of it.

Then we are singing again, a traditional hymn, singing seriously, for the joy: *When the trumpet of the Lord shall sound and time shall be no more.* A lot of people have been away from a place and gone home to rediscover what's there and have been welcomed by the ones who never left, or who have already returned.

I have been told it is the sweetness of mother's milk that causes our sugar craving, and that we humans evolved as fruit eaters in the trees. It is a sorry place that cannot produce a sweetness for its animals—maple, molasses, sorghum, honey. In south Georgia our sweetener is cane syrup, boiled from the pressed juice of sugarcane. The syrup has a curious taste that a lot of people can't stomach. But those of us raised on it, who never had Aunt Jemima, who didn't know anything else, we sop it up with hot biscuits and pour it over griddle cakes and wet our cornbread with it. We boil it up and pour it over popcorn.

The making of syrup is laborious. The cane has to be grown and cut, its juice squeezed out through what's called a grinder, although nothing is ground up. The machine is really a roller. The juice is boiled down meticulously, the syrup bottled. It's easier to store-buy. With the loss of small farms, we were lucky to see a syrup boiling at all. Our farm's syrup boiler hasn't been fired in thirty years, and the grinder is gone.

Tommy Davis, whose farm this was, knows how to make syrup. He is a sweet-faced man of sixty, wearing overalls. He has worked hard for syrup making—planting the cane and harrowing it and fertilizing it. He chopped it (best done the day it's to be pressed), hauled it to the shelter, and pushed the stalks through the grinder. Years ago, a mule harnessed to a lever would have walked around and around, spinning the gear that pressed the cane. Tommy has hooked up an electric motor to his.

For a long time, he didn't make syrup, but a few years ago he decided to take it back up. He is standing by the boiling syrup when I tear away from the singing and go inside.

"Glad you came," he says, sticking out his hand. "Sue said you might."

"I haven't been to a cane grinding since I was a girl," I say. "There aren't many of them anymore."

He tells me it takes three hours to boil off a making, and this one has been going two and a half. The juice is cooked in an iron kettle about four feet in diameter, mortared into a chimney. In the old days, you had to build a good fire under the kettle, build it of fat lighterd, the resinous heartwood of old-growth longleaf pine, and keep it roaring, but Tommy has welded a propane stove under his. He uses twelve gallons of propane in a cooking.

"Have you had any juice yet?" he asks.

"No."

He lifts a flap of blue tarp at the back of the longhouse and leads me outside.

There is the big grinder and, in the shadows outside the reach of light, a trailer loaded with sugarcane. Tommy flips a switch and feeds two or three six-foot stalks through the metal rollers, holding a paper cup under the outlet. Cane juice runs down, cloudy as fresh lemonade, and thin.

He hands it to me and I drink deeply.

"Years," I say. "It's been years."

To tell the truth, I always thought sugarcane juice too sweet. It's like drinking sugar water. But it's one of those tastes that's becoming endangered, like the taste of blackberry cobbler, and when you get a chance to drink it, you drink it. Some of us talk about past times and rattle on about what holds a community together. The Tommy Davises of the world don't say a word but set to work. They make a cane grinding happen, year after year. They harrow and plow and plant and fertilize and weed and water and harvest and grind and cook. Tommy returned to syrup making because it was dying out, the way our small towns are dying out and our farming communities and our longleaf pine forests. The way family time is dying out. Events like this keep us connected. Tommy's not standing by, watching what's important vanish.

Back inside, a couple of people lean over the hot vat with wet cloths, skimming dregs—black specks of cane—off the foamy top. Rhythmically they rinse the cloths in a metal bucket and skim again, carefully dabbing at the foam, filtering impurities. There is no hurry; they are slow and steady. Parents keep small children back.

I observe awhile, then try my hand at skimming dregs, swabbing and rinsing, careful not to scald myself. The bucket fills with skimmings. "That's the part that'll make you drunk," they say, laughing. "It'll make dogs drunk."

Now Tommy is eyeing the kettle, not leaving it. It is about time to dish up, and there's one moment when the syrup's ready, when the yell comes to shut off the gas. He can't miss that moment, he can't be too early or too late, and he can't be unprepared for it. He clothespins a clean piece of white cotton over the top of a steel vat with a valve at the bottom—the cloth will catch the dregs that the skimming didn't.

The syrup is bubbling madly and reddening now. Tommy lifts a dipperful and lets it run back into the vat. It isn't quite ready. Too thin. But much more heat and it would burn and ruin the entire cooking. Nobody is talking. Everybody is watching, waiting for the perfect moment. Tommy's wife, Jeanette, grabs a long-handled dipper made from a bucket and a slat and sets to dipping and pouring the syrup back into itself to dissipate heat. Young neighbor Kenyon seizes another dipper. Tommy concentrates.

Finally he unhooks from the wall a hand-sized instrument that tests viscosity.

The syrup is thin yet. In a few minutes, he tests again, and it is ready. In a flash the syrup is ladled into the cloth-lined vat, Tommy working on one side and Kenyon on the other. I have learned that this batch is Kenyon's syrup. He grew the cane, and Tommy is boiling it down for him.

When they are done, a scum of white taffy sticks to the rim of the boiler. People edge up to eat it.

"Dog candy," they explain.

Kenyon hands me a length of cane stripping about as long as a fork. He motions for the man beside me, his father, to show me how to use the stripping to spoon up the candy. It is delicious, warm, without the bitterness of molasses. If our history had a taste, this would be the good part. I could eat mountains. I eat more than anybody else. I make sure the entire rim is clean of dog candy before the men start washing the kettle.

Meanwhile, another relative is draining the vat into quart jars. Someone else sticks on labels, "Pure Cane Syrup Made by Tommy Davis." Toward the end, Kenyon hands the valve operator a tall, pretty bottle, and the man fills it. Kenyon screws the lid on and hands it to me.

The bottle is hot in my hands, filled with dark syrup that by night appears almost black but that will lighten to the exact amber of a tannic creek when held up to the morning sun. The thick syrup runs slowly toward the neck of the bottle when I upend it. A golden bubble travels down the bottle's length and disappears.

"It's beautiful," I say to Kenyon, and hand the bottle back.

He keeps his arms by his side, a bashful and happy look on his face. He shakes his head.

"I can't take your syrup," I say. "You've worked too hard for it." I again hold the bottle toward him.

He shifts sideways. "You're not taking it," he says. "I'm giving it to you."

"Let me pay for it. I'll gladly buy it."

"Your money's no good here," he says.

"Thank you," I say. "I'll remember where it came from."

I've talked about the syrup and not enough about the people. Once I pass Sue and she leads me to rabbit, roasting on a grill, from animals she's raised and butchered. The piece she gives me is delicious. Jeanette brings in a baker of hot biscuits that we proceed to drown in syrup and eat. Later I go out and shuck oysters with Walter and Uncle Mike. Everybody wants to talk, to catch up. Linda asks me to send family information and photographs for her genealogy project. She and Walter live in Orlando now.

Everywhere I turn, people are asking how long I've been back and where I am staying and how the folks are, and remembering my grandmother, and telling me stories of their own lives, how their son was killed and they are raising their granddaughter, or how they love the home place but their life is too tied to Atlanta or Dallas to leave. Every time I turn around, somebody is hugging me and telling me to come see them *when the roll is called up yonder.*

It's sweetness keeps people together. Sweetness. The sweetness of our tongues, of kind words, of praise, of invitations extended and invitations accepted, and the sweetness, too, of acts of imagination and love. Forgiveness, tolerance, and the courage to reach out. Every morning I pour the syrup on thick. *I'll be there.*

JANISSE RAY

The Meat of the Matter

To the Unconverted

JAKE ADAM YORK

This is the meal equally set.—Whitman

Mud Creek, Dreamland, Twix-n-Tween,
the joints rise through smoke
and glow like roadhouses on Heaven's way.
Or so the local gospels raise them,
every tongue ready to map the ramshackle
of shacks and houses, secret windows
and business-sector hip in some new
geography of truth. If the meek shall,
then a rib-mobile may shame the fixed pit
in a reading from the book of skill,
the grill-less one cook himself to legend
rib by rib. The great chain's links
are live and hermetic as bone
and where cue burns hotter than politics,
every mouth's the forge of change,
all scholars temporary and self-proclaimed.
One says he half-sublimes each time he eats
a rib and expects to go in a puff of smoke
when he finds the perfect pig:
he wanders like a ghost, his eyes
trying everything, a genuine R&D,
and once a day he proclaims the latest find,
a homegrown Moses canting
a vernacular Talmud changeable as wind.
A word could crumple him, some backyard
master slapping mustard on a country rib
to turn the state of things entire.

So every word reverberates and mystery's
sown again. Rib or rump, dry rub or ketchup,
the eternal terms turn and barbecue's rooted
or pulled anew. Theories proliferate
like flies after rain, but that's the usual business
where Georgia and the Carolinas river in,
the wind spirits Mississippi or Caríb,
and piedmont's melted to the uplands
in open hearths and coke ovens, stitched tight
in cotton fields, where a kudzu vine's
the proper compass. Beef or pork,
catfish, quail, or armadillo,
we've tried it all, loved it with brushes,
kiss of vinegar, tongue of flame,
so whatever it may not be,
we've covered all it is. Vegetarian
exception opens eggplant, means tofu's
the next horizon, purity an envelope
that's always opening. So summer afternoons
and Saturdays when the fires go up,
smoke rises to a signal and shapes
the single common word,
hand-made silence talking on every tongue.

Of Possums and Papaws

JOEL DAVIS

Possum doesn't taste like chicken—no, sir. It tastes neither fowl nor foul. And like everything else that has ended up on my Papaw's table over the years—from squirrel to bull testicles—I have eaten possum several times. The secret to dining with my maternal grandfather is to chew quickly, swallow fast, and only then ask what it was you just ate.

Now my reputation as a ravenous possum eater is probably undeserved, stemming as it does from certain apocryphal tales of my childhood: family myths telling of epic dinners at Papaw's house during which I gobbled portions of our nation's most identifiable marsupial between chants of "more possum, Papaw, more possum!"

Still, truth be known, I have smacked my lips several times since upon a meal of our much maligned *Didelphis marsupialis*. After discussing these meals with Papaw, I have come to realize that these days, a lowly possum will likelier end up as a speed bump on our public highways than as an entrée on the tables of our well-fed populace. "People don't hardly eat 'em no more," Papaw says. "I don't know of anyone around here that still eats 'em."

Papaw still eats them, though—eats them and enjoys them, too. "They're all good," he says. "I'd rather have a possum than a groundhog." The thought of all the poor people who never have—and probably never will—eat a possum dinner inexplicably saddens me, and so, on this lukewarm autumn day, I have undertaken the task of writing a guide for those who wish to partake of the plethora of possums to be found in our fair land.

The first step on the journey to a meal of possum is the most profound one. This step involves catching a possum. Now, there are two schools of thought on how to catch a possum. One approach is to cruise the back roads of your neighborhood at night in the comfort of your car until you glimpse your prey scuttling across the road and either run over him or jump out and chase the rascal down. If you choose the latter option, take a tire iron with you. Of course, while hunting possums from your car is convenient, it probably isn't legal—and it lacks a certain panache.

The traditional way to catch a possum is to take to the woods with your hunting dog some moonlit night during possum season, which extends from November to February in Tennessee. Possums love the taste of a ripe persimmon. So the best time and place to catch a possum is in a persimmon tree after the fruit has ripened, which is usually around the first frost. "Yeah, boy," Papaw says. "Coons like the persimmons, too."

When I asked Papaw about persimmons, he drove me up the hill on his farm, and we gathered some prematurely ripe persimmons from under a lonely tree. Afterward, while driving over to his brother Joe's farm to look for a possum to catch, I tried a persimmon or two and was struck by the distinct mellowness of the fruit. The texture of the pulp was soft and smooth against my tongue and the roof of my mouth.

At any rate, after you've located a possum in a persimmon, or in any other tree, the question is "what now?"

"You just climb the tree and shake 'em out," Papaw says. "They're out on a limb, so just shake it so they'll turn loose. I'd have to shoot one out now, though, 'cause I can't climb."

"I can climb," I say, remembering family myths of my half-squirrel heritage. Later that day, I found myself teetering along the limbs of a hollow tree. Papaw had caught possums out of it before so it seemed like a good place to check. No possums. On the way out, we did harvest a dozen golf balls that were hidden in the undergrowth like the eggs of some half-crazed fowl.

If you have better luck at finding a possum, Papaw advocates catching the critter alive in order to fatten it up. So leave your gun at home, grab a stick, and take your courage. Despite the impressive dental hardware that the average possum possesses, it is a relatively meek and slow opponent. Just don't underestimate it, and remember to grab it by the tail or back legs. Grabbing a possum by the snout is not considered prudent.

After capturing your future supper, the next step is to put the animals in a clean cage and feed them well, says my Mamaw. "We put them up in a cage for about six weeks and feed them food we like to eat," she says. "They'll eat milk and bread and vegetables—they love vegetables. We feed them up like that for a while, and then we kill them."

But how to kill a possum? The next few steps are not for the squeamish. To kill the possum humanely, Papaw suggests laying a stick across the animal's neck, standing on both ends of the stick, and picking it up by the hind legs. This will break its neck and minimize the suffering.

To dress the possum, immerse it in very hot, but not boiling, water for one minute. Afterward, scrape the skin with a dull knife to remove the hair. Be careful not to cut the skin.

Next, slit the carcass from the neck to hind legs with a sharp knife and remove its innards (this should prove to be the most popular step so far). Wash the possum thoroughly inside and out with hot water and remove the head and tail. Cover it with cold water mixed with a cup of salt, and let it stand overnight. The next day, throw out the salt water and rinse the possum in boiling water. After cleaning the possum, the most basic recipe is to fill a pan half full of water, place the possum in it, and cover it. Then parboil the possum by heating the pan at high on top of the stove. After the water begins boiling, turn the temperature down and continue parboiling it for one hour; the time varies slightly with the size of the animal. When the meat begins falling apart, the possum is ready for the next step: Place the possum in a roasting pan and surround it with peeled sweet potatoes. Add salt and pepper to taste. Bake the critter at about 350 degrees until it's brown, then pepper and salt it.

At this point, the novice possum eater must make peace with his or her gustatory expectations. No matter how fervently the eater might wish otherwise, friend possum's dark and greasy meat does not resemble chicken or pork in taste or texture. It tastes like possum. According to my decidedly undereducated palate, it resembles pot roast—a greasy, slightly stringy, and benignly gamey pot roast. As to what to serve with possum, you can eat it with pinto beans or green beans or potatoes, Mamaw says.

In the end, while possum is much maligned, it can still provide a tasty meal, and at least for me, a possum dinner is the stuff of which fond memories are made. So take a chance. Go find a persimmon tree some moonlit night and settle yourself down to wait for our old friend, the possum.

A Passion for Bacon

PETE WELLS

Throughout most of my twenties, for reasons that would probably make me laugh today if I could remember them, I was a vegetarian. For nearly a decade, I wouldn't go near a porterhouse or a lamb chop or a sparerib. I always made an exception for bacon, though. People thought I was kidding when I explained that bacon wasn't a meat, it was a condiment. But I was serious: Bacon seemed to me like pure flavor—not animal, vegetable, or mineral but some intensified, distilled essence of sweetness, salt, and smoke. I'm not sure I was wrong, either. A recent cookbook was titled *Everything Tastes Better with Bacon*, and it's true. Everything is better with bacon. Even vegetarianism.

It stands to reason, then, that Dan Philips is one of my few heroes. Philips is the founder of the Grateful Palate, a wine importer and mail-order epicurean foods company perhaps best known as the perpetrator of the Bacon of the Month Club. The Bacon of the Month Club works like the Book of the Month Club, except that the book club mails you some fat best-seller that sits on a shelf until your next yard sale, while a pound of bacon from the Grateful Palate usually finds itself in a hot skillet before the mailman can say good-bye. One customer wrote Philips to say that each time a new shipment arrives, her husband dances around the box. The Grateful Palate now offers more than thirty artisanal bacons from all over the United States, and collectively they outsell everything else in the catalog, including stunning bottles of Australian Shiraz and more esoteric treats, like crimson pumpkinseed oil from Austria.

Philips, a native Californian, grew up eating bacon almost every day and still does, but he was nonetheless surprised by the size and excitability of the audience for it. He knew something powerful was at work, but he wasn't sure what. I don't know much about bacon, other than how it tastes, he told me recently. Then he said that he was thinking of calling on some of his favorite producers to see if he could learn why their bacons are so different from one another. Western Kentucky and Tennessee are particularly rich in makers of country bacon—pork bellies that are cured with salt and sugar, hung to dry, and then saturated with hickory smoke.

This suggested to Philips a road trip, starting in Louisville and meandering south-by-southwest down country roads in search of knowledge, wisdom, and pork products. I didn't beg. Perhaps I did drop a few dark warnings about the dangers facing the solitary hunter of breakfast meats in isolated rural areas. A few days later, Philips sent an e-mail inviting me to ride shotgun on his bacon safari. I have a few stipulations, he wrote: (1) I must always be addressed as Captain Bacon. (2) No stopping for cheap hookers. (3) You must bathe at least once every day. Other than that, I'm easy to travel with.

I met Captain Bacon at 6 A.M. in front of the Seelbach Hotel in Louisville. With full cups of coffee and empty stomachs, we charted a course for Bremen, Kentucky, where Charlie Gatton makes a product he calls Father's Country Bacon. As we crawled along a two-lane blacktop past cornfields and convenience stores (Marlboros $2.10!!!), I mentioned a legendary country-ham producer I'd heard of down in Trigg County, hinting strongly that I might go on a bathing strike unless I was promised I'd leave the state with a ham in my suitcase. "Don't worry," he said. "All the bacon guys we're going to see also make hams." The two meats are cured and smoked in essentially the same way, he explained, but then hams are aged for months, while bacon is ready in a couple of weeks. "If the same people make both things," I asked, "then how come country ham gets talked about as an artisanal product, while bacon is just bacon?"

The Captain thought it over. "I don't really know," he said. I think it's because people buy hams for Christmas, for Easter. A ham is an event. Bacon is more of an everyday thing. But toothpaste is an everyday thing, and so are socks. Neither could lure me to the back roads of Kentucky before sunrise. Bacon is an everyday thing, but a mystery, too—an everyday mystery.

About three hours out of Louisville, we turned at a sign that read "Gatton Farms: Home of famous country hams, bacon & smoked sausage." On our left was a white shingle farmhouse planted in the shade of a 100-year-old cypress tree. To our right was a white fence whose pickets were topped by miniature silhouettes of hams. The door of a low-slung red brick structure swung open, and Charlie Gatton Jr. stepped out to welcome us. A born salesman, Gatton took over his family's cured meats business two years ago, after his father died. Since then, he has experimented with new products, like smoked rib eyes, and new ways of reaching customers, including a website and appearances on the Home Shopping Network. "Bacon is good for you," he tells viewers. "When you cook it, most of the calories melt away." The Home Shopping phone operator who hopes for a relaxing day at work is in for a bitter disappointment when Charlie Gatton gets in front of the cameras.

Gatton told us cheerfully that we'd come on a good day. Just that morning, he'd received more than a ton of fresh bacon from his packer in Missouri. "Dan, would you like to help us cure some?" he asked. Clearly, Philips couldn't refuse and still call himself Captain Bacon, so he followed Gatton to a fluorescent-lit back room where half a dozen men worked while Hank Williams Jr. sang "Family Tradition" on the radio. The sides of bacon, cut from the bellies of freshly slaughtered hogs only the day before, were piled up in rubber bins on the floor. Another bin was filled with Gatton's curing rub: salt, brown sugar, white sugar, and tiny amounts of nitrite, a preservative that helps the meat keep its alluringly rosy complexion. "You just rub the cure all over with your hands," Gatton said. "No, don't brush off the extra. You want to leave some on there."

Philips coated a slab with the sand-colored rub until it looked like a boogie board after a day at the beach. Then Gatton laid it down in an empty bin so the salt could begin sinking into the meat and drawing out the water. As the meat dries, its flavor gets more concentrated, giving country bacon the depth and intensity that sets it apart from its gentler, brine-cured cousins. "Our bacon loses about 12 percent of its weight in water when we cure it," Gatton said. "Supermarket bacon has water added, with needles that pump it full of brine. When I go on Home Shopping, I'll cook a strip of supermarket bacon. It shrinks to half the size of ours."

Back out front in a small retail shop decorated with fourteen blue ribbons from the Kentucky State Fair, the Captain had a private word with Gatton while I chatted with Gatton's wife, Lori. She doesn't have her husband's polished spiel, but she is a steadfast believer in the mystery of bacon. Whenever she leaves Kentucky, she packs a little plastic bag of Father's Country Pepper Bacon, cooked and crumbled, because she has discovered that some restaurants of otherwise high quality "don't put any bacon on their salad at all," she told me. "And if I can't have bacon on my salad, I just don't care about it."

We said our good-byes and started for Owensboro to spend the night; nobody has yet thought to build a hotel in Bremen, Kentucky. In fact, nobody has built much of anything in Bremen except barns and grain silos and squat brick houses and places of worship. One church we passed had the kind of sign on its front lawn that you see outside car lots and flea markets. "To go nowhere fast," it read, "follow the crowd."

"This area reminds me of where my mother grew up," the Captain said. "She was from eastern Kentucky. Appalachia. Her grandfather made bacon, and she used to cook it for me every morning. We went back a few years ago to find her house. It's mountainous there, but somehow it looks a lot like this—kind of bleak." "Where was your father from?" I asked. "Hungary. He was an Orthodox Jew. He's the reason I got into wine and food. He was a doctor, and he thought he needed to cultivate an interest in the finer things, so we always had expensive wines at dinner. When I was fourteen, I took a wine-tasting class, just so I could know more about it than he did. I was always very competitive with him."

That this rivalry with his Jewish father set young Dan Philips on a path that has now brought him to his mother's home state in search of the flesh of the swine struck me as material that would keep a psychoanalyst busy for years. We set out early the next morning for Greenville, Kentucky, home of the Scott family. As we glided south past soybean fields and horse pastures, Captain Bacon phoned for directions. "She said we look for the turn where it used to say Scott Road, 'until someone stole the sign,' " he said. Scott Road, when we finally found it, led us straight to Scott Hams, and to Leslie and June Scott. Like most small smokehouses, the Scotts' operation grew out of a family farm; Les's grandfather cured hams and bacon at hog-slaughtering time each winter. Les, a talkative man in a cap from the American Cured Meat Championship, raises bulls now as a hobby. "Kept pigs once," Les said. "We had 'em down on the other side of that hill there. The guy who built the pen for us said, 'Don't worry, the smell will never reach you all the way up here.' Well, the very first day we had those pigs, the wind was blowing straight toward the house. It was a real hot day, so we had all the windows open."

The Scotts showed us the parts of the process we'd missed at Gatton Farms. We saw the refrigerated lockers where the bacon ages for two weeks after it's rubbed with the dry cure, and then the smokehouse where it hangs on wood scaffolds for another week in the company of smoldering hickory logs and sawdust. Les Scott's cure is as simple as they come: brown sugar and salt. His bacon can shade in color from pink to nut brown, since Scott uses no nitrites. The Captain asked him why. "My people didn't do it," Les said flatly. "My dad never did it back on the farm. So I don't do it."

I had now sampled the two smokiest bacons the Grateful Palate sells, and there was no mistaking one for the other. Gatton Farms's was complex and "gnarly" (the Captain's word); and its flavor lingered and developed like a Polaroid coming into focus. Scott's was more straightforward, lucid: If it were a painting it would have been called "Still Life with Smoke, Salt, and Pork." Les Scott's bacon is cured about ten days longer than Charlie Gatton's and gets a little less smoke. It doesn't have the white sugar Gatton's has, either. But I wasn't sure that the cure and the smoking technique were the whole story. Les said he believed there's more going on, that bacon is changed by the age and the shape and the smell of the rooms where it's made. "I think each smokehouse has its own personality," he said.

Tripp Country Hams is about an hour north of Memphis in Brownsville, Tennessee, one of those small Southern towns centered around a courthouse square. Charlie Tripp works out of a cavernous facility built by his grandfather, who hauled the sand for the building's mortar in a mule cart. The building started life as a meat locker, where, in the days before electric refrigeration, farmers could store what they'd butchered. Somewhere along the line, Tripp's father "started curing a few hams," Charlie said. Today, Tripp's bacon is a favorite among Grateful Palate customers—perhaps because Tripp puts cinnamon and cayenne pepper in his dry cure. Philips asked if his family has always had the recipe. Tripp shook his head. "No. We were doing it one way, and it made 'a good bacon,'" he said. Good, not great. "But there was this old man who used to have a stand on the side of Highway 70, and he did a little curing. He said, 'I've got a recipe that makes a delicious bacon.' So eventually he gave it to me, and that's the one I've been using ever since."

The genius of this mystery man's secret formula became clear a few minutes later, when Charlie Tripp invited us back to his house, an antebellum mansion across the square. His wife, Judy, had baked biscuits and fried some ham and bacon. In the bubbling oil, the spices floated free of the bacon's edges and coated the entire slice. The low burn of cayenne, as many snack companies know, has the effect of making you want to eat more and more, and that's just what we did.

Our bacon safari over, we turned back down Highway 70 toward Memphis. The Tripps had warned us not to drive so much as one mile above the speed limit unless we yearned for an extended vacation in Fayette County, so we had time to soak up the roadside scenery. The far western end of Tennessee begins to look and feel like the Mississippi Delta. Trees are smothered in kudzu, cotton fields flat as a concrete floor extend to the horizon, and tilting frame shacks promise cold beer in roughly painted letters. This is the landscape that bred the blues. The blues and bacon: both born of poverty, both looked down on by people who feel it's worth drawing a distinction between high culture and low.

"When Charlie was talking about that old man by the side of the road, I started thinking about Robert Johnson," Captain Bacon said. "The way Johnson said he'd met the devil on the highway, and the devil showed him how to play guitar." Johnson is the great Mississippi bluesman who turned up in Delta juke joints in the 1930s with a fluid, dexterous guitar style no one had seen before. According to legend, he summoned the devil at midnight at an intersection about 100 miles south of here and traded his soul for guitar lessons. There is, naturally, a rival theory, which holds that Johnson simply went away for a year and practiced. This is the theory I subscribe to, and in fact I believe it's conde-scension of the worst kind to suggest that a poor black refugee from the Mis-sissippi cotton fields could make himself into a towering musical figure only through the intervention of sorcery. But then I listen to "Me and the Devil Blues" or "Crossroads," and my scalp shivers like the leaves of an aspen when a storm is coming, and even the rationalist in me is tempted to say that the song, if not the singer, is in communication with the supernatural.

I'm also inclined to be a rationalist about bacon, attributing everything to techniques of curing and smoking. But if I eat a slice of bacon made by Charlie Tripp or Charlie Gatton or Leslie Scott, I wonder if Scott isn't right about the personality of the smokehouse, not to mention the man in the smokehouse, and maybe even the figure by the side of the road who whispered an ancient spell in the ear of the man in the smokehouse. Somewhere in these streaky bands of pig meat is a powerful sorcery that can make a grown man dance around a card-board box, corrupt a pure-minded young vegetarian, and transform the son of an Orthodox Jew into Captain Bacon.

Dan Philips phoned me a few weeks after our trip to say he'd been listening to a lot of blues and eating even more bacon than usual. He'd just received a package in the mail: first-run samples of Grateful Palate private-label bacon, cured and smoked by Charlie Gatton following a recipe that Philips had whis-pered in his ear on our visit. Philips said he thought it turned out "pretty damn good" and offered to send me a pound. But no matter how many times I asked, he wouldn't tell me exactly how it was made. That, he said, would have to remain a mystery.

Mad Squirrels and Kentuckians

. . . .

BURKHARD BILGER

A September dawn, windless and clear, with the sky going to lavender behind the high branches. At the bottom of a hollow, Steve Rector and I wind our way along an ocher creek bed, stepping slowly from rock to rock to avoid the crackling leaves. These beeches should still be cloaked in emerald so early in the season, this creek overflowing its banks, but western Kentucky is in the throes of the worst drought in half a century. The only puddle in sight has been claimed by a box turtle, and camouflage clothes are our only cover.

Rector crouches down ahead of me, balancing his sixteen-gauge Winchester on his shoulder, and comes up with a handful of broken shells: beechnuts, gnawed open by little mouths. "I came through here on Sundee, but there wasn't any cuttin's at all," he whispers, moving on. In the distance a woodpecker's hammering dopplers through the forest. Then it happens. Using his shotgun as a crutch, Rector tries to clamber up the bank, but his feet slip just as his body goes horizontal. He reaches for a sapling, but it isn't there, and all 300 pounds of him come crashing down at once. For a moment he just lies in the dirt, his heavy jowls and drooping eyes looking more than usually defeated. "Well," he says, groaning back to his feet, "I guess I must have that mad cow disease after all."

How many other squirrel hunters, I wonder, are thinking the same thing this morning? True, England and its agonies are half a continent and an ocean away. The epidemic that killed fifty-six British people, sent 2.5 million cows to the incinerator, and poisoned Europe's already queasy trade relations should be no more than a distant rumor. No American cow has died of bovine spongiform encephalopathy, and British beef has never found a market here. Still, panic has a way of finding new victims.

In August 1997 two neurologists published an odd letter in the *Lancet*, a prestigious British medical journal. A disturbing pattern had come to their attention, they wrote. In the previous four years, five patients in western Kentucky had been diagnosed with Creutzfeldt-Jakob disease (or CJD), of which mad cow disease is a variant. All five patients had one trait in common: They ate squirrel brains. Given that some forms of CJD can be transmitted by the eating of infected brains, and that most mammals seem able to carry the disease, the connection made sense. "Caution might be exercised," the authors concluded, "in the ingestion of this arboreal rodent."

To a country primed for the next epidemic, this was perversely welcome news. As the terror of AIDS slowly subsided in America, fears of future viruses were beginning to flare up. Books like *The Coming Plague*, *The Hot Zone*, and *Deadly Feasts* were joining best-seller lists, and disease movies weren't far behind. Now here was the perfect fuel for all that smoldering paranoia. Mad squirrel disease, if it existed, was as fatal and as exotic as any novelist could wish, yet most people were no more likely to get it than the plague. If AIDS once seemed an affliction cooked up by country Baptists to punish city dwellers, here was the urbanites' revenge: a disease, common only among squirrel brain–eating hillbillies, that turned its victims into demented fools. What could be more appropriate?

The feeding frenzy was brief but exceedingly gleeful. The *New York Times* began by garnishing the story with some suitably gothic details. "Families that eat brains follow only certain rituals," the paper reported, then it quoted Eric Weisman, one of the authors of the *Lancet* letter. " 'Someone comes by the house with just the head of a squirrel and gives it to the matriarch of the family. She shaves the fur off the top of the head and fries the head whole. The skull is cracked open at the dinner table and the brains are sucked out.' " Squirrels killed on the road, the *Times* added, "are often thrown into the pot." Soon Jay Leno and David Letterman were riffing on squirrel brains in their monologues, and columnists across the country were chiming in. "This report raises some troubling questions," wrote syndicated humorist Dave Barry. "(1) Since when do squirrels have brains? (2) Have squirrels and cows been mating? How? (3) Does a person who eats roadkill rodent organs pretty much deserve to die?"

Steve Rector first heard about it in the coffee room at work. He was putting some squirrel heads into the microwave for lunch, he remembers, when one of the guys mentioned the mad cow disease story in the Owensboro paper. "I figured that if it was really bad, like the bubonic plague, it would be on TV," Rector says. So he started to watch the evening news, scan the local obituaries, and look for signs of strange behavior in local squirrels. Though he never saw or heard anything more, he was spooked enough to lay off brains for the first time in thirty years. But that was last year. Like most of the squirrel hunters I interviewed, he couldn't stay away for long. "I just thought, you gotta die of somethin," he says. "First it was cigarettes cause cancer, then pesticides, and then the water you drink. But I been eatin' squirrel brains since I was six years old, and I ain't dead yet."

It's midmorning now, and our vest pockets have yet to hold any dead squirrels. But as we circle back to the truck, Rector stops suddenly and gestures for me to hang back. Peering at the crest of a distant hill, he slowly raises his shotgun to his shoulder and shoots twice in quick succession, the reports ripping the air around me. Then he hustles up the slope toward a skinny maple tree.

Rector is no champion marksman. At forty-four he has developed astigmatism and can't use a rifle without a scope. His reflexes have slowed down, his heart beats irregularly, and his fingers go numb in the morning cold. Yet when he reaches the tree, his face breaks into a boyish grin. "That was a hell of a shot," he says, reaching into the leaf litter, "sixty yards if anything." He pulls out a young squirrel, its tiny chest still heaving. "Smell of 'im," he says almost tenderly, lifting the warm body to my nose. "Isn't that just like . . . the woods?" Then he takes the animal by the tail and beats its head methodically against the tree. "Don't want to do that too hard," he says after a couple of whacks. "Else I'll spoil the best part."

If hunters around here seem uncommonly suspicious of authority (medical or otherwise), if they clam on to their traditions even at peril of their lives, they have good reason. Ninety years ago, when Rector's grandfather was cutting the giant scaly-bark hickories out of these bottomlands and rafting them to the mill, it was said that the land would make its people rich. But eastern land speculators reaped most of the timber and mining profits, and a tobacco monopoly took what was left. When the virgin forests were gone, Rector's grandfather went to work as a sharecropper and then a coal miner. When his son turned twenty-two, he joined him.

They dug vertical shafts back then, 200 feet down, and up to four miles long, with thin wooden props and little ventilation. They used black powder to blast out the coal and steel picks to chop it up, praying that their carbide lamps wouldn't ignite a pocket of gas. After as many as seventeen hours underground, they emerged black as crows and got paid in company scrip, redeemable only at company stores. The result was best summed up by Merle Travis, whose father and brothers worked in the same mine as Rector's grandfather:

You load sixteen tons and what do you get?
Another day older and deeper in debt.
St. Peter, don't you call me 'cause I can't go.
I owe my soul to the company store.

When Rector was a little boy, and a life underground seemed his inevitable lot, he used to have a recurring dream. He was standing on a high hill overlooking a strip mine, waiting for his father to drive by so he could wave to him. Far below, the mine pit had filled with rain, and the acids in the coal had turned the water bright blue. "I was always wearin' a red shirt and blue jeans, and every time I'd just fall off that edge toward that Bahama blue water," he says. "I'm terrible scared of heights, and I'm not too good a swimmer, so I swear that fall took forever."

Rector always woke up before he hit the water in his dream. But in real life it was the coal business itself that saved him. "Don't bother," the owners told his father when he went looking for a job for his son. "The mines are almost played out. You're better off lettin' that boy finish high school." So Rector took a job as a meat cutter at a supermarket, while his father stayed on at the mine. His grandfather would die of consumption eventually, exacerbated by black lung disease. "The last two years of his life he had to sleep sittin' up in a chair," Rector says. "Couldn't get his breath otherwise."

These days Rector lives just off Paradise Street in the town of Greenville, in Muhlenberg County, Kentucky. His ranch house is small and nondescript—"just a plain old country house," as he puts it—yet to a fan of folk music, staying there is like staying down at the end of Lonely Street at Heartbreak Hotel. It constantly brings to mind the refrain of a song, this one from "Paradise" by John Prine:

And Daddy, won't you take me back to Muhlenberg County
Down by the Green River where Paradise lay?
Well, I'm sorry, my son, but you're too late in asking
Mr. Peabody's coal train has hauled it away.

There are three things that every Rector man has always done, an oral historian once told Steve: hunt, make moonshine, and play guitar. Rector never did take to moonshining (maybe it was seeing his great-uncle's pajamas with the small hole in front, where the bullet went in, and the giant hole in back, where it came out). But he more than makes up for it with his other hobbies. In a county that calls itself the "Thumb-Picking Capital of the World," Rector's command of the guitar has earned him an honorary street sign, and his love of hunting is nearly as legendary. At the age of six he went hunting with his daddy, carrying a BB gun to kill crippled squirrels. At ten he had his own shotgun. "And then pretty soon I was huntin' all the time."

In New York or Boston, where squirrels eat handouts and scamper impudently above park benches, squirrel hunting can seem like poor sport. But in Kentucky, squirrels know the meaning of fear. They leap to the canopy at the first sign of movement. They *baaaaa* to one another, like lambs on speed, sounding the alarm. They flatten their bodies against trees, rotating slowly to keep the trunk between them and the hunter, or just dive into the nearest knothole. "I'd say they're pretty damn smart," Rector says. "I don't know how many pairs of my socks I've burned up trying to smoke 'em out."

Rector's father taught him a few squirrel-hunting tricks, but most of what he knows he learned from his cousin Jimmy Vincent. Tall, skinny, and agile as an otter, Jimmy was nine years older than Steve and half-orphaned by the state: his father was in prison for killing a man. When he was ten years old, another boy shot him the right eye with a BB gun. ("It didn't bust it," Rector says. "It just went behind the eyeball so he couldn't see with it anymore—it had a funny shine to it, like it was made of glass.") But Jimmy didn't let that stop him. He learned to aim over his left shoulder instead and still killed more squirrels with one eye than most did with two.

"Jimmy was like the Chet Atkins of squirrel hunting," Rector says. "He had a sixth sense about 'em. He could smell 'em through the leaves." If the woods went suddenly quiet, Jimmy would pick up a nut and scratch it with his fingernail—an "all clear" sign to the squirrels. If a knothole was within reach, he'd cut a cross in the end of a green stick, poke it in the hole, and twist until it got caught in some hair; then he'd pull out the squealing animal. If a squirrel was hiding on the far side of a tree, he'd tie a string to a sapling and shake it on one side while he circled to the other. "Back when I hunted with my daddy, he used to just say, 'Walk around there, boy, and check that bush,'" Rector remembers. "It wasn't till later that I realized he was usin' me as his string."

All through their youth, Jimmy and Steve kept the family continually supplied with squirrel meat. It was said, in those days, that squirrel soup could cure a cold, but its healing properties were mostly in the form of raw nutrition. What game there was in Kentucky was small, and coal company wages could pay for meat only once a week. So the two boys would get up before dawn, kill a mess of squirrels, and make it to class by 7:30. (In elementary school they hung the tails from their bicycle handlebars; in high school, from their car antennas.) "I remember one time Jimmy and I killed ninety-nine squirrels in a stretch of five days," Rector says. "My mom just pressure-cooked 'em all and put 'em in jars with barbecue sauce. That way, all winter long we could have squirrel sandwiches whenever we wanted."

Alien as they sound, such habits have shaped countless American boyhoods. Squirrels are usually a hunter's first kill, historian Stuart Marks writes in his book *Southern Hunting in Black and White*, and they nest in his memory ever after. "I'd rather kill me six fox squirrels than a ten-point Boone-Crockett buck,"

Steve says, and he'd rather see a squirrel run free than waste any part of its meat. Besides, he says, all of it tastes good.

After our first morning of hunting, we dropped by to see the owner of the woods, Juanita Adkins. Small and neatly put together, with wide glasses, bright white hair, and mischievous eyes, Adkins is eighty-two years old but sharper than most neuroscientists. She took up painting a few years ago, and her farmhouse is hung with skillful oils flanked by the blue ribbons she's won for them at county fairs. Standing in her living room, admiring her animal paintings, Steve asked her if she'd ever eaten squirrel brains. Adkins looked at him as if he were a little dim: "When I was growin' up," she said, "that's all I'd ever eat was the brain."

There was a time, not so long ago, when neurologist Eric Weisman would have laughed at the thought of eating squirrel brains; a time when he would have dismissed it as yet another puzzling local custom, in a state that seemed to have an endless supply of them. Then a squirrel brain eater showed up at Weisman's Neurobehavioral Institute in Beaver Dam, Kentucky. And soon Weisman was asking all his patients if they had the same habit.

At the age of fifty-four, Marvin, as I'll call him, was still robust, articulate, and sharp enough to run his hometown as mayor. True, he'd gotten fired from his day job recently for forgetting to fill out the left side of sales forms. And yes, he did hit that nun's car. But these were all misunderstandings, he said. For some reason, he just didn't see the nun coming from the left, even though it was broad daylight. The crash didn't hurt him much—just a fender bender. But when they took him to the hospital in Bowling Green, he couldn't seem to keep from nodding off.

"They did a sleep study on him after that, but the problem didn't go away," Weisman remembers. "They said it was a stroke at first, and then a brain tumor. Then they sent him to me." During the tests that followed, an odd pattern emerged: if Weisman asked Marvin to draw a clock, for instance, he would cram all the numbers on the right side of its face. "He had what we call a nondominant hemisphere syndrome," Weisman says. "The left side of the world just didn't exist for him." An EEG revealed a strange, periodic disturbance in Marvin's brain waves, and an MRI scan revealed that the right side of his brain had atrophied. But what was the cause? "I just didn't have a good answer," Weisman says. "And then I saw him jerk."

Some eighty years before, a German physician named Hans Gerhard Creutzfeldt had seen the same twitch in one of his patients. A twenty-three-year-old orphan, she had once cheerfully worked as a maid at a convent; now she refused to eat or bathe, grew paranoid, and assumed strange positions. And there was worse to come. Bouts of wild laughter grew into ceaseless screams; chronic tics amplified into waves of epileptic seizures; periods of stupor devolved into cata-tonia and then death. When Creutzfeldt autopsied the patient's brain, he found masses of fibrous brown glial cells—designed to repair damaged tissue—spread through it like spackling on an old plaster wall.

Even today, no one knows for sure what causes such damage. Most doctors blame bits of rogue protein called prions. But others finger stealth viruses, known as virions, or insidious, corkscrew-shaped organisms known as spiro-plasma. Whatever its origin, the disease that was eventually named for Creutz-feldt and his colleague, Alfons Jakob, is among the most mysterious in all of neuropathology. Invariably fatal, CJD chooses victims across gender, race, class, and geographic lines. It can incubate, unseen, for decades and predominantly strikes the middle-aged and elderly. Over the years, forms of it have been found in sheep (scrapie), cows (bovine spongiform encephalopathy), and certain can-nibals in New Guinea (kuru). Mad cow disease and kuru have further been shown to infect those who eat infected meat, particularly brains. But true CJD strikes rarely and randomly, killing one person in a million. "It's like plane crashes," Weisman says; "it only seems to happen to nice people."

Not long after Marvin's first visit, his mind began to seize up with increasing violence, like an engine that first runs out of oil, then grinds down its bearings, and finally throws a rod. What had looked like hiccups gave way to full-fledged spasms, and his mental lapses spread to his whole brain. "If you said, 'With the pen touch the comb,' he could do it fine," Weisman says. "But if you said, 'Touch the comb with the pen,' he wouldn't understand." Meanwhile, other patients were arriving with related symptoms. There were a few who couldn't walk straight, one with mysterious back pains, and two with full-blown dementia. Over the next five years Weisman alone treated six people in the early stages of CJD.

"I don't even like to look at those charts," Weisman says. "It makes me want to cry." Yet there is something of this magpie in most neurologists—something that can't resist the odd mental disorder, the shiny fragment of a mind that somehow casts light on all of human consciousness. The coauthor of the *Lancet* paper, Joseph Berger, calls himself "a collector of unusual patients," and Oliver Sacks has made a career of the same pursuit. Weisman says he was never interested in publicity. But the eerie glow of these rare cases—cases related to a disease that was then much in the news—must have been hard to resist: will-o'-the-wisps beckoning him out of a long exile.

Born in 1957 to a Jewish family in the suburb of Peabody, Massachusetts, Weisman had once seemed destined to become a Boston intellectual, if not a

Brahmin. His father was an artist and businessman who sculpted the heads of swan boats in the Boston Public Gardens. His mother was a soprano with the Boston Opera. (When she retired, she was replaced by her understudy, Beverly Sills. Later she went on to earn her B.A. in archaeology from Harvard—valedictorian at seventy-one.) By the age of six, Eric was drawing pictures of brains. By the age of sixteen, he was taking a course in neuroanatomy at MIT.

He entered Harvard the summer after his junior year of high school, dreaming of becoming a brain surgeon. But when fall arrived he declined to stay on. "It was so competitive," he says. "People were stealing my research, pulling pages out of reference books so no one else could read them." He enrolled at Bard instead, took up dance, and started a rock band. But his grade point average slipped too low to get him into an American medical school. He toyed with going to a school in Belgium but decided on Grenada instead—just in time for the U.S. invasion. ("The local kids were throwing rocks at us, but we got to meet General Schwarzkopf.") In the end he earned his medical degree in Brooklyn. But though he went on to an internship and residency in Mobile, Alabama, and a fellowship at Boston University, he had long since ceased to be the golden boy. In 1987, when a headhunter offered him a job in rural Kentucky, he took it.

It was in Alabama that he overheard a conversation that would later change the course of his life. "We were cutting this brain from Texas or Oklahoma one day," he remembers. "It had CJD, so the pathologist turned to his resident and asked him what kind of history it had. Was its owner a farmer or a factory worker? Did he eat sheep brains, cow brains, or pig brains?" The pathologist, it turned out, was veteran CJD researcher Frank Bastian, the originator of the spiroplasma theory. When he got to the last question, the resident answered, "yes." As a matter of fact, the patient ate squirrel brains.

Twelve years later, relaxing on a terrace overlooking the Ohio River, Weisman seems at first glance to have settled in quite nicely. His hair is long, black, and fashionably unkempt, his body stocky and sunburned. While jazz fusion pulses from massive speakers behind us, he pads around barefoot, in khakis and a striped cotton shirt open halfway down his chest. "I don't know if you know, but neurologists don't usually live like this," he says, gesturing back at his swimming pool and deck chairs, his two-story home with its skylit cathedral ceilings and mantelpiece hung with an English fox-hunting scene. "Guys like me, in New York, we usually have one-bedroom apartments."

Yet as breezy and sunlit as it seems, this house has become a fortress of sorts, and Weisman is in a state of siege. He may be a card-carrying member of the Kentucky Colonels, the state's prestigious fraternal organization, but he's been tarred and feathered by the local press. He may have one of the finest homes in

Owensboro, but his own neighbor—an eater of squirrel brains, Weisman suspects—won't talk to him. He may be married to a former candidate for Miss Kentucky, but by now she's ready to move to Boston herself. "You aren't going to get me killed are you?" Weisman asked the first time I called. "I've gotten death threats, you know." The next time, he answered the phone by saying, "Squirrel brains," as if uttering a secret password. When I asked him how he knew who was calling, he said he had caller ID.

All this trouble, Weisman says, all this bitterness and innuendo, is a result of good medicine and bad media. It began a year or so before Marvin died, when the other dementia patients were beginning to crop up. Weisman was in his office one day when Joe Berger called to ask him if he had seen any CJD cases lately. Berger, who is chair of the neurology department at the University of Kentucky Medical Center in Lexington, had seen a few cases of his own by then, and he had a hunch that they might be tied to farming somehow. By then, however, Marvin had told Weisman that he liked to eat squirrel brains, which had reminded Weisman of the CJD patient in Alabama. When he suggested the connection to Berger, something clicked in the other man's memory as well. In the late 1980s, while still at the University of Miami, Berger had had a CJD patient who had eaten squirrel brains, too.

The coincidence, as it turned out, was not quite as great as it seemed. Nationwide, 3.2 million people hunt squirrels and 25 million of the animals are killed every year in Kentucky, Ohio, and Tennessee alone. (Burgoo, the Kentucky state dish, used to require squirrel meat.) When Berger surveyed 100 local people, he found that 27 had eaten squirrel brains. Given those numbers, one could argue that there should have been more victims if infected brains were the culprit. Besides, squirrels had never been found to carry CJD, and it's hard to imagine how they would have passed it on: they eat only fruits and nuts—not one another's brains.

Still, by then the mad cow epidemic had accustomed researchers to macabre, wildly improbable tales coming true. "All I know is, everyone with CJD I saw ate squirrels," Weisman says, "and not that many people eat squirrels, and not that many people have CJD." Squirrels may not eat meat in the woods, he adds, "but in the city they go after beef by-products all the time—like the suet that people put for birds." As for the rarity of mad squirrel disease, that jibes with a long incubation period. The fact that most CJD victims in western Kentucky are elderly, Weisman told the *New York Times*, "makes me think there may have been an epidemic thirty years ago in the squirrel population."

There was only one way to test the hypothesis: capture some squirrels and check them for the disease. But even as state wildlife biologists were setting out traps, the squirrel brain story was running wild—much to the state's dismay. It wasn't so much the threat of mad squirrel disease that rattled Kentuckians as the hillbilly portraits it inspired. Some admitted to eating brains, but few could remember presenting a squirrel head to the family matriarch, as Weisman told the *Times*, and fewer still remembered scraping squirrels off the highway for dinner. "Is there anything as gullible as a Yankee?" columnist Keith Lawrence wrote in the *Owensboro Messenger-Inquirer*. "Somebody start printing up the bumper stickers now. 'I brake for squirrels. Mmmm-mmmm good.'" The *Kentucky Post*, meanwhile, berated the eastern media for its "snobbish perception that the Bluegrass State is filled with shoeless, toothless, inbred, mouth-breathing, roadkill-eating hijacks so primitive as to chow down on anything that walks, crawls, or slithers." It wasn't long before Weisman's referrals were drying up, and the father of a hockey player he coached was taunting him during practice.

Sitting in his sunroom, recalling the controversy, Weisman hunches his shoulders, and his features darken behind his glasses and beard. He doesn't like to talk about it, he says—this is the first interview he's granted since the story came out. But the words stream out anyway in a low, embittered monotone. He alludes to anti-Semitism and says his colleagues abandoned him. He calls parts of western Kentucky "strongholds of white supremacy" and asks if Rector is a member of the Klan. He insists that the *Times* misquoted him, that he never said Kentuckians eat roadkill.

"How could they say I don't know anything about local culture?" he says, jabbing a cigarette at a framed picture of a young woman on the wall. "My own stepdaughter was the first International Barbecue Festival Queen! I watched her put on her costume and makeup in this house before the parade."

"Look at this," he says, pointing to a stuffed red squirrel slightly flea-bitten, standing there like a supplicant. "My wife bought that for me for my birthday." Then he adds offhandedly, "She grew up eating squirrel brains, you know."

Across the room Beverly sits primly on the sofa, as if patiently awaiting this revelation. When I first came she was wearing a T-shirt and jeans, but while Eric talked, she disappeared into the bedroom for a makeover. She has on green silk pants now and a purple batik blouse. Her hair is pulled back in an elegant knot, and rouge and fresh mascara highlight her beauty queen cheekbones and her kind, slightly asymmetrical eyes. "It's true," she says with a half smile. "I used to go squirrel hunting with my dad when I was a little kid. The brains were kind of a delicacy." She hasn't eaten them in thirty years, she adds, and she doesn't quite believe they can cause disease. When the letter was published in the *Lancet*, she was listed as a coauthor.

They make an odd pair, sitting on opposite sides of the room: New England intellectual and Kentucky farm girl, Jew and gentile, yoked together by their dissatisfactions. When they met at the regional medical center, Weisman was living in a one-bedroom apartment, eager for his next move; she was an intensive care nurse, dreaming of medical school and the wider world beyond it. Instead of leaving after their marriage, though, they bought this house and opened the Neurobehavioral Institute. "The circumstances kind of set me up," he says. "I had to show people that I could set down roots." When Eric needed help, Beverly came on as nurse and sometime bookkeeper—deferring medical school indefinitely.

Every morning now he reads the *Boston Globe* and the *Boston Herald* online. Every night he watches the Red Sox on TV, noting the scores on sheets of paper taped to the refrigerator door. (Beverly has become a fan now, too, he says.) He plays drums in his music room, travels to conferences, and keeps Kentucky at arm's length. "If I didn't have cable TV and a computer, I probably would have moved by now," he says. "But this way, it's almost like I'm living in Boston. It's just easier to find a parking spot." Does he ever feel isolated? I wonder. No, he says, pointing his thumb across the river to Indiana. "I've got the North right there."

The day's kill has been skinned and gutted by now, washed clean of blood clots and flies, and soaked in water for a few hours. Standing at his kitchen sink, Steve Rector pats the pieces dry and salts them generously while his basset hounds, Buford and Macey, look on. They get to eat the tails but not the meat, he says, rubbing Macey's belly with his foot—"She's so fat, there's enough room in there to fit another dog." But hope springs eternal.

We killed two gray squirrels and one red squirrel this morning, though two of their heads were too shot up to keep. Glistening against the porcelain, the rest of their limbs could be mistaken for rabbit or dove, but never chicken: the bones are too delicate, the flesh too dark and tightly muscled. Rector coats them in self-rising flour, then fries them in an electric skillet filled with hot oil. When the squirrel is nicely browned on both sides, he moves the pieces to a pressure cooker. "This is the healthiest meat there is," he says, throwing a few handfuls of flour into the bubbling oil to make gravy. "It hardly has any fat or cholesterol at all." Then he adds more salt to the mixture, shakes in a substance called Kitchen Bouquet ("just to turn it brown"), and pours it into the pressure cooker with the meat. When the top starts jiggling, he says, it'll be done in fifteen minutes.

Standing there, girding myself for the coming meal, I try to imagine myself as John Lawson, an early American explorer whose diaries I've been reading. In 1700, when Indian guides led Lawson through the Carolina wilderness, he happily feasted on raccoon, opossum, and bear fat. Beaver is "sweet Food," he declared, "especially their Tail," and skunk meat "has no manner of ill Smell, when the Bladder is out." Among the Indians, Lawson noted, a meal in great demand consisted of "two young Fawns, taken out of the Doe's Bellies, and boil'd in the same slimy Bags Nature had plac'd them in, and one of the Country-Hares, stew'd with the Guts in her Belly, and her Skin with the Hair on."

Squirrel meat is one of the last holdovers from those older, immeasurably wilder days. Until 1996 even the *Joy of Cooking* had some recipes for it, complete with a drawing of a boot standing on a squirrel's hide and a hand reaching down to yank out the meat. Now mad cow disease and other epidemics, real and imagined, are chasing the wild game from our diet once and for all. "I can serve Chilean sea bass any day," one Southern chef told me. "But if I serve largemouth bass from a local lake, the health department could shut me down." In fact, most restaurants in the country can't serve game legally unless it's raised on a farm, and fewer and fewer people prepare it at home. In 1997, when the *Joy of Cooking* was overhauled, the squirrel section was quietly deleted.

"I watched my grandmother eat squirrel, and my mother eat squirrel, and I eat squirrel," Rector says. "But my son, he won't touch it. 'Daddy,' he says, 'that looks too much like a rat to me.'" Like everyone else around here, he's a deer hunter now. "There was a time, back in the sixties, when Kentucky didn't have any deer, and you could hunt squirrel just about anywhere," Rector says. But the coal company stripped everything out that squirrels would eat—60,000 acres of black oak and black walnut, mulberry, dogwood, and hickory in this area alone. The first thing that grew back was honeysuckle and saw brier: perfect browse for deer.

When Steve and Jimmy Vincent were kids, it seemed as though the land had no limits, and its rhythms were the only clock they followed. They'd drive anywhere they wanted, split up for a few hours, and meet back at the truck when the katydids hollered. But when the deer came in, local farmers got smart. "First they started charging deer hunters a dollar an acre. Then the next year it was two, then three, then eight. Pretty soon, the deer hunters were kickin' me off the land, when I was just tryin' to shoot squirrels." Nowadays, Steve has only four places left to hunt—one of them next to the power plant where he works, shoveling coal ashes with a front-end loader. "I'm a dinosaur," he says. "Nobody hunts squirrel anymore." But he still manages to put a hundred squirrels in the freezer every fall.

It's been six hours since we last ate, I'm reminded, and for the past half-hour we've been enveloped by the smell of frying meat. Perhaps that explains why I'm suddenly more open to the thought of consuming rodent. "I was watchin' the

Discovery Channel the other day, and it was sayin' rat is a delicacy in some places," Rector says, emptying his pressure cooker on a plate. "It's just a different concept. It's like we look at a cow and think that's somethin' you eat, and we look at a horse and say that's somethin' you ride. But a horse probably tastes even better than a cow."

I hesitate for a second, staring at the creamy mass of jumbled limbs. But when I take my first bite, the meat is tender and its taste straightforward—sweeter and richer than rabbit, I think, though it's hard to tell through the Kitchen Bouquet. By the time Rector reaches for the only head, I almost envy him.

"Here's how you eat one of these," he says, lifting up the skull with his fingertips. Seen in profile, it looks like the head of a monstrous ant: streamlined and mechanical with buck teeth in front and incisors curving down the sides like whiskers. First Rector nibbles off the neck meat, then the cheeks, then he pulls off the lower jaw and plucks out the grayish-blue tongue. When all that's left is in the braincase, he picks up a teaspoon and smacks it down smartly on top.

Inside, beneath the eggshell-thin surface, lies a pink organ about as large as the first joint of my thumb, stained inky black between its lobes. If some infectious agent lurks there, no pressure cooker could have killed it: brain tissue from a mad cow can pass on the disease even after baking in a 700 degree oven. "Ya want some?" Rector asks, holding the glistening brain toward me. Before I can answer, he pops it into his mouth. "Too late," he says.

Late one morning, after another few hours of hunting, I head for Louisville and Lexington, leaving western Kentucky behind. "There's more difference between your life and mine than there is between mine and Jesus'," an opossum hunter once told me, and today I have to agree with him. The clock jumps forward an hour as I drive east, but as small town gives way to cityscape, it feels like a millennium or two have passed. Along the highway, at first, there seem to be more pedestrians than drivers: broken-down old men waving flags around concrete barriers; women with bad backs and distended bellies, holding up signs that say "SLOW." But the construction clears eventually, and the faces give way to gleaming headlights, hurtling headlong for modernity.

"Let me give you a sense of the culture shock," Joseph Berger tells me later, reclining in his office high above the campus in Lexington. "When we first moved here from Miami, my wife went to our little grocery store one time and asked the proprietor if he had any Danishes. 'Ma'am,' he told her, 'we don't have Finnish, we don't have Swedish, we don't have Norwegian, and we certainly don't have Danish. But if you'd like a Twinkie, it's over there.'" He points toward an imaginary counter and bursts into an infectious giggle, his small round face and dark brown eyes turning more impish than usual.

Born and raised outside of Harrisburg, Pennsylvania, Berger spent most of his adult life on the East Coast, first in Philadelphia for medical school, then in Florida for seventeen years. When he got the offer from Kentucky, he says, he first had to find it on a map, but the chairmanship of a department was too much to turn down. Sure, it took a while to get used to the place. "When we first moved here, I was having my bread baked and half-frozen and brought in from Chicago. My meat was all imported, and I had those French cookies that I particularly liked—Petite Beurres—shipped in from friends in France." But there's been a sea change in the past four and a half years, he says, a "tremendous maturation" in the city: "There's no fine French restaurant yet, but we do have some decent nouvelle cuisine, as well as Mexican and Japanese restaurants." A few stores have even started carrying Petite Beurres.

The squirrel brain letter was just an accident of circumstance, it seems, a spin-off from old interests colliding with new surroundings. Berger had seen more than twenty cases of CJD in Florida—a surprising number, given its rarity—and become the medical director of the Creutzfeldt-Jakob Foundation, but he'd never known so many to have so odd a common trait. "In putting this letter together for *Lancet*, I did it almost tongue in cheek," he says. "Had I known how prevalent squirrel consumption was, and how volatile the issue would be, I probably wouldn't have bothered to report it." On further consideration, he says, the risk of getting CJD from squirrel brains is "vanishingly small." If he were offered a squirrel brain, he'd probably decline. "But if you feel funny refusing it, go ahead and eat the damn thing."

Berger's ambivalence is understandable, if a bit convenient. Since his letter was published, only one other squirrel brain eater in Kentucky has been found to carry CJD. In 1998, at Berger's request, the state department of wildlife killed fifty squirrels in western Kentucky. By then, however, fears of CJD infection were so widespread that lab technicians in Kentucky refused to autopsy them. (More recently, in Louisville, a man suspected of having CJD was hastily buried, only to be exhumed at a senator's insistence, autopsied, and declared free of the disease.) Frank Bastian eventually agreed to examine the squirrels at his lab in Mobile. But he found no evidence of disease in their brains: no spongelike holes, no profusion of glial cells, no signs of any infection at all.

Fifty squirrels are hardly a representative sample, Weisman is quick to point out. "Even if you are looking at the right squirrels, you might still miss it," he says. "What are you supposed to look for? No one has ever seen mad squirrel disease before." Bastian agrees. Until he searches the brains for prions and spiroplasma, he says, the negative autopsies "don't mean anything at all."

But when I quoted Bastian to Ermias Belay, the epidemiologist in charge of

CJD studies at the Centers for Disease Control in Atlanta, he let out a long, low chuckle. "Well, it means something to me," he said, then chuckled some more. After the *Lancet* letter appeared, Belay called the Kentucky Department of Health to check the state's CJD rate. "It wasn't a hell of a lot different from other states," he says. "That doesn't rule it out, but you would expect it to be higher." Next he called a squirrel expert, who told him that squirrels live less than five years on average, making them poor candidates for a slow-incubating disease like CJD. Finally, he took a closer look at Berger and Weisman's material.

Cause and coincidence are hard enough to tease apart for most disease clusters, Belay says. But for CJD it's almost impossible. "What does it matter if you have two cases in the same neighborhood, when you know that they probably contracted the disease twenty or thirty years ago, when they lived in different states?" The *Lancet* letter blundered blithely into such statistical pitfalls. Berger and Weisman hardly examined the countless other common traits that surely connected their five CJD patients. Squirrel brain eating seemed so exotic, so reminiscent of what caused mad cow disease, that they felt compelled to single it out. Yet if their surveys were representative, more than a million Kentuckians have eaten squirrel brains at some point in their lives. Fewer than that, Belay points out, have green eyes. "If those same CJD cases all had green eyes, would you then say that green eyes are associated with CJD?"

Truth be told, Belay's office is less concerned about CJD from squirrels than CJD from deer (though even that doesn't worry him much). In southeastern Wyoming and north-central Colorado, deer and elk have been found to carry a form of the disease known as "chronic wasting disease," and many more Americans eat venison than squirrel brains. But though a few deer hunters have contracted CJD, and though the *New York Times* ran a story on the topic similar to the one on squirrel brains, Letterman and Leno never quite got around to working mad deer into their monologues. Chances are they'd eaten some venison lately. And deadly diseases are never quite as funny when you might get them yourself.

These days the epidemic of epidemic stories seems to be dying down at last. Reporters have moved on to newer, fresher fears, and even mad cow disease seems to be petering out: only ten new human victims were reported in 1999, and only 1,600 cows caught the disease—down from around 6,000 in 1997. The *Lancet*, for its part, is unlikely to publish a follow-up letter about squirrel brains—much less a retraction. "It's very hard, in science, to prove that something never existed," Belay says. "And when you do, people are not usually interested."

Kentuckians, in any case, have long since made up their own minds. Only a year after the controversy erupted, Rector gave a squirrel-cooking demonstration at the Kentucky Folklife Festival in Frankfort. When he was done, he says, a local health inspector had to shoo people away to keep them from having a taste. "One elderly lady came up to me afterward," Rector remembers. " 'If I can't eat this squirrel,' she said, 'can I just take this biscuit and dip it in the gravy?' "

A year later, at the same festival, I wait under an open tent for Rector to give another demonstration—this time of guitar playing. Up and down the mall of the state capital, quilt makers, basket weavers, and wood whittlers are earnestly expounding their craft. Coal miners, at the "Narrative Stage," are telling stories from underground, while cooks in the "Foodways Area," stir an enormous kettle of burgoo. The whole scene is both authentic and deeply contrived, edifying and dispiritingly predictable. But for a day, at least, it turns the tables on popular culture: tradition matters more here than the marketplace, and a good story has more authority than any scientific study.

When Rector shambles on stage for the day's last session, he hardly seems to notice that the tent is almost empty. Though the festival guide calls him "a key figure in the music of his region," Rector knows by now that his style is too eclectic for the average folk fan. Settling gingerly into a small folding chair, like a walrus on a rubber ball, he lays his acoustic guitar on his knee and silently fingers the fret board. He talks awhile about his teacher, Mose Rager, who invented the thumb-picking style, and about his idols, Merle Travis and Chet Atkins, who perfected it. Then he feathers a few harmonics to verify his tuning, plucks a chord or two, and he's off: "Bed-Bug Blues" at full throttle.

In the later stages of mad cow disease, patients may twitch so badly that they can barely hold a coffee cup. But Rector seems to be doing all right. Though his fingers are stubby and thick-knuckled, with nails so ragged that he has to wear paste-ons for concerts, they look as nimble as acrobats dancing on steel tight-ropes. While his thumb snaps the bass line and the heel of his hand thumps and dampens the soundboard, the other fingers play the melody and ornaments. They contort themselves into odd chord positions, then skitter down the strings for solos; they swing wide for bent notes, then hop up the fret board again side by side. During one particularly tortured run, a nail pops off and flies into the crowd. But Rector doesn't miss a lick.

For the next forty-five minutes his set follows an ascending curve of virtuosity. He plays a few more blues tunes for the traditionalists in the crowd, then gradually chucks in the rest of popular music: "The Shadow of Your Smile" and the theme from "Popeye," Duke Ellington, Elvis Presley, and John Philip Sousa, with his pinkie playing the piccolo part. Though his eyes stay glued to the fret board—out of shyness rather than necessity—a look of rising delight plays across his clenched features. "I haven't practiced this one in a while," he mumbles, and promptly seems to make a series of mistakes. Then I realize that he's really playing two songs at once: "Yankee Doodle" in the bass and "Dixie" in the treble—the perfect anthem for Kentucky, whose soldiers fought for both sides in the Civil War.

Watching Rector's fingers travel up the guitar neck, seeming to grow more confident the more difficult their position, I remember riding in his truck after our last hunt together. He'd shown me most of his childhood hangouts and hunting spots by then, but before I left he wanted me to see the Rochester Dam, the one John Prine sings about in the last stanza of "Paradise":

> When I die, let my ashes float down the Green River
> Let my soul roll on up to the Rochester Dam
> I'll be halfway to heaven with Paradise waiting
> Just five miles away from wherever I am.

Those words always remind him of his cousin, he said. Jimmy never could get used to losing his old hunting grounds. Without a guitar or children to distract him, he couldn't stand to keep going to the same small patches of forest every week, where once he'd had the whole countryside. "You know that Indian?" he once told Rector. "The one in the pollution commercials that's always cryin'? I feel just like that Indian."

After his wife left him, Jimmy twice tried to kill himself, but both times he was too drunk to succeed. He used a long-barreled shotgun the first time and blew out part of his jaw. He aimed at his heart the next time and blasted off a piece of his shoulder. The third time he finally got it right.

One by one, Rector said, his heroes had died around him: Jimmy and Merle, Mose and Chickenhawk Murphy. "Chet's had cancer five times," he said, "and the last time they took a tumor the size of a hot dog out of his brain." (Chet Atkins died in 2001.) Now, as we drove within sight of the river, he admitted that he was worried for himself—and mad squirrel disease had nothing to do with it. "My doctor tells me I've got the heart of an old man," he said, "and I've been passing a lot of blood. They want me to get a colonoscopy, but I know how that works: you get all cut up, and then you still die."

We parked on the shore and looked out at the drought-stricken river, its sandstone ledges and muddy shallows, dark bluffs and sunken caverns exposed to the sun. And I thought about how rarely we face the true topography of our fears. Though death winds its way through every living moment—in the cars careening past us and the chemicals coursing through us, in the thickening of our arteries, the withering of our cells, and the uncertain courage of our hearts—

we submerge its traces almost completely, letting our hopes and routines wash over its implacable shores. Each generation has more time to confront its mortality, and each generation concocts more outlandish threats—whether from Alar or aliens, fluoride, power lines, or mad squirrels—to defer the confrontation, to preserve the delusion that death can still be defeated.

Rector said that he might not live through the year, and his pale, possessed features showed that he meant it. But then, too, I could tell he was still riding his luck, hoping that colon cancer was just another death threat he could escape through inattention. "You know, I never did understand that line about his soul rollin' up to the Rochester Dam," he said, pointing at the gray-green waterfall below us. "To do that, it would have to float *upstream*." Then he gunned the engine and turned his truck toward home.

The Oyster Shucker's Song

DAVID CECELSKI

I grew up by the salt marshes and brackish creeks in a quiet North Carolina tide-water community that lies between the Neuse River and the Newport River at a place where they are both great saltwater bays on the edge of the sea. Oysters were just a part of my life. When I was a young boy, we still picked up oysters on the rocks off Mill Creek, or the flats off Harkers Island, and opened them, and downed them, standing knee deep in the water without a thought to pollution or getting ill. Come the first cold snap in autumn, we relished oysters as the high-light of dinners that my grandmother Vera served every Sunday after church.

I don't much remember my grandmother buying oysters when we went to town in Beaufort on Saturday mornings. (We treated those trips sort of like a ceremonial rite that went from the A&P to the Rose's Five and Dime to my great-great-aunt Rosa's home across the bridge in the Promised Land.) Instead, our neighbors and cousins shared oysters the way gardeners elsewhere foist their overabundances of tomatoes and yellow squash and pole beans on unsuspecting souls. Many a time, we would come home from town and find a wet burlap bag full of Newport River oysters waiting on our back porch, a gift from some cousin or neighbor who had been out on the river that morning. We'd shuck them and roast them in a pit that we dug in the field, or eat them raw, or fried, or steamed in a big pot. My favorite oyster dish in those days was oyster fritters, and my grandmother turned a few oysters, a handful of cornmeal, a dash of salt, a little water, and of course the oyster's own juices into the finest oyster fritters in God's creation. Sitting down to a plate of her oyster fritters was all the lesson that I'd ever need to convince me that humanity's highest arts could be fashioned out of the simplest things in life. I could eat a mess of them right now.

No matter how we fixed them, the taste of those Newport River oysters harkened to far-off saltwater places and distant origins, to raucous, abundant life, and to a profound yearning that all of us who grew up in that time and place felt for the saltwater marshes and the open seas beyond them. Roasting oysters out in that field or pulling those fritters out of the Crisco in my grandmama's cast-iron frying pan reached, too, into my young heart and touched a place I certainly couldn't put into words in those years, and that I better not put into words in public at this particular moment. All I'll say is this: Back then I could never quite grasp how all my elders could seem so bent on denying me access to every other sensual pleasure in life I could imagine (and many more I could not) yet could knowingly leave me alone in a kitchen with oysters from the Newport River! If trying not to awaken a young boy's appetites for the sensual things in life was the point, it seems like they should have known better.

In those days we talked about oysters with scarcely less seriousness or exactitude than I have heard that Inuit people discuss the fine points of ice and snow. When, say, my cousin Edsel dropped off a half-bushel of oysters on our porch while we were away, my grandmother and my great-aunt Irene and maybe my mother would carefully shuck a few and sample them and then venture where they had come from by their flavor. I don't mean what state or region of the country they came from either—I mean what creek or bay. To this day, I believe that I can distinguish the difference between an oyster from Cedar Island and an oyster from the Newport River, though they are scarcely more than a half-hour's drive apart. Of course, *any* oyster from Cedar Island or the Newport River was a *good* oyster, the question was just how good. But if, on those rare occasions when we did buy oysters at the fish market, we ate an oyster that was just this side of rank, we would somberly nod and say, "Well, it's not bad for a Virginia oyster." (I don't really know if all those poor oysters were really from Virginia, but we certainly thought as much.) And on the other side of things, if we tasted an oyster that seemed to raise our souls nearly to celestial heights, we would nod and "ooohhhh" and finally proclaim, in a breathless whisper, "must be from Mill Creek way."

Mill Creek is a little community five or six miles from my family's home place. It is bordered by Harlowe Creek and the Newport River; it's on the way nowhere, really, but isn't too far from Beaufort if you were going to visit. The oysters from Mill Creek have been legendary for their abundance and the grandeur of their flavor since the nineteenth century. It seemed only fitting, then, that in 1973 the local fire and rescue squad founded the region's first oyster festival. Originally mostly a local affair, it now attracts as many as 10,000 visitors. Every first Saturday in November, the rescue squad volunteers serve up platefuls of fried fish and brimming kettles of clam chowder, but I recommend you head straight to the oyster shucking shed. If you are lucky, you will taste the saltiest, most delectable oysters in America—those taken from the Newport River.

I know that you who are from the coast, or perhaps have a favorite watering hole down there, probably think that your local oysters are better than the

Newport River's. I know that all of you folks from around Rose Bay, up in Hyde County, or Bay River over in Pamlico County, or Stumpy Point way out in Dare County, are mighty proud of your oysters, and I'm not saying you don't have a lot to be proud of. I know that any of you old-timers from Brunswick County will boast on your oysters, too, and I will concede that they are mighty fine. And down at the New River, below Jacksonville, you people—bless your misguided hearts—act like you invented the oyster. But even though I know you are all in grave error—Newport River oysters are unquestionably the best—I do not mind you standing up for your homegrown shellfish, no matter how wrongheaded you are. I am more than happy to argue oysters with anybody so long as it involves plenty of shucking and slurping.

There is only one problem: Our oysters have practically vanished. When my buddies and I get to comparing oysters, we are arguing about oysters that we used to have but do not anymore. A century ago, Carolina watermen harvested nearly 2.5 million bushels of the tasty bivalves annually. In recent years, our watermen and women harvested less than 2 percent of that total, a mere 42,000 bushels. We do not have a single oyster cannery left. Coastal restaurants import oysters from the Gulf of Mexico. Even our most intimate little oyster bars, some of them in business for three or four generations now, rely on oysters from the Gulf states or Mexico. Rare, too, is the oyster lover these days who can put aside fears of pollution and sewage and eat an oyster raw out of one of our bays like we used to. And while none of us likes to advertise the fact, even at the Mill Creek festival the fire and rescue squad has to look far beyond the Newport River to feed us hungry hordes of oyster lovers.

What happened to our oysters? The answer is complicated and involves a mix of ecological, economic, and management factors. Without question, though, the turning point in our state's oyster fortunes came in the 1890s. You will never hear a more colorful chapter in coastal history than that of the oyster boom of that decade, but you might also never hear of a period that sounds more like our own.

In 1880 the U.S. oyster industry was concentrated in Chesapeake Bay. That year, Maryland watermen gathered more than 10 million bushels of oysters, a hundred times the amount harvested in North Carolina. A Norfolk, Virginia, company opened a steam cannery at Ocracoke Island in 1877, apparently the state's first, but it was hardly typical. A New Bern newspaper's reaction made that clear: "Anyone who has visited this locality," wrote a correspondent for the *Newbernian* on May 12, 1877, "will readily understand the startling nature of their innovation. With its steam engine, its energetic Northern managers, and the aggregation of the floating labor of this place, the industry and enterprise exhibited all present a marked feature in this hitherto Rip Van Winkle locality." Ocracoke, one might have pointed out to the newspaper's correspondent, at least had an oyster cannery; New Bern, at that time, did not.

Up until that time, most Carolina watermen tonged for oysters just to feed their families. From very early in the nineteenth century, and probably quite a bit earlier, Outer Banks fishermen also bartered unshucked oysters for corn with mainland farmers every fall, traditionally trading a pound of corn for a pound of oysters. The shallow draft, wide-beamed schooners of the day—locals called them "corn crackers"—worked their way from Portsmouth Island, Bay River, and the other great oyster rocks up coastal rivers to trade at every wharf and town. In port towns like New Bern and Wilmington, oysters could be bought every day during oyster season from hawkers who moved up and down the streets at dawn. A few draymen carted oysters all the way into the Piedmont, and with the completion of the coast's first railroads in the 1840s, a few dealers began to send oysters as far inland as Charlotte. But oysters still had so few markets that Pamlico Sound watermen often raked up smaller ones and, not bothering to shuck them, sold them for a few cents a bushel to lime kilns. The lime from oysters was used as a wall plaster, to make bricks, as fertilizer, to preserve fishing nets, to inter the dead. Oyster shells found wide usage in building and construction: the walls of Fort Johnston, built in 1802 to protect the mouth of the Cape Fear River, consisted solely of what its slave builders called a "batter" of burnt-down oyster shells and pitch pine, for example.

The Carolina oyster industry began its ascent in the 1880s. With Chesapeake Bay stocks already diminishing and America's population soaring, the Baltimore canneries began to look south. Previously limited from sending oysters any great distance by the lack of transportation or preservation methods, the advent of new preservation technology—primarily steam canning and ice making—and the new availability of railroads and steamships opened local waters to a national market for the first time. Bair Brothers opened a branch plant in New Bern in 1881, but it was the Moore and Brady oyster cannery at Union Point, there in New Bern right at the juncture of the Neuse and Trent Rivers, that became the first real success. By 1888, Moore and Brady hired 500 shuckers at peak season, making it the city's largest employer. Its workers shucked as many as 2,000 bushels a day. Virginia canneries also began to send "buy boats" south. They bought oysters from Carolina watermen (rendezvousing with them directly off remote locales like Portsmouth Island, Brant's Island, or Cedar Island Bay, so the oystermen did not have to leave the oyster grounds to sail into port), then carried the oysters back to Norfolk for shucking, canning, and selling as "Chesapeake Bay" oysters.

The potential for the Carolina oyster industry seemed limitless. In 1886 a nautical surveyor named Francis Winslow charted 10,000 acres of oyster beds in state waters. His report on the Newport River estuary—right off Mill Creek— was typical. Winslow described, in his words, "large and thickly stocked beds . . . extending nearly across the river." He counted a whopping 403 acres of oyster beds in the Newport—so many that he found it more practical to sketch on his charts where oysters were *not* than where they were.

An oyster boom hit like a gold rush in the winter of 1889–90. Spurred by new laws opening the state's oyster rocks on an unlimited scale and prohibiting the shipment of unshucked oysters out of the state, the Baltimore companies built large canneries in Beaufort, Vandemere, Washington, Belhaven, Southport, New Bern, and Elizabeth City. "Men who had never before used an oyster tong could be seen repairing to our oyster banks," W. T. Caho, the state's shellfish commissioner, exclaimed. "All along the marshes," he went on, " . . . could be seen the camps of hundreds and thousands who had never before engaged in the oyster business."

Fishing crews from Maryland, Virginia, Delaware, and New Jersey stormed the state's oyster beds. A visitor at Stumpy Point reported that as many as fifty Chesapeake schooners could be seen in Pamlico Sound in a single glance. A little west of there, a newspaper reporter described 150 to 200 "canoes and small boats" oystering in Hyde County, where Chesapeake schooners loaded their catches onto barges and carried them back to Norfolk and Baltimore. "It is a real God-send to numbers of poor people," the reporter wrote. The Chesapeake schooners overwhelmed the oyster beds and the local oystermen. The newcomers also introduced oyster dredges and longer, sturdier tongs into the local industry. The new gear opened up the deepest waters of Pamlico Sound to oystering for the first time.

The oyster boom brought new life to coastal villages. One of the enduring fallacies about our coastal past is the region's provincialism and isolation. In fact, through most of modern history just the opposite was the case. While the North Carolina coast often seemed a backwater to people in-state, shipping, fishing, and the maritime trades generally tied the Outer Banks and our entire coastal region to the far-flung corners of the Atlantic—far more so than the small towns and cities in-state. These maritime occupations made the coast in many respects more cosmopolitan, diverse, and sophisticated than inland towns like Raleigh or Charlotte, particularly prior to the coming of the railroads. "The fact is," as a nineteenth-century visitor recalled of Beaufort, "communication with New York, Boston, Philadelphia, and Baltimore was more direct and frequent than with New Bern." New Bern, of course, was only thirty-five miles west of Beaufort.

This was certainly true during the oyster boom. Waterfront streets thronged with local laborers, Chesapeake oystermen, and "Bohemian" oyster shuckers— Serbian, Dalmatian, Polish, and other eastern European immigrants recruited from ghettos in Baltimore and New York City. According to Kathleen Carter, a historian at High Point University and the leading authority on the oyster boom, the tiny town of Elizabeth City alone boasted at least eleven oyster canneries and 1,700 oyster workers in 1890. "It was a jolly time—a new revelation," reported the *Economist Falcon*, an Elizabeth City newspaper. "Population and money followed in perpetual stream and prosperity was felt in every fiber and pulsation of business. New people, new faces, new ways, new manners. . . . The song of the oyster shucker was heard in the land." The streets of coastal towns would be paved, literally, with oyster shells.

Prosperity bred controversy. Tempers flared between local tongers and Chesapeake dredgers. Reports of oyster poaching, smuggling, and fraudulent leases were widespread. Battles over private property rights and the public's rights to oyster grounds were hard fought and often nasty. To conserve the rocks, the North Carolina General Assembly prohibited oyster dredging after the 1890 season, but many Chesapeake oystermen refused to heed the law. In 1891 the governor sent the Pasquotank militia, armed with a howitzer, to prevent Chesapeake "pirates" from oyster dredging. As late as 1895, reports of Chesapeake schooners sneaking bargeloads of oysters to Baltimore were still coming from Pamlico Sound.

Local oystermen also protested the monopoly held by the Chesapeake Bay companies. They did not want North Carolina oystering to follow in the footsteps of the Chesapeake industry, which was, as shellfish commissioner W. H. Lucas warned in 1893, "in the hands of the large corporations, and the oystermen are nothing more than slaves in the employ of said large syndicates." A petition from a group of Hertford citizens echoed Lucas's sentiments. In June 1892 they wrote, "We can't see the justice in any arrangement that deprives the whole people of a divine blessing intended no doubt by the Almighty himself at the creation for their mutual good and enjoyment, that the pockets of a few may be filled with gold."

The Chesapeake canneries moved south to the Gulf of Mexico when the Chesapeake watermen—most of whom worked directly for the canning companies—were finally stopped from oyster dredging. Tonging did a better job of preserving the oyster beds, but it could not supply the canneries adequately, and the number of canneries fell to two by 1898. The state's oyster boom continued in a new guise, however, as sixteen establishments eventually packed raw oysters on ice. Belhaven, Elizabeth City, Oriental, New Bern, Beaufort, Davis Shore, and Morehead City all had packinghouses.

The oyster boom quickly depleted the Carolina coast. This hurt the poor first. A ten-acre leasing system helped prevent big companies from monopolizing the oyster beds, but it took the beds out of the public domain and put them into private hands, and usually the hands that had money and political clout. A poor family that relied on oyster beds in a backyard creek or nearby bay to stave off hunger in a hard winter all of a sudden might find that they could not legally harvest oysters in their own neighborhood without violating another individual's lease. In 1890, when the Pamlico Oyster Company charged five Ocracoke watermen with trespassing on oyster grounds that their families had worked for generations, you can imagine the local watermen's bitterness. In 1911 Jordan Carawan of Mesic, in Pamlico County, expressed a common sentiment when he petitioned the General Assembly, arguing that the leasing system, as he put it, "deprives poor people of oysters to eat and catch for a living."

The oyster boom also took a heavy toll on oystermen and oyster shuckers. Spurred by the new markets, oystermen worked through the heart of chilly winters in small, open skiffs and often stayed in remote, windswept camps, usually only coming home on weekends, if then. "The injury to health from exposure is so great that few ever reach old age," observed Ernest Ingersoll, a fishery biologist. Oyster shuckers—mainly women and children—had it no easier. The work was hard, the oyster houses were unheated, and the day's work often began at four or five in the morning and lasted well into the night. When oyster shuckers pressed for better pay or working conditions, the companies frequently imported migrant workers or seasonal workers from other towns, as in 1893 when the local shuckers at the Weitzel and Delamar cannery in Beaufort refused to work for the proffered wage of less than 13 cents per gallon of shucked oysters, or roughly a dollar a day. The company responded by recruiting shuckers in James City and New Bern and bringing them in by railroad. Many a coastal youngster had one ardent hope: to grow up and earn enough money to get Mama out of the oyster house.

By 1909, the oyster boom was over. It had peaked in the winter of 1898–99, when Carolina oystermen harvested 2.45 million bushels. By 1906, state geologist Joseph Pratt was already reporting a 50 percent decline in oyster harvests. It was the beginning of a long downward spiral for the state's oyster catches. From 1890 to 1908, the industry gathered more than 4 million pounds of shucked meat every year. From 1920 to 1960, a good annual harvest fell to 1.5 million pounds.

From 1960 to 1990, a half million pounds was a good year. In more recent winters, our watermen and women gathered less than 230,000 pounds, and our busiest packinghouses shucked oysters trucked in from Texas and Louisiana.

Ecological changes since 1960 have made it difficult for oysters to recover from generations of overharvesting. As filter feeders, oysters are notoriously sensitive to water quality, and estuarine pollutants have risen dramatically in recent decades. Both wastewater drainage and industrial pollutants have taken their toll. Oysters are also highly sensitive to changes in salinity levels. The drainage of pocosins and other coastal wetlands for agribusiness and corporate timbering, in particular, has increased freshwater runoff into our estuaries, tainting many of the great oyster bays. Land clearing, channelization of water-ways, and new ditching has also heightened the amount of silt flowing into the estuaries, another damper on the health of oyster beds. Many of the old-time oystermen I know also blame the drag-lines on shrimp trawls for damaging oyster beds and tearing up the hard bottoms where oysters once flourished. In addition, since the late 1980s, shellfish diseases have invaded coastal waters. While harmless to humans, they have proven catastrophic to oysters.

Nowadays, I hate to admit, you probably won't find a single Newport River oyster at the Mill Creek festival. But I still go, and I still hear the call of the oyster shucker's song from day's past, and I am still drawn home to the great salt marshes and the quiet tidal creeks where I grew up. I still stay as much of the year as I can at my family's home place, and now and then I still come home from town and find a wet burlap bag full of oysters on my back porch. I do not have to be told where they are from. My community has changed a great deal, like nearly all such places, and that soggy bag of oysters is a much-needed reminder to me that not everything has changed, and that not all my neighbors are yet strangers, and that a few oysters can still be found in the Newport River. A burlap bag full of oysters won't feed the crowds at the Mill Creek festival, but it is enough to remind me of other days, and it is enough to give a soul a glimmer of hope that one day the great oyster beds will return to those saltwater bays and brackish creeks that are lodged so deeply in my heart.

The Harvest

The Fruit of Temptation

FRANK BROWNING

I was raised surrounded by apples.

My earliest visual memory is of the swaying limbs atop a row of Golden Delicious trees. It was summertime, and the Kentucky sky hung hot behind those high twigs, their leaves leathery-green on top, soft as down underneath. Rows of Goldens stood next to a dirt road that separated the orchard from our front yard. Beyond the top row an acre of apple trees marched down the slope toward the gravel highway, the ground beneath them blanketed by rye and fescue and orchard grass, Queen Anne's lace, orange milkweed, and buttercups. The apples, a little bigger than shooter marbles, played hide-and-seek with a child's eyes unless, on a June afternoon, a late thundershower drenched them and the last golden sunlight showed them off like Christmas balls. They were in that way both ordinary and magical, as common as toast, as elusive as dreams.

Not until adolescence, when I began to accumulate the images of English and American poets (Yeats's "silver apples of the moon . . . golden apples of the sun" and Millay in her moist earth listening for "drenched and dripping apple trees") did I learn how widespread were the lures and mysteries of the apple. Apples were simply the family trade. A bad apple crop meant the car wouldn't get nonessential repairs and my mother wouldn't make her annual trip to New York to visit her sister. Pedestrian stuff. At the same time, our crop set us apart from the tobacco growers and dairymen who made up most of the county's farmers. We and the other apple grower one ridge away were somehow a touch strange and ever so slightly suspect.

It seemed to have to do with pleasure. No one else in our part of the world grew anything for money that gave so much plain delight. The annual act of taking the first apple, roundish, blushed with crimson, the flesh beneath its skin firm and sturdy and ready to explode upon the tongue, announced by a fragrance so clear and subtle that the memory centers deep within the brain let loose an avalanche of nearly forgotten summer tastes, memories that are themselves inseparable from the expectations of eager youth—this plain act of snapping the fruit from the branch or lifting it from a wooden crate and drawing it up toward the ready mouth was an affirmation of the senses. To eat into the apple, to press the edge of the teeth past the taut, unwilling skin into ready white meat, to feel the spray of tart and honeyed juices rain down against the tongue and wash over the palate, was to know again how exquisite are the treasures of the ordinary earth. Apple season—not the apples of summer best left for sauce pots and jelly jars, but the apples that fall in September and October, when the sun is sliding south—is the time for harvest mischief. It is the time of last temptation before the cold and darkness, and the growers are the agents of temptation.

You understood about apples and temptation when the preachers arrived Sunday afternoons.

Along with hundreds of other country and city people, they would rattle up the rutted mountain road to our orchard. Like everyone else, they and their families would park under oak trees, get out of their cars, and amble into our dirt-floor sales shed. No matter how full the outside air was with dust and goldenrod pollen, inside the shed the perfume of fresh apples was overwhelming. "Whew, shore does smell like apples, don't it!" they'd say, and add, "Lands'a mercy. Never saw so many apples!" even though they had been walking into the same sales shed, buying the same varieties, for twenty years. Wood-slatted bushel crates of apples were stacked four high and three deep: Jonathans, Cortlands, Grimes Goldens, Golden and Red Delicious, Winesaps, Rome Beauties, and even rare old apples called Winter Bananas, Black Twigs, and King Davis. Each variety was marked with the apple's name and price.

The preachers would walk in after church to choose their apples. The ordinary apple customers would mill about for fifteen or twenty minutes, sniffing, punching, peeling, slicing the fruit, make their selections, and carry their bounty off to their cars and pickups in gunnysacks or big brown bushel bags tied with twine. The preachers would do the same thing, up to the point of purchase. But because it was Sunday, they would ask us to set their apples aside in the rear packing room. Then they would return Monday to pick them up and pay us.

I suppose the authorities could have closed us down for violating Kentucky's blue laws. No one else, except for the town pharmacist, opened on Sunday. The supermarkets were closed. So were the gas stations. By the time I was old enough to ask questions, my father assured me that apple orchards were special. Without Sunday sales, apple growers couldn't stay in business.

As a practical matter, Sunday was the only day most of the country people were free to come buy apples. Until the 1960s, few women drove cars, and their husbands were busy workdays. Farm work started at six-thirty or seven o'clock in the morning and ended well after sundown. Inside the household, there were also strict regimes. Monday was wash day. Saturday was town day, and each square (there were only two) was packed with men in denim overalls standing around jawing while their wives bought groceries. Saturday night was bath night. Sunday, after church and chicken dinner, was the time "to drive out to the mountain" to get apples. City people who had come from Lexington or Cincinnati took the day as an autumn outing; they usually bought anywhere from a peck to a bushel and a half of fruit. Country people, who were most of our customers, packed off from two to ten bushels, and often they returned a month later for a like amount. So Sunday was the practical day to buy apples. Still, there was something else: because it was Sunday, and because the apples were both wholesome and primordially forbidden, the whole experience bore just a trace of an illicit adventure. Driving up that scary mountain road with the steep cliffs (maybe 150 feet down), spending money just after the sermon was over, letting the kids loose to romp in the orchard, looking over the city folk in their fancy hats and polished Pontiacs (or, for the city folk, pointing at the pickups and listening to the hillbilly twang), and complaining politely about how the prices seemed "awful high this year": all this made coming to get apples unlike any other shopping experience.

Most of our customers grew plums and cherries and blackberries in the backyard or along old fence rows. Bananas and oranges were store-bought food. But apples, at least good apples, occupied a special place, geographically and culturally. To grow them, you had to use poisonous chemicals with odd names— arsenate of lead, Malathion, captan. You also had to have special equipment to spray the chemicals onto the trees. Tobacco, the crop that most Kentucky farmers grew, was little more than a high-class weed whose cultural practices had been passed along from generation to generation. Serious apple growing took book knowledge, which itself brought to mind the lessons of Eden, which of course is all about the invitation to temptation.

Of all the fields that farmers tend, the apple orchard seems to me the most inviting. Others have their own unmistakable beauty. Cornfields betray geometric patterns that can be as mesmerizing as Navajo rugs. Bean fields run on in endless dark green lines against the sunburnt soil. Wheat fields press their swaying fingers to the wind. Orange groves fluff themselves up like fuzzy columns of deep green porcupines, but they never show their structure, never invite tomboys to shinny up their trunks and crawl along their bare scaffold limbs. Apple orchards wander along hillsides. They meander around boulders and roadways. They make room for wet spots where trees won't grow. They encourage guests to stop in and visit a while.

Once lured inside, visitors come upon fantasy hideaways full of imaginary furniture. Sturdy lower limbs become fast horses leaping from the trunk. High in the top, twisted branches make crow's nests and pirate perches. Halfway up hang the swaying wooden hammocks of August daydreams, where faces made of leaves and clouds tell tales of impossible voyages. Apple trees promise temptation to the young fertile mind. Autumn journeys into the orchard seem to stir the memory of all those temptations to lassitude. With winter only a month or two away, the trek to the orchard carries just the slightest feeling of a fling. The preachers knew that, too, and maybe theirs was the finest fling of all, as they stepped inside the fruit shed and then concocted a transparent scheme to avoid a technical violation of the law of the Sabbath.

A few years ago, when my brother and I took over the farm, we began to press cider. Cider is a misnomer in America. Cider, as the English or the French or the Spanish or even our colonial ancestors knew, is, properly speaking, a fermented drink, the wassail of English caroling, the beautiful, bubbling, champagne-looking stuff that Bretons sip with crispy crepes. But since real cider all but disappeared in America a hundred years ago, the word has been given to fresh, whole apple juice.

Our entry into cider making taught us even more about apples and temptation. When we started out, no one in fifty miles had made cider for decades. It wasn't part of the diet. The only apple juice our customers knew was the de-natured yellow liquid produced by industrial juice bottlers and served to children in school lunchrooms. Yet when we told them we had cider and offered them a sample cup, a sinner's smile would often spread across their faces. "You better be able to drive," the wives told their husbands. Our orchard is in a dry county where Prohibition has remained in effect since the depression. But the memory of moonshine is strong.

Our county and the county just east of us were two of the best white-lightning spots in Kentucky all the way through Prohibition. Bars and nightclubs in Covington and Newport, down on the Ohio River across from Cincinnati, were among the nation's biggest moonshine consumers. Even into the 1970s and 1980s. Mostly their patrons wanted sour mash or corn liquor. But a good many had a taste for applejack, which our respectable customers understood was just a few days down the fermentation trail from the fresh, vitamin-packed whole juice we drew from a spigot in our converted milk cooler.

One of our neighbors—he lived only four or five miles away—was Asa Muse. Asa was the last of the county's great moonshiners. Asa's grandfather, F. T. Muse, also known as Uncle Toll, had prospered all through the Great Depression on applejack and corn whiskey. F. T. grew corn, much of which he ground and turned into sour mash, and he tended an eighteen-acre apple orchard. Half his apples went into the big copper still that he kept up on the southern tip of Pea Ridge, above his house. Red Delicious, Asa told me, made the best applejack.

Asa had already retired when he told me about his moonshining and about how when he was fourteen his grandfather sent him up the hill into the woods with a .38 special and told him to shoot anybody who came around. Asa made a lot of money, he said, in the applejack and moonshine trade—maybe a quarter million dollars, a quarter of which he allowed he's tucked way (but not in the bank). He'd never gone to a jail, though he was tried three times. "In the forty years I made whiskey, I've been in jail twelve hours. They tore up three stills, and they'd come and arrest me. I'd get me a good lawyer. I beat 'em three times." He laughed, his stubbly jowls jiggling like an old basset hound's. "They didn't like that very well."

Asa's great-grandfather had hauled his family over the Appalachian Mountains from Virginia and had been awarded a 20,000-acre land grant early in the nineteenth century. They had fought Indians, cleared ground, and established a mill to grind corn. The village just down the hollow from Asa is still called Muses Mills. From the beginning, Asa said, the family had a knack for making liquor. As profitable as it was, though, and as much land as they held, it all seemed to slip away—so that by the time I was growing up, the name Muse carried the sweet-sour fragrance of wildness and decay.

Our apple orchard was three or four miles from the site of the Old Muse orchard. We never cooked up any applejack, and I was well into middle age by the time I met Asa. Yet I always felt an odd connection with the Muses. While we were regarded as respectable, educated, and, in local terms, prosperous, and they were the raucous mountain men (nobody ever spoke of the Muse women) who got everybody drunk on Saturday night, both the Brownings and the Muses were tainted by their association with forbidden fruit.

Though others might violate the Sabbath by spending their money on Sunday, theirs was a minor sin, and an easily forgivable one. But as the people who had planted the trees, harvested the fruit, and then offered it, we were the authors of their temptation. In this deeply religious mountain country, where a substitute schoolteacher once eyed a novel on my desk as though it were a satanic cookbook, we Brownings were seen as never too far from sin. Even the children who brought apples to school in their lunch boxes were somewhat suspicious. One became horrified when in sixth grade I explained that we made all our trees with grafting knives and tape. "Only God makes trees!" she insisted, no doubt left in her mind that if what I had said was true I must be associated with the forces of Satan. Fundamentally, however, they were extremely practical people. My classmate's mother continued putting apples in her lunch box, and Sunday has remained our busiest sales day.

I certainly understood that in the Department of Sin and Temptation we were not in the same league as the Muse boys with their moonshine stills. Nonetheless, I've always been sure that we were somehow kindred spirits. As a child, I never knew that they, too, grew apples and cooked applejack. A half century would pass before I learned those stories and began to experiment with making my own apple brandy. The kinship I sensed had more to do with finding the dangerous magic in ordinary things: the white lightning in the corn kernel, the sales day on the Sabbath, the alterations in God's nursery. Just as there was fire in the cornstalk, so there was magic beneath the gold and crimson skin of that insufferably wholesome apple.

A Pawpaw Primer

COLLEEN ANDERSON

It's early autumn, a warm afternoon. Leaves are beginning to fall on my favorite hiking path: the old carriage trail that begins near the Kanawha River in Charleston, West Virginia. The path makes a few switchbacks on its way up the mountain and ends at the sandstone mansion Governor William MacCorkle built for himself in 1905. I'm walking hard, working up a good sweat, enjoying the end-of-summer light through the thinning leaves.

Then I smell it for the first time this year—the sweet, fruity aroma that says, "It's fall." The smell of ripe pawpaws.

I smelled pawpaws in the fall woods for years before I knew what they were. You probably have, too. Wafting on a warm breeze, the sweetness is almost audible—a lilting music with an overtone of melancholy, a hint of the exotic, a suggestion of gypsy. All that from a pale green, hard-to-see-for-the-foliage, squishy, kidney-shaped fruit that often turns blotchy and black as it ripens.

The pawpaw, *Asimina triloba*, is North America's largest edible native fruit. Its range extends as far north as southern Ontario, as far south as northern Florida, and as far west as eastern Nebraska. The Appalachian region, including the entire states of Kentucky, North Carolina, Ohio, Tennessee, Virginia, and West Virginia, is the heart of pawpaw territory. *Asimina* is the only temperate genus in the otherwise tropical and subtropical family, Annonaceae. All eight members of the genus grow in North America, but the pawpaw is the northernmost and, by far, the most widespread.

Nobody knows how long pawpaws have been growing in North America or how they got here in the first place, but fossil records indicate that they predate *Homo sapiens* by tens of thousands of years. However, it is probable that humans were responsible for dispersing the tree throughout its present range. Native Americans were the first on the continent to prize the nutritious fruit. In 1541 Spanish explorer Hernando de Soto noted the tree being cultivated by Native

Americans and related seeing baskets being woven from strips of pawpaw bark. Nearly 200 years later, explorer John Lawson reported in his 1709 book, *A New Voyage to Carolina*, that pawpaws were "as sweet, as anything can be. They make rare Puddings of this Fruit." Pawpaws surface again in a September 18, 1806, journal entry of the Lewis and Clark expedition. Although the party had run out of provisions, they were "perfectly contented" with subsisting on nothing but pawpaws and a single biscuit per man.

Around 1827, naturalist and painter John James Audubon chose a pawpaw tree as the background for his painting of a yellow-billed cuckoo. In a somewhat more dubious claim to fame, pawpaw bushes served as the backdrop for the 1882 triple murder of Randolph McCoy's sons during the Hatfield-McCoy feud along the West Virginia–Kentucky border. In the 1950s, singer Burl Ives popularized the traditional song, "Way Down Yonder in the Pawpaw Patch." And about a dozen towns in the United States, including one in my own state of West Virginia, bear the name of the tree.

Early in the twentieth century, pawpaws surged in popularity. Orchards were established in Michigan and West Virginia by 1910, and in 1916 the *Journal of Heredity* sponsored a national contest to find the best fruits. The journal pointed out that the fruit has several drawbacks: a thin skin and a tendency to bruise easily (characteristics which contribute to its perishability); low yields per tree; the inconsistent flavor of wild pawpaws; and the plant's large and plentiful seeds, usually as many as ten or twelve per fruit. The contest resulted in the identification of seven new superior clones and fourteen already existing varieties. More were added during the next thirty years.

But interest in the pawpaw was eclipsed by the public's taste for another fruit that became widely available around the turn of the century: the banana. The banana was everything the pawpaw wasn't: seedless, tough-skinned, easy to peel, able to travel well and ripen slowly. The mass market spoke, and the pawpaw was relegated to the background.

That brings us to the topic of taste. What do pawpaws taste like? In West Virginia I often hear the fruit called the "West Virginia banana." In Michigan it's the "Michigan banana," and the lucky folks in Indiana, of course, get to rhyme. In fact, pawpaws taste only a bit like bananas. The taste has also been compared to peaches, mangoes, papayas, and vanilla custard. None of these is even close. Pawpaw is a pawpaw is a pawpaw.

And what a taste it is: dense, sweet, distinctly tropical, sometimes floral, sometimes slightly astringent, and with an aftertaste that can, to certain palates, be unpleasant. The creamy yellow flesh is the texture of custard. You either love it or hate it.

So far, the pawpaw's early drawbacks have prevented its acceptance as a commercial fruit, but around the country a number of scientists (and more than a few devoted amateurs) are working on breeding a better pawpaw. One of those scientists, geneticist R. Neal Peterson, has championed the pawpaw since the early 1970s. A native of St. Albans, West Virginia, he was a student at West Virginia University in Morgantown when he first tasted the fruit. His natural curiosity and love of plants led him, at first tentatively and then passionately, into an avocation that would eventually give rise to comparisons with Johnny Appleseed. Among the dozens of researchers now working on various potential uses for pawpaw—as food, ornamental tree, cosmetic base, organic pesticide, and anticarcinogen—he is acknowledged as one of the earliest, most well informed of contemporary pawpaw researchers. And he has certainly been one of the most dedicated: While an agricultural economist at the U.S. Department of Agriculture in Washington, D.C., he did all of his pawpaw research at his own expense and on his own time. We who know him well sometimes call him "Mahatma Pawpaw."

It's been my good luck to have known Neal Peterson since before he discovered his avocation. I have watched his interest lead him to long-abandoned orchards in search of superior fruit; watched him learn, mostly by trial and error, the delicate arts of hand-pollinating and grafting; seen him eat the first fruit from a six-year-old, 700-tree orchard; watched him clean and disinfect seeds from hundreds of pounds of overripe fruit; and heard him cry when an entire year's harvest of painstakingly hand-crossed fruit was accidentally discarded by an assistant cleaning out a refrigerator.

Peterson's persistent hard work, combined with knowledge and intelligence, has enabled him to achieve a great improvement in pawpaw quality. From 1,500 seedling trees collected in 1981 from historic collections, he identified three wonderful varieties in 2002 that he calls "Shenandoah," "Susquehanna," and "Rappahannock" and that he has recently made commercially available to the public.

In the name of science, and to please my old friend, I have eaten pawpaw bread, pawpaw ice cream, pawpaw chutney, pawpaw sorbet, pawpaw zabaglione, and more ripe pawpaws than I care to count. Once he talked me into driving a cooler full of pawpaws to a natural foods exhibition in Chicago, where we spooned out the delicacy to eager tasters. On the way back, we stopped at an experimental farm to load a rented truck with 300 small pawpaw trees on their way to another research facility.

In 1994 I attended the first international conference on pawpaws, held at the University of Maryland's Research and Education Center in Keedysville, Maryland, and organized by Peterson. By then the fruit had attracted admirers who traveled from as far away as Russia and China. By default, I have ended up as secretary of the nonprofit organization Peterson started, the PawPaw Foundation, and I serve as the coeditor of its semiannual newsletter. I never intended to learn this much about any plant, but I'm glad it happened. Peterson's enthusiasm, sense of humor, and gentle but persistent teaching have opened a door for me, not only to pawpaws but to growing things in general.

The way pawpaws grow, like so much else about this plant, is odd. In the wild they tend to be found in moist, shady, well-drained places, often beside rivers or creeks. Germinating seedlings cannot tolerate full sun, and this trait typically relegates pawpaw trees to the shade. Pawpaws under these conditions tend to develop into spindly understory trees with few widespread branches, and they generally bear little or no fruit. Paradoxically, pawpaw trees in the open (if you can protect them from the sun for the first year of their lives or can transplant them) grow in a handsome pyramidal shape, from fifteen to thirty feet tall, and bear much more fruit. The trees are easily recognizable by the foot-long oval leaves, glossy green and distinctly veined, that droop from the branches. In fall they turn a buttery golden color.

The trees blossom in spring, shortly after dogwoods bloom, with small, bell-like flowers that turn from pale green to a rich brown or dark purple color. The flowers have three outer petals and three smaller, fleshy inner petals. The odor of the mature blossom is repugnant to humans—a musky, rotting meat smell—but apparently the scent is attractive to flies and beetles, the tree's pollinators. And because the trees are not usually self-compatible, they require for cross-pollination another nearby, genetically different pawpaw tree, or a person willing to hand-pollinate.

Pawpaws may have drawbacks, but they have one quality any gardener will appreciate: a chemical compound in the pawpaw makes it resistant to nearly all garden pests. One of the few pests is worth tolerating for its beauty: the zebra swallowtail butterfly, whose larvae eat only pawpaw leaves.

The fruit ripens in early fall, usually between late August and early October. Fruits grow singly or in clusters—sometimes as many as nine on a single stem, or peduncle—close to the branch. They vary from plum-sized to mango-sized and tend to be oval or kidney-shaped. As they ripen, pawpaws may turn yellowish, and dark brown or black spots may appear. These blotches do not affect the flavor. The fruit is ready to eat when it is fragrant, slightly soft to the touch, and easy to separate from the peduncle with a gentle tug.

So, what do you do with a ripe pawpaw? Most pawpaw lovers think it's best to eat the fruit where you find it. (If it has already fallen from the tree, you may have to brush away a few ants.) Finding and eating the first pawpaw of the season is an annual ritual. Cut or break the fruit in half and scoop out the pulp with a spoon, if you just happen to have brought one along. I like them even better with a squeeze of fresh lime juice, a tangy complement to the heavy sweetness of the fruit.

A little bit of pawpaw goes a long way. Eating a lot of pawpaws at once, I can report from unhappy personal experience, will cause diarrhea. Still, it's easy to see why Native Americans valued the fruit so highly. It is exceptionally rich in calories, protein, minerals, and essential amino acids.

Fully ripe pawpaws don't keep well. Expect them to last only a couple of days at room temperature or up to a week in the refrigerator. Underripe pawpaws can be kept longer, up to three weeks refrigerated, and then finish ripening on the counter. You can freeze the pureed pulp with skin and seeds removed, and some people freeze the whole fruit. When cooking with pawpaws, you generally get good results by substituting them for bananas in breads, cakes, custards, puddings, and muffins. There are also a number of published pawpaw recipes. The most comprehensive collection, *Cooking with Pawpaws*, is free from the Pawpaw Research Program at Kentucky State University in Frankfort, Kentucky. The program offers a dozen other publications about pawpaws, including some that go into detail about current pawpaw research, cultivation methods, and techniques for evaluating the fruit.

Not the least of the pawpaw's blessings, for me, is the people it attracts. Pawpaw fans, even those with official titles and strings of college degrees, are invariably quirky, opinionated, passionate, and subject to spontaneous outbursts of glee. Maybe it's the fruit's eminently rhymeable name (which perhaps arose from a confusion with the papaya). Maybe it's the pawpaw's underdog status in the commercial fruit-growing world—pawpaw proponents, even the most devoted, cannot really take themselves too seriously. Whatever the reason, I've noticed that conversations about pawpaws have a tendency to end in wordplay and laughter. Ray Jones, a California grower and avid fan, once published a list called "Pawpaw Facts." Topping the list was the observation that "pawpaw" spelled backwards is "wapwap." For pawpaw lovers, serious science and unbridled silliness are not mutually exclusive.

But make no mistake, there is serious science going on. At twelve universities throughout the pawpaw's native range, researchers are conducting regional variety trials—long-term cooperative experiments to evaluate twenty-eight pawpaw varieties and clones. In 1994, under the leadership of Desmond Layne, Kentucky State University was named the primary repository for the preservation of *Asimina* germplasm, or the plant's genetic material, which can be preserved and propagated. Layne has since moved on to Clemson University (coincidentally, one of the regional variety trial sites), but the research program at Kentucky State continues strongly under the leadership of Kirk Pomper, who is also president of the PawPaw Foundation. The university has also received grants for research on tissue culture, the most efficient means of preserving and propagating plant clones, and for the analysis of isozymes, the enzymes which permit the identification of plant tissue by variety. Before his retirement a few years ago, Jerry McLaughlin conducted pioneer research at Purdue University on chemical compounds in pawpaws that show great promise as a treatment for certain types of cancer.

Perhaps, as Neal Peterson occasionally and shyly suggests, pawpaws will end up saving the world. Why not? In the meantime, they will continue to quietly blossom and bear, sweetening each fall with the incomparable aroma that signals summer's end.

COLLEEN ANDERSON

Going for Peaches,
Fredericksburg, Texas

NAOMI SHIHAB NYE

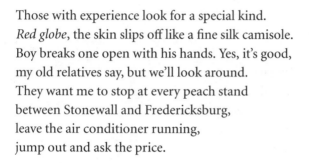

Those with experience look for a special kind.
Red globe, the skin slips off like a fine silk camisole.
Boy breaks one open with his hands. Yes, it's good,
my old relatives say, but we'll look around.
They want me to stop at every peach stand
between Stonewall and Fredericksburg,
leave the air conditioner running,
jump out and ask the price.

Coming up here they talked about
the best ways to die. One favors a plane crash,
but not over a city. One wants to make sure
her grass is watered when she goes.
Ladies, ladies! This peach is fine,
it blushes on both sides.
But they want to keep driving.

In Fredericksburg the houses are stone,
they remind me of wristwatches, glass polished,
years ticking by in each wall.
I don't like stone, says one. What if it fell?
I don't like Fredericksburg, says the other.
Too many Germans driving too slow.
She herself is German as Stuttgart.
The day presses forward, wearing complaints
like charms on its bony wrist.

Actually ladies (I can't resist),
I don't think you wanted peaches after all,

you just wanted a nip of scenery
some hills to tuck behind your heads.
The buying starts immediately, from a scarfed woman who says
I gave up teachin' for peachin'.
She has us sign the guest book.
One aunt insists on re-loading into her own box,
so she can see the fruit on the bottom.
One rejects any slight bruise.
But Ma'am, the seller insists, nature isn't perfect.
Her hands are spotted, like a peach.

On the road, cars weave loose patterns between lanes.
We will float in flower peach-smell
back to our separate kettles, our private tables and knives,
and line up the bounty,
deciding which ones go where.
A canned peach, says one aunt, lasts ten years.
She was 87 last week. But a frozen peach
tastes better on ice cream.
Everything we have learned so far,
the stages of ripening alive in our skins,
on a day that was real to us, that was summer,
motion going out and memory coming in

Tales of Dough and Dowry
Fried Pies in Tennessee

. . . .

JOHN T. EDGE

Up above Memphis, Tennessee, near the border with Kentucky, roadside vendors hawk fried apple pies tucked in glassine envelopes. Filling stations stock them by the register. Vegetable stands stack them alongside flats of tomatoes in the summer, by slat baskets of sweet potatoes in the fall. They're omnipresent, like Crock-Pots of boudin in southwestern Louisiana and bags of boiled peanuts in the South Carolina midlands.

Traveling the back roads of America, especially in the Upper South and Midwest, I spy fried pies with regularity. Near Knoxville, Tennessee, I once tasted a fried pie with a distinctive crust that owed its amber color—and no small measure of its flavor—to the use of flat Coca-Cola as the sole liquid in the dough. I've eaten saccharine Mennonite pies in Kentucky and Amish variants in Ohio that, appropriately enough, tasted just a tad chaster.

In Alabama, somewhere outside Jasper, I once bought a "Sonshine" fried apple pie, wrapped in a crude sleeve. I was in the parking lot, halfway through demolishing the crescent of crust and stewed apples, before I realized that the name of the maker was not a misspelling but a testimony of Christian faith.

I have talked to people who call these treats "preaching pies," in tribute to their ability to placate a child squirming for escape from a Sunday morning sermon. I've heard huntsmen who know the warmth of secreting a hot one in the slash pocket of a tweed jacket on a cold morning. I've heard the plaints of McDonald's aficionados who remember a day when their lozenge-shaped apples pies were fried instead of baked, and all was right with the world.

During a recent run through Tennessee, I met two women—and tasted two pies—that offered opportunity to move beyond matters of nomenclature and provenance. Their life stories offer a glimpse at why the act of making apple pie can take on a larger significance. The pies crafted in this corner of Tennessee are not necessarily unique, but I do believe that they are representative of something that approaches profundity.

Ivon King's husband went in a week. Cancer, they told her. And then he was gone. That was back in 2001. "You can't tell what's coming," she says. "I took something from that. I surely did."

King is in her early seventies. Her hair is gray and silken, her white face is furrowed like fine wale corduroy. I stand behind, watching as she rolls out dough with a pin; cuts it into circles by guide of a coffee saucer; and, after plopping a tablespoon of stewed apples bottom-center, crimps the half-moon closed with a fork and slides it into a cast-iron skillet set over a countertop electric coil. On a typical weekday, she works four hours in the makeshift kitchen at the back of Jerry Kendall's Fruit Market in Union City. During that time, she will make forty pies. Kendall sells her pies for a $1.50. King gets a dollar for every one sold.

"I have always cooked" she tells me, flipping a browned pie with the aid of two spatulas, and sliding it back into the hissing fat. "And I always knew about fried pies. We took them to our school when I was little. The rich children might bring a saltine four-pack and peanut butter and a marshmallow. I thought they were better off at the time, but there was this one girl always wanting my fried pie. I always had one in my box."

Ivon's brother was the one who suggested she fry pies. He knew that, with her husband gone, she would need money to supplement her Social Security income. "The Amish folks around here sell [fried pies] on a route, delivering them from place to place," she tells me. "But I didn't want to move around. This place suits me well," she says, looking back over her shoulder past me, eyeing the concrete floor and particleboard ceiling of the fruit shed.

When the pie turns the shade of a timeworn penny, Ivon scoops it from the skillet and, after blotting the crust with a paper towel, sets it on the counter before me. If I had any sense or self-control, I would wait for the pouch to cool. But patience is not *my* virtue. I bite. The crust gives easily, yielding first to an inner layer of softer dough and then to a cinnamony goo just this side of apple sauce.

Between bites and sharp intakes of cooling air, I tell Ivon how much I like her pie. She smiles. I ask her about the texture of the apples, about how she manages to cook them just so. I ask if she relies on a special variety of apple, and if the apples she uses are raised in her employer's orchards.

She laughs and points her foot toward a box of Sun Maid–brand dried apples. "That's all we use," she says. "When I was coming up, my parents would core and slice apples and dry them on the tin roofs of old outbuildings.

Of course, that was a long time ago, back before my mama passed away. You know she left us when I was a senior in high school. Gone, like my husband. Just gone."

Fifty or sixty miles southwest of Union City, near the burg of Darden, Margo Hayes fries pies, too. Like Ivon King, Hayes turned to pies when confronted with an unspeakable loss. But her husband didn't die. She just wished him dead.

"I grew up over in Decatur County, but I'd been living in Nashville for a long time when I came back this way," she tells me, not long after I polish off my first apple pie and order a peach for good measure. "I had been married twenty-four years when I found out my first husband was keeping another apartment and another woman. That man was taking her the tomatoes I raised in our garden. My tomatoes, raised with my own two hands. Can you imagine that?"

Less than a year passed before she met Jim, her second husband. In 1988, not long after she bought a cinder-block country store out on the highway east of town, he fell through the front door. "He had broke his leg," she tells me. "He broke it bad, and I was there to help get him to the hospital. I helped him get well, too. And then I married him."

Today, Jim and Margo Hayes work side by side in the café. She boasts that her fried frog legs "can't be beat," and locals brag on her midday plate lunch. But after I eat two or three of her fried pies—and revel in the biscuit crust that enrobes each—I'm unable to entertain notions of further caloric intake.

It seems that I'm not alone in my passion for her pies. Jim tells me that, upon his last count in November 2003, Margo had fried 627,686 pies. (In a manner that makes me think that they're aiming for the *Guinness Book of World Records* or girding for the day when the taxman cometh, he notes each pie sold in an old ledger and can, if inclined, enumerate sales by apple, peach, and chocolate varieties.)

At first, Jim's accounting of fried pie sales gave me pause. It didn't fit with the notion of quaintness I had ascribed to their enterprise. I figured that since Margo—with her cumulus of white hair and well-rouged face—looks as grand-motherly as Ivon King, she would think herself to be an accidental business-woman who merely applied what she knew as cookery as a means of supporting herself.

Margo's entrepreneurial ambition reveals itself, though, when I dare pull out my camera and attempt a picture of her crust-rolling technique. "You got $10,000 handy?" she asks, her face fixed with a stern expression. "That's what I charge for a lesson. Ten thousand. Now do you want to get out your checkbook, or do you want to put that camera away?" I see the barest of smiles crease her lips. But I pocket my camera and retreat to a nearby table with a cup of coffee and another pie.

I sit at that table for a while. Margo tells me about some of her favorite customers, including a man named Pompey Mayo, who would drive over from Lexington to buy a dozen pies at a time. "He hid them under his bed," she recalls. "Ate one every morning and one every night." We talk some more. Though it's obvious she was fond of Mayo, her sentimental impulses are few. Mostly she talks of how she has mastered the art of fried pies and of how many gross they sell to the truck stop, up on the interstate.

Soon I come to know that it would be just as wrong to sentimentalize Ivon King as it would be to trivialize Margo Hayes. Both women, it seems, have come to consider their way with a pie and a skillet to be a kind of dowry, an indemnity against past—and future—loss. Though operating on far different scales, they know that, if all else fails, they can fry pies; they can survive dishing fried dough and stewed apples.

The Pumpkin Field

WILLIAM JAY SMITH

An Army Lieutenant observes the Cherokees he
guards on their passage to the west, Arkansas 1838

What a grand lot they were,
 the Cherokees I first saw in June,
lined up in their Georgian camp
 to greet the chief on their departure,
elegant blankets hanging loose
 about their shoulders, ramrod-straight,
dark eyes darting from high-boned
 copper faces under bright turbans
and striped caps pulled down at an angle,
 some in long robes, some in tunics,
all with sashes or wondrous drapery,
 they stood, framed by bearded oaks,
Old Testament patriarchs
 pausing on their way to the Promised Land.

Then in October, where I'd been sent ahead
 to patrol their passage here in Arkansas,
they came from a cold and threadbare wood,
 thin pines bent and tipped with sleet,
eyes glazed and blank,
 half-naked, barefoot,
bones poking through
 their scarecrow shredded clothing,
and stumbled through layers of mist
 onto a scraggly open field

where in wet and tangled grass
    fat pumpkins lay in rows
like painted severed heads.

Oblivious to all around them,
    skeletal automatons,
the Cherokees plunged ahead
    until a farmer on the edge
bade them halt
    and, breaking off a pumpkin,
invited them to take
    whatever his poor field could offer.

Flies swarming to their target,
    they darted up and down the rows,
black hair flying,
    long-nailed tentacles
protruding, they ripped apart
    the pumpkin flesh
until their brown and vacant
    faces merged with jagged pulp,
seeds foaming from
    their hungry mouths, and all I could see,
as on some battlefield, was
    everywhere a wasted mass of orange flesh.

A light rain then began to fall
    as if the shredded pumpkin fiber
drifted down around us:
    I felt ill
and sensed the cholera
    had set in. The farmer guided
me inside his cabin
    and put me down in a dark corner
where between the logs
    I could empty my stomach.

All night long I lay there
    while wind roared
and rain beat down
    and through it I could hear the sloshing

of the weary feet,
    the creak and rattle of ox-carts,
the cursing of the drivers,
    cracking their long whips to urge the oxen on,
the whinnying of horses
    as they struggled through the mud.

"What have we done to these people?"
    I cried out . . . And then a silence fell;
across the dark I saw
    row after row of pumpkins carved and slit,
their crooked eyes
    and pointed teeth all candle-lit within,
not pumpkins but death's-heads they were
    with features of the vacant
hungry faces I had seen,
    stretching to infinity
and glowing in the dark—
    and glowing still when I awoke—

as they do now, and as they always will.

Stand Buy Your Yam
The Lure of the Southern
Produce Stand

DEB BARSHAFSKY

Since I associate roadside stands with rural Georgia, I headed south out of Augusta to see if I could unearth a gem—a little plywood shack with whirligigs and Better Boys that would make my eyes pop. I drove up Deans Bridge, down Tobacco Road, and out Windsor Spring. Out, out, out. Past Jesse Carroll's swimming hole (when did that become a funeral home?), past the hand-lettered "Baby Chicks $1" sign, past Whispering Pines Baptist Church. All the way out to the township of Hephzibah where Windsor Spring intersects with SR 88. No tomatoes. No whirligigs. But a lesson. Well, two lessons. The first: Time marches on. This after the heart-wrenching realization that Hephzibah Junior High, the grand old building in which I toiled side by side with my sister, deciphering the mysteries of adolescence and algebraic equations, has been leveled. The second, and infinitely more germane: Roadside markets are never where you think they should be. If you don't know where they're located, looking for them is futile, like searching the night sky for shooting stars.

It's 9:30 A.M. and Jack Collins is still setting up at Gibbs Produce, a roadside fruit and vegetable stand that punctuates the string of used car lots and tattoo parlors leading into Fort Gordon's Gate 1. "I had laryngitis all week, didn't feel too well, so I let my carrots get away from me," he says. Culling carrots is something of third career for Collins, who retired from both the U.S. Army and Johnson Controls. "When you get good enough with the remote control that you can change channels with either hand without looking at the keypad, it's time to get up out of that chair."

So for three years Collins has worked for Milo Smith, first selling produce out of the bed of his pickup and now at Gibbs, since Smith purchased the stand from the previous owner in April. "I was trout fishin' when he bought it. Had a job when I got back." I suspect that produce stands are a growing employment sector for senior citizens. Even my neighbor Mrs. Potter (Nanny) sells peaches from a pickup, deftly dissecting Blakes for her regulars under a brightly colored floral umbrella. Grocery stores are clean, well-lit, well-stocked shrines to all things edible, but you don't get somebody's grandmother putting a piece of peach in your mouth. You do get somebody's teenager who needs a photo album at the cash register to tell the difference between a butternut squash and a daikon radish.

Keep your mountains of waxed peppers, your polished and neatly bagged Granny Smiths, your presliced and packaged cantaloupe. One of the simple realities of life is this: Vegetables grow in dirt. Handling a basket of soil-smudged crooknecks with my Keds firmly planted in Georgia red clay just feels right. No neon. No barcodes. No bonus cards. No simulated thundershowers. Just me, the bounty of Mother Earth, and a wasp hovering over the sweet potatoes.

I look around—at the homemade "Hot Chow-Chow," Collins's weathered hands as he chops carrots, the crudely rendered dancing, shell-enclosed seed of a leguminous bush on the boiled peanuts sign—and I think I comprehend the lure, the intrigue of a roadside market. I ask him, "Mr. Collins, what do you think it is that brings people here? Why do they come?" He looks up, gazes at Gordon Highway, and my breath catches in my throat. "Prices," he says, returning to his carrots, leaving me to romanticize with the wasp.

Produce at a roadside stand is cheap. Dirt cheap. And the dollar bill seems to be the common denominator, the universal unit of commerce for edible commodities in all colors, shapes, and sizes. For one dollar, you can score four cucumbers. Or one pound of okra. Or three pounds of squash. Five pounds of cabbage. Four bucks and you're hauling home an impressive armload of produce. I priced out a similar harvest at Publix: $9.39. The lesson here? Expect to pay at least double if you opt for the bright and shiny environment of chain grocers. Plus, you're afforded the pleasure of peeling off those pesky little stickers (#4428 on my otherwise perfect persimmons).

But a dollar buys a lot more than mere product at roadside markets. Bob Martin dispenses prices, cooking instructions, buying tips, and rhetorical questions ("Have you ever seen a more beautiful strawberry?") in a seamless litany at his market on Davis Road. The pace here is a little slower than across the street at CGs, the market of choice of most West Augustans. But Gary, the "G" in CGs, has handsome produce. He magnanimously offers samples and often tosses in extras. On most mornings, you'll find the paved lot he borrows from a dance studio brimming with BMWs, Suburbans, and Mercedes jockeying for position—the Fresh Market of Augusta's roadside stands.

But on the other side of Davis Road, I share Mr. and Mrs. Martin with a shaggy shepherd that's lurking around the periphery of the market. Martin's pitch sells me on a small basket of sweet red peppers (yes, one dollar), three ears of corn (also one buck), and a watermelon (not one buck). "You've got to listen for a hollow sound," Martin instructs, leading me to his intricately stacked pyramid of melons. "Thump real hard, like this." He thumps and apparently the sound pleases him, for that's the melon he hoists to his shoulder and deposits in my backseat. A few more cars stop, a Taurus and a dusty blue Chrysler. Mr. Martin approaches the open window of an elderly lady gesturing at the peppers. One buck, I think, as I pull onto Davis, with the better part of my dinner rolling around in the seat behind me.

When rock-bottom prices are a given, nay a very tenet of the roadside market, who thinks to shop around? I thought my $6 watermelon a veritable coup (try $9.99 at the big store). But then I stumbled upon a truckful of them on the northbound side of Peach Orchard Road, near a small hand-painted sign heralding the Lifting Up Jesus Ministries. Homemade signs must be all the rage these days (recall the aforementioned baby chicks and dancing peanut). Here, in magic marker on cardboard, I read "MELLONS. YOUR PICK.. $5." The proprietor, Bill, rises at my approach, gesturing at his study in green, artfully arranged in the bed of a pale yellow, gravel-pocked truck.

"Bill . . . ?"

"Just Bill."

I remembered a tidbit that Mr. Collins from Gibbs shared about selling out of a truck. License required. I tentatively inquire, "How do you pick a spot for selling?"

"Aaw, I thought you was gonna ask me how you pick a melon."

I grin.

"Look here," he says, thumping a melon. Hard. "See. Sounds holler." And then he lapses into an impassioned narrative of the close call Georgia's watermelon crop had with gummy stem blight. I'm still grinning, and I ask again, "So how do you pick a spot?" Just Bill just grins back and raps the melon one more time. "You try," he says. "Hard, like this."

Farmer's Market

MARCIA CAMP

It isn't okra cut small and tender the way
   we know it should be, or
tomatoes whose imperfections declare them
   simon-pure, or
peas bursting from their purple hulls
(their remembered anthem sung on summer-
   morning streets,
"Peas . . . " with soft refrain, "already shelled")—
we come for none of these, though we ask the
   price at each tailgate.
We're here to see hardy faces (our parents and
   grandparents with different features)
smile a warranty on produce knowing hands and
   bent backs coaxed to life.
We tender crisp dollar bills, drop quarters
   into calloused palms and
purchase affirmation.
For we need to hear the vernacular of hill,
   prairie and delta in
words carefully weeded from our city talk,
have our nostrils sting from manure on boots,
smell musk of frying bacon lingering in work shirts.
Only here can we feel Dallis grass switch our ankles,
   blackberry briers claw our legs,
hear the night call of the whippoorwill,
   see its red eye pierce the dark, and
know that we did not dream childhood.

Of Sorghum Syrup, Cushaws, Mountain Barbecue, Soup Beans, and Black Iron Skillets

FRED SAUCEMAN

Walk with me through a field of sorghum cane in late summer. Pull back the leaves of a cushaw plant in early fall. Inhale hickory from smoldering fresh hams after the first frost in Bullock's Hollow. When summer's crops are canned and frozen, claim a spot at the counter for a cold weather bowl of stew-seasoned soup beans. And end this jaunt through my native northeast Tennessee as we take down a century-old iron skillet off the pegboard for some bacon-greased and buttermilked fried chicken.

Arland Johnson describes sugar groups with the authority of an organic chemist. He analyzes the strength of metals with the precision of a mechanical engineer. He speaks of soil and sun with the detailed knowledge of an agronomist.

This retired Eastman Chemical Company maintenance worker and his wife, Novella, apply all that independently acquired knowledge to the production of sorghum syrup, at their hillside home near Limestone, Tennessee.

The Johnsons' operation may well be the largest producer of the sweet, dark amber syrup in East Tennessee. Since getting into the business for a hobby back in 1982, they have grown to the point where some 8,000 quarts of syrup drip down the metal troughs in Arland's self-constructed, self-contained cottage industry.

Drive by their place in midsummer and you'd probably think you were looking at a twenty-acre stand of corn, but an up-close inspection, a squeeze, and a smell will tell you differently. The Johnsons grow sorghum cane. There are around fifty varieties on record, with Early Orange, Topper 76, and Umbrella performing the best in this climate.

From the middle of September to the first of October, Arland keeps his four-wheel-drive, high-rise tractor rolling and his corn binder hot, as the mature cane is harvested from the field and hauled up the hill. It's then fed through press rollers to extract the precious juice, which is cooked down and boiled by a 200-horsepower, gas-fired boiler, under constant watch, until all the impurities are gone.

"There's no other food industry like sorghum," Arland says. "Sometimes you're dealing with five or six sugar groups, plus you've got starches and other things that'll get out of balance and cause a problem cooking. So you've always got to be on your toes. The milder you can get it and the lighter you can get it, the better."

The terms "sorghum" and "molasses" are often used interchangeably, but Arland is quick to point out the difference. Molasses, he says, is a by-product of the making of sugar and can often be a blended product, even containing as much as 20 percent Karo syrup. Sugarcane does not grow well in the mountain South, so the syrup produced in southern Appalachia is properly called sorghum, from sorghum cane.

"Even your sugar people, if they make a pure syrup from sugarcane, they don't call it molasses, they call it ribbon cane syrup."

The sign alongside Providence Road at the Johnsons' place in rural Washington County reads, "Mother Nature in a Jug." This sorghum syrup is a natural, pure product with no additives, and the Johnsons have no qualms about allowing their growing grandsons, Joseph and Bradley, to dip their fingers into a cooled run.

Once a year, Arland and Novella make the trip to either Nashville, Tennessee, or Bowling Green, Kentucky, for some "continuing education" at the National Sweet Sorghum Producers and Processors Association convention, attended by about 300 farmers. Tennessee and Kentucky produce more sorghum syrup than any other states.

"Since I've been going, about fifteen years, I've seen a big improvement in the syrup that's been brought in and talked about," Arland says. "The quality of it is really coming up."

Sorghum is one of America's oldest foods and was the primary sweetener during colonial times. Like many Southerners, the Johnsons drizzle it over hot biscuits and cornbread. Arland even stirs it into peanut butter. Novella's baked beans, gingerbread, and ham glaze all profit from healthy glugs of sorghum syrup.

Arland has concocted a fine East Tennessee–style barbecue sauce, with both sorghum and honey as sweetening agents and upwards of eighteen spices and herbs.

"Most people who try it really like it. It's unusual, and it's not real hot. I sell it out of our home now, but I'm talking to a grocery store chain about stocking it. People I sell it to come back and say they can eat it on cereal. It just reaches out and grabs you."

Arland Johnson comes by his love for sorghum syrup honest. Raised in a sharecropping family around Newmansville, in northern Greene County, he remembers his grandfather growing sorghum cane. His mother even learned to drive an A Model truck by hooking it up to a cane mill and circling around to grind the stalks, as horses used to do in earlier times. For craft demonstrations today, Arland occasionally hooks up a horse to teach people about the old ways.

The shelf life of sorghum syrup is about two years, but Arland and Novella's customers never seem to have any jars around that long.

"Oh, Lord, I don't know how much butter's been made in that thing," says Uncle Sam Melear, age ninety. Apple butter, pear butter, and peach butter have gurgled and steamed and popped out hot on bare arms stirring down the sides of the brass kettle Sam bought back in 1941.

He gave less than $40 for the whole rig, stand and all. "I bought it off a Whetsel woman. Her husband had died and she'd broke up housekeeping and was going to Florida."

Butter boiled down from the fruit of the family's trees has been lovingly ladled into recycled pint jars as long as Sam can remember. He's kept up with what's been cooked in that coal-black vessel. He used to loan the kettle out to friends who'd pay him back in fruit butter, but he had to threaten Isom Hensley one time that if he put any more cinnamon in the apple butter, he'd have to find a kettle somewhere else.

Dear as those fruit butters are, for the Conkin and Melear clan, the product that brings them back together around the beginning of fall each year is cushaw butter, crafted in a similar way, but from a crooknecked, green-and-white-striped squash that grows on a vine, like a pumpkin.

Mention cushaws to gardeners in Appalachia, and you'll invariably hear how they're preferred over pumpkins for pies. Loyal Jones, retired director of the Berea College Appalachian Center in Kentucky, says there's another advantage, too.

"If you were growing those big old pumpkins on one of these hillside corn-fields, it might come loose and roll down and kill somebody, but those cushaws, they won't roll. They'll hook around a cornstalk or something and stay in the field."

Jones says cushaw is an Algonquian Indian word, and the plants were grown by Native Americans long before white settlements were established in America. His brother once sent him some seeds from North Carolina, and he's shared them with neighbors all around Berea.

This year's cushaw-butter making in the East Tennessee town of Mount Carmel began with a pile of oak, the remnants of a Memorial Day storm that tore through the Bloomingdale community in Kingsport.

By 7:30 in the morning, all the Conkins and Melears are assembled, the cabana's up, and the coffee's done.

Cubed cushaw is dumped into the kettle, and slowly the water is cooked out through constant stirring. The poplar stirrer is about eight feet long. A rectangular piece of board, perforated with holes, is attached to the end. The tricks are to keep the liquid moving, never let the wood touch the kettle, and use hardwood, not pine.

Before any sugar is added, the Conkins dip out and can cooked cushaw for pie filling. Then the fire is stoked, the boiling continues, and along about noon, out of deference to Uncle Sam, the cousins season up the first turn, without cinnamon.

The heavy responsibility of spicing the butter falls to Leonard Melear. There isn't a measuring spoon in sight as he sprinkles in pumpkin pie spice, then nutmeg, cinnamon oil, and vanilla extract.

"What's it need?" he hollers, and the opinions fly like late summer yellow jackets as plastic spoons dip into the warm, golden butter. Oblivious to requests that he cease the seasoning, Leonard goes through the cycle of flavoring again. The cousins glance at each other silently as it looks like Leonard's about to go for the pumpkin pie spice once more, but Jean Davis says "Enough," and it's canning time.

The cousins take their assigned roles with the precision of a military drill team, and soon the brass kettle's empty, and Jennifer Woods calls out to Dennis Conkin, "Come over here, we need a man for that last little twist of the jar lids."

As always, the pie filling, the butter with cinnamon, and the butter without will all be given away to family and friends.

"We call ourselves 'the Cousins,' and we're all involved, from J. W. raising the cushaws to Leonard providing the place," says Dennis Conkin.

J. W. planted nineteen hills last spring, just after the last frost, and raised forty-two cushaws. "And it stayed so wet I didn't even get to plow them," he says. "All you need is good ground and a little fertilize. Cushaws are easy to grow. The leaves on them will shade themselves and keep it moist down under there."

Diabetes has afflicted a couple of family members. Leonard only eats about a pint of butter now in a year's time, and Uncle Sam none at all, but it's the getting together that really matters to this southern Appalachian family.

"I've got sugar, shucks fire," Sam laments, "but this means a lot, Lord yeah."

This pharmacist's prescription for well-being calls for fire, smoke, and spice. Larry Proffitt leads a dual life. He dispenses medications and advice to the citizens of Elizabethton, Tennessee, at Burgie Drugs while keeping the hickory fires going over in the next county at Ridgewood Barbecue, a business his parents, Grace and Jim Proffitt, began in 1948.

A good memory is one element that links Larry's two careers. Going through pharmacy school at the University of Tennessee in Memphis, Larry memorized massive amounts of information in biochemistry and organic medicinal chemistry courses. Stored within that memory today are the unwritten directions for Ridgewood's mountain-style, tomato-based barbecue sauce.

With the deaths of Larry's brother Terry in June 2002 and their mother, Grace, less than a year later, now only Larry and his daughter Lisa, a registered nurse, know the recipe.

"We came over to the restaurant one Sunday afternoon, when everything was closed, and I wrote the procedure and ingredients down for her," Larry recalls. "She said, 'Do you really remember the recipe?' I said, 'Do you remember your Social Security number? I've known this recipe since I was sixteen. It's been in my head, and now it's going to be in your head.'"

In the quiet of the empty restaurant, Larry took his daughter through the steps to make thirty gallons of the sweet-and-sour sauce and then went outside to retrieve a pack of matches. He took the written recipe to the sink, turned on the water, burned the paper, and washed the ashes down the drain.

"There goes the recipe," he said. "I hope it's in your head, because it's only in mine and yours now."

There it will reside until the next generation, when Lisa and Mark Peters's twin son and daughter witness the same ritual and commit the nearly two dozen ingredients and their measurements to memory.

All the hickory logs that fuel and flavor Ridgewood barbecue are harvested within a few miles of Bullock's Hollow, and the Proffitt farm, which has been in the family since 1856, is covered with towering hickory trees of varying ages. The restaurant itself is constructed from hickory planks off that farm.

Ridgewood's pit, like the restaurant, backs up to a heavily wooded, steeply inclined hill along a gently curving two-lane road where ivy-wrapped tulip poplar trees scatter shade across the hollow. The construction of the pit is a closely guarded, proprietary secret, and the door to the house that encloses it is permanently padlocked. Jim Proffitt burned down several pits over the years before settling on his final design of fire bricks and stainless steel. Even with that configuration, the entire structure, wooden beams, chain-link gates, blackened screen wire, and all, must be rebuilt periodically because of the intense heat.

Ridgewood is one of the few barbecue restaurants in the South that does not serve pork shoulder. For over three decades, the only cut of pork the Proffitts have smoked is fresh ham.

"Any country boy knows the difference," says Larry. "In the country, we turn the shoulders into sausage. Shoulder has a different taste. It's like the difference between breast meat on a turkey and thigh meat from the legs. The shoulder and the ham taste different. The ham is far superior, and it costs more."

Trucked down the highway from Bristol, the hams come boned and rolled in cotton netting, about 120 of them a week. They're smoked for about nine hours, then rubbed with a spice blend and chilled in a cooler. The next morning, the darkened hams are sliced, revealing meat that is almost white. Seconds before troweling massive piles onto platters or sandwiches, cooks reheat the meat on a grill and sauce it. Chopped, pulled, or minced are not options—only sliced.

Meat isn't apportioned with a kitchen scale. Cooks just know how much to reach for.

"I'm sure we're not making any money on some of the sandwiches because those ladies get heavy hands," says Larry. "When I eat out, I don't care what somebody charges me as long as they give me something good and give me enough of it."

Still, Ridgewood's barbecue pork sandwiches, dressed with a cool, crunchy, minced layer of coleslaw, ring up less than what some of the gas and electricity converts are charging.

The beverage of choice at Ridgewood is Southern sweet tea, the strongest drink in the house. "This used to be a beer joint when it first opened," Larry recalls. "There were beer joints everywhere up and down the road. In 1952 Sullivan County went dry, and our other owners bailed out. One went to work for Ford in Detroit, the other for Bemberg, where they made rayon yarn over in Elizabethton."

In the early days, every year, Grace and Jim Proffitt borrowed the money to take their family on a vacation. In Daytona Beach, Florida, they saw people smoking chickens and came up with the idea to start serving barbecue back at home in the hills. For awhile, they barely survived. Couldn't buy a car until 1950.

Jim kept his job at Bemberg while Grace ran the restaurant because, she said, "I've got two boys to put through college."

Grace grew up in Easley, South Carolina, and had met Jim in Johnson City, Tennessee, where her father ran a rock quarry.

"Mother had patience," says Larry. "She was determined to succeed and wouldn't give up."

Even with the coming of the new four-lane that wrapped around Bullock's Hollow a mile and a half away, Grace never panicked.

"Everyone told her we'd go broke since the road had passed us by," says Larry. "My mother said 'We'll make it. We don't owe nothing.'"

Temporarily, back in 1987, it looked as though those predictions would come true. Business dropped off sharply the first year after the new four-lane was finished. But Grace kept the faith and the fires. She'd saved enough money to get the family through, and the business recovered. In fact, the new road provided better access, even without a Ridgewood sign on the highway.

"Stay with the pig until he makes a hog," Grace Proffitt always said. This determined pioneer philosophy is as fundamental as the fire and smoke that have mingled with the Tennessee mountain air at one of the nation's most heralded barbecue restaurants for over half a century.

Jerry and Donna Hartsell carry on a great and lasting legacy within the aging, sign-covered walls of the Bean Barn on the corner of East Church and Cherry in Greeneville, Tennessee.

Six days a week, they cook beans, and they cook them with lard. They cook beans the way Romie and Zella Mae Britt taught them to, in a pot as old as the place. Romie and Zella Mae are both gone now. He died in 2003 at age eighty-nine. She passed on in 1999, around Easter time, at age eighty-three.

Romie got a real kick out of the Greeneville newspaper's attempt to kill him off early one time. I had mentioned him in an interview, and the reporter mistakenly inserted "the late" into the story, about the time Romie, then a vigorous eighty-six, was about to get remarried.

Romie and Zella Mae Britt were inventive, resourceful people. They were country people who had known hard times and were determined not to live through them again. And they did an ingenious thing. They combined two simple dishes, common to East Tennessee country kitchens: soup beans and beef stew.

They called the result "Beans All the Way," and they were proud of their creation. And they were proud of Jerry and Donna for keeping it alive, as they've done for nearly twenty-five years. Jerry's sister, also named Donna, is married to Romie and Zella Mae's son Danny, so the business remains within the same family that started it over fifty years ago.

Beans All the Way begins with a spoonful of beef stew in the bottom of the bowl, always with a potato cube. Then the bowl is filled with the lard-seasoned pinto beans and topped off with chopped onions. It's an incomparable blend of farm flavors, and I'm surprised some Manhattan hotshot hasn't discovered it, slapped on a French name, and served it in a ramekin for $10. At the Bean Barn, a bowl will cost you all of $1.79, and that includes a square of Jerry's white cornbread. Choose light bread and you get three slices, right out of the bag, and four with the heel.

Just as you'd match a Cabernet with a Black Angus fillet, the beverage that pairs the best with Beans All the Way is buttermilk. Jerry and Donna stock two kinds, one for cooking and one for drinking.

The Bean Barn is a creaky-floored, bare-light-bulbed, bowed-ceiling type of place. Behind the cash register, you can trace the history of the business through layers and varying styles of linoleum, all the way down to the dark hardwood. It's a place where diners pass around the daily paper and where extracting a tooth-pick out of an old hot sauce bottle is a postmeal ritual, whether you need one or not. Suited Main Street lawyers, electricians fresh off power poles, backpack-toting high schoolers, and denim-clad tobacco farmers occupy the swiveling stools and wooden benches for beans.

In addition to All the Way, you can get just soup beans, beans with stew, beans with onions, or beans "super soupy."

Jerry and Donna have done a little inventing of their own, and they, too, put together two foods that are typically served separately. The Hobart Special, named for Jerry, is a double cheeseburger, with grilled, hickory-smoked ham, and the best red tomato they can buy.

The Hartsells cook about ten pounds of pintos at a time, putting them on while the breakfast eggs sizzle atop the old grill, and keeping them slowly sim-mering right through lunch. The Bean Barn, originally called Britt's, rarely advertises, but one time Romie and a disc jockey from radio station WSMG stuck a microphone down into the pot to lure listeners with the bubbling of beans.

Beans and cornbread have gotten their share of ridicule over the years, espe-cially from folks who never had to eat them to survive. Romie and Zella Mae Britt rose above all the kidding and the jokes and taught their descendants that beans and cornbread are dishes to be celebrated. Today, when the Hartsells serve you up a bowl of Beans All the Way, lipping full, they do so proudly, and without apology, just as the dignified and virtuous creators of the grand and noble dish would have wanted it to be.

When I want to reconnect with my Southern mountain past, I take a black iron skillet down from the pegboard wall and open the flour bin.

Nothing says Southern cooking any better than a black skillet. Ours are about a century old. They hold, deep within their dark molecules, silent memories of floured, fried fatback on cold Depression mornings. Pineapple upside-down cake from better times. Brown biscuits glossy with lard. The legacy of cracklin' cornbread.

My contribution to the collective memory of the black skillet is buttermilk-fried chicken. In that skillet, in my kitchen, products of the Southern farm are most at home. Bird and buttermilk and bacon grease. White Lily flour and whole milk for gravy.

I think of those who, by necessity, had to make chicken gravy with water, and I remember those who still say it tastes better that way.

Redeye gravy has slickened and shined that skillet for decades. It's hard-times cooking. Making do with what you have. Gravy made with ham grease and water and maybe a little leftover coffee. Mountain folks still make it that way these days—not always because they have to, but because they want to.

As flour and oil brown in that iron skillet for a roux to color and thicken my gumbo, I remember Leah Chase down in her New Orleans restaurant kitchen, telling me a roux ought always to be the same color as she. Each time I make one, I think of her coffee-colored Creole complexion.

Flour-thickened gravies, sauces, and soups—cooked in black cast iron and ladled over the whiteness of rice, mashed potatoes, and biscuits—unite the South, from Appalachian mountain church suppers to New Orleans Sunday jazz brunches.

Those two stark and elemental things, a black skillet and a handful of flour, speak of permanence and simplicity in a time of complexity and change. The dishes created by the chemistry of black iron and soft winter wheat bring continuity and connection.

In the South, our skillets go unsoaped. We wish never to destroy that patina no scientist could ever replicate. We don't soap for another reason, too. Somewhere, deep in our being, we know our skillets tell the story of our past: once grasped by soft and youthful hands cracking their first henhouse egg, now lifted off the wall slowly by old, arthritic hands. Hands that still recall, from the first year of marriage, the heft of flour to make a perfect blackberry cobbler, one that stayed black-iron warm all morning.

FRED SAUCEMAN

From the mineral it feeds into our culinary artistry to the very aroma that forever drifts from its experienced planes, the black iron skillet is central to an understanding of the South. It is solid, insistent, and binding—the repository of age-old ingredients and stories of survival and celebration. It is an eternal gift of the American Southland, both covenant and comfort across the generations.

A Garden in Kentucky

JANE GENTRY

Under the fluorescent sun
inside the Kroger, it is always
southern California. Hard avocados
rot as they ripen from the center out.
Tomatoes granulate inside their hides.
But by the parking lot, a six-tree orchard
frames a cottage where winter has set in.

Pork fat seasons these rooms.
The wood range spits and hisses,
limbers the oilcloth on the table
where an old man and an old woman
draw the quarter moons of their nails,
shadowed still with dirt,
across the legends of seed catalogues.

Each morning he milks the only goat
inside the limits of Versailles. She feeds
a rooster that wakes up all the neighbors.
Through dark afternoons and into night
they study the roses' velvet mouths
and the apples' bright skins
that crack at the first bite.

When thaw comes, the man turns up
the sod and, on its underside, ciphers
roots and worms. The sun like an angel
beats its wings above their grubbing.
Evenings on the viny porch they rock,
discussing clouds, the chance of rain.
Husks in the dark dirt fatten and burst.

Of Fall Days and Harvesting, and Falling in Love

JEAN RITCHIE

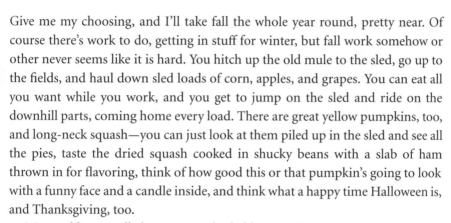

Give me my choosing, and I'll take fall the whole year round, pretty near. Of course there's work to do, getting in stuff for winter, but fall work somehow or other never seems like it is hard. You hitch up the old mule to the sled, go up to the fields, and haul down sled loads of corn, apples, and grapes. You can eat all you want while you work, and you get to jump on the sled and ride on the downhill parts, coming home every load. There are great yellow pumpkins, too, and long-neck squash—you can just look at them piled up in the sled and see all the pies, taste the dried squash cooked in shucky beans with a slab of ham thrown in for flavoring, think of how good this or that pumpkin's going to look with a funny face and a candle inside, and think what a happy time Halloween is, and Thanksgiving, too.

We would carry all the corn up the ladder into the barn loft, sort out the nubbins for the cow and mule, and store the full good ears in the other loft room against the times we'd shell and go to mill. Bam, the mule, was the proudest thing and got so he wouldn't eat nubbins, and then he had to have six or seven of these good ears a day, too. Dad said he reckoned Bam figured, here he was doing all that work plowing and helping raise that corn, and then hauling it down from the fields, so that he might as well get the best of it—no more than his due. One winter I remember Dad fed old Bam so well that we had to borrow corn from Aunt Mary Ann, enough for a turn or two, to do us for cornbread until the crop came in that next summer.

On Saturdays we'd get up before the birds and go a hickory nut hunting, taking flour sacks and coffee sacks and stay all the long day rambling about in the hills. Mom would go with us, and was the best climber among us, too. We'd race and chase up ahead of her, and get so winded that we'd have to fall down and rest. By the time we'd start on, she'd be up with us. She'd never stop until she got to the top of the ridge, then she'd stand still and puff a little, fanning herself with a cowcumber leaf and looking all around her.

"Lord, children, look what a pretty sight it is. I guess it's Indian summer. My dad always said you couldn't find anything so fair as an Indian summer day. The air right hazy soft and the sunshine yaller as firelight, and the hills all manner of fine colors."

Whenever Mom talked like that and looked away off, it made me feel like she was talking to someone far away there where she was looking, someone I knew and yet did not know. I'd get around and pull at her apron so she would notice me. I'd get the same feeling whenever I went to church with her, and they started singing those old long slow lonesome songs. She'd sing, and the tears would start in her eyes, and she'd forget all about me there beside her. It was like she had gone off and left me, it was the lonesomest feeling. Once I asked her why all the church songs sounded so sad, and why it was she always cried in church. She said:

"Folks in church cries for joy, not because they are sad. The singing, well, 'pears to me like our songs are the only real good music I ever did hear. Lot of churches you go to now, sing them little flibberty-te-jibbity songs, sound more like dance pieces than meeting songs. Our meetinghouse songs are different. I purely love them in my heart, love to dwell on the words of them, relish the tune of them. To me they are more like worship and God than any other music."

I guess the way she felt in church and the way she felt in the midst of the fall hills must have been somehow akin to each other, but I couldn't appreciate that at the time. I was only worried because she wouldn't look at me. Anyway, she finally would notice, in a minute or two, and ask me how many hickory nuts we had found.

"Is that all you got? Swear to goodness I thought you'd know where the good trees stand. Take over in the holler yonder, that old twisted tree that was struck by lightning, see if it's got any this year. I'm satisfied that's the one allus bears the best of any around here."

Walnuts we'd gather too, long walnuts and black walnuts. They tasted the best of any kind of nuts when we made fudge on winter evenings after supper. The very best taste of all, though, was to crack out a handful of black walnuts and eat them with a piece of cold cornbread, first a bit of nut and then a bite of bread. That's the main best eating in the world!

There was no end of good things about the fall. Often we'd get out of school in fodder-pulling time, for the teacher couldn't say much when your own mom and dad said you had to stay home and pull fodder. Then there was the excitement of storing up the apples in under the floor so that the whole house smelled like a party all winter long. Or helping to make jelly out of the grapes and apple butter out of the apples that wouldn't keep, and getting to scrape all the pans. Or looking for the prettiest bunch of fall leaves to put on the teacher's desk at school. Or getting a new pair of shoes because it'd soon be cold weather.

More partying, too, in the fall. I guess that was the time when the reasons for parties were most plentiful. Stir-offs, pie suppers, corn gatherings, and other kinds of workings with one thing and another about the harvest, always winding up with everybody playing games and singing and running a few sets.

It was in the fall, just before my fourteenth birthday, that I first fell in love.

I was a big, healthy, gangly girl, not slim and not pretty. I was good in my books and everybody thought well of me, but the boys never winked at me or pulled my straight red hair. They never said much of anything at all to me, come to think of it. Seemed like they were afraid of me, and I was scared finally to death of them. I was so bashful that whenever a boy looked at me sideways, my tongue would cleave to the roof of my mouth and my face would turn ever which color. The worst of it was that everybody saw how bad I felt about it and every living soul I knew began to tease and torment the life out of me over the boys. Seems like that would just fly all over me, and I'd light into them, who-ever'd tease me, and I'd just want to kill them, scratch out their eyeballs, and pull out their hair by the roots.

Mom would say, "Now what you reckon makes her act thataway? Why she's been claiming the boys all of her life, bragging about how this one and that one was her sweetheart. What's got into her now?"

Then she'd be bound to tell about the time when I was just five years old, I came running into the kitchen house where she was stirring up some bread for supper.

"Well Mommie, I know who it is I'm a-going to marry when I get big."

"You do now! Lordy mercy, who is it?"

"Nobody but Little-Bill Browning."

"That's a mighty fine thing to know, little girl. How'd you find out about it?"

"He ast me!"

Now, here I was going on fourteen and in my heart I wanted more than anything to be noticing the boys, but they just didn't like me. They all acted like it plagued them to talk with me, like I wasn't good enough for them, and they were ashamed to be seen with me. I thought I knew why it was. It was on account of the way I looked. I wasn't little and slim like the other girls were; I never had any new clothes. Everything I wore had belonged to several other people before it got down to me.

I began to act as though I couldn't stand the boys, would fight anyone who named one to me, and said nobody'd ever catch me walking and talking with any of them. That was another thing—I couldn't talk. In my mind I could have charming talks with rich handsome men, having them fight duels with each other over me, right and left, but whenever I undertook to say any of those smart things to the boys I knew, the pretty words came out all wrong. The boys would look at me and say "yes" or "no," if they bothered to say that much, and then they'd go away.

One day in October I was sitting at my desk in school, studying my lessons, when someone eased into the seat beside me. I looked up, thinking to see Helen or one of the other girls, but there was Cleve Hamilton with a grin all over his face and a twinkle in his blue eyes, acting like he wasn't a bit afraid of me. Cleve was the only boy in school who didn't have to do a blessed thing to get girls to notice him. They were all so crazy about him that he just had to look at them once, and they'd take the big-head for a week.

He was the best basketball player in the whole school. He was tall and slim but with plenty of muscles; he had the curliest light-colored hair, and every move he made put you in mind of a streak of lightning. I thought he was the prettiest thing in the world, but I hated him because he was stuck-up, and I never even thought of wanting him to talk to me because I knew he never would.

My first thought was to jump up and run away. He put his arm around the back of my seat.

"Howdy, Cleve," I said. My insides were on fire. I tried to hide my red face with the geography book. Cleve peeped over the edge. He had to whisper because it was in time of books.

"Tell me what in tarnation you studying about so hard?"

"Geography."

"Never saw anyone study so hard as you do. Here shut up that fool book and talk to me."

I determined that I wouldn't let him scare me to death, so I looked him right in the face and eyes and asked him what it was he had to say.

Cleve let out a big laugh, and the teacher frowned and said, "Shhh!"

"Well, don't look so all-fired mad, I ain't going to ask you to shoot yer granny. I just want to be friendly like."

He came closer so nobody could hear but me, and the look on his face put me in mind of a little boy.

"Honey, I like you, and you won't ever look my way at all. Maybe that's the reason I like you, but what's the matter, don't you like menfolks or are you just bashful?"

"I'm ugly!" I whispered. I don't remember ever saying that to anyone before, and I felt right good about it. Cleve looked like I was crazy.

"Why, honey, you're not ugly. What makes you say a thing like that, you-you-redhead!"

"It's awful to be a redhead. Little young uns follow you around, say,

Redhead, gingerbread,
Five cents a cabbage head!"

Well, in no time we were both laughing and joking, and everything I said was coming out just right. Came time for the geography and for the first time I didn't know a one of the answers. A funny thing about that was, Mr. Hall didn't seem to mind. Once I looked up quick and caught him smiling down at Cleve and me, for all the world like he knew a good secret.

That evening I went home from school and threw down my books and took to the hills to hunt cows without anyone telling me to go. I raced through the woods like a deer, swinging on grapevines and tree limbs, and laughing and making speeches on top of high rocks, and cutting such a shine that I was ashamed of myself, but that nor nothing else could stop me. The old cow was waiting for me at the gap, and I let down the bars with a great clatter and hollered, "HEIGH!" at her so loud that she must have thought I was plum crazy, for she swung her old head around and looked at me a minute and then heisted her tail and made the dirt and rocks just fly getting down that hill road, her bell clangety-bang-banging like the devil was after her.

I marched down the road behind her with my stick over my shoulder, singing to the top of my lungs. I never usually hollered out on a song like some folks around did, but now I purely felt like it. A funny thing was that I was singing, the best I remember, "Come All Ye Fair." The words of that song surely didn't match my feeling, but maybe the tune did, or maybe it was just because it was a song you could really holler out on, and to me at that time it seemed like the finest song in the world.

Come all ye fair and tender ladies,
Take a warning how you court young men;
They are like a bright star in a summer's morning,
They'll first appear and then they're gone.

They'll tell to you some lovely story,
They'll 'clare to you their love is true,
Straightaway they'll go and court some other
And that is the love they have for you.

I wisht I was some little sparrow
And I had wings and I could fly,
I'd fly away to my false truelover,
And while they'd talk I'd sit and cry.

But I am not no little sparrow,
I have no wings and I can't fly;
So I'll sit right here in my grief and sorrow,
And pass my troubles by and by.

If I had a known before I courted
That love had a-been such a killing thing,
I'd a-locked my heart in a chest of golden
And a-bound it down with a silver pin.

Young man, ne'er cast your eye on beauty,
For beauty is a thing that will decay;
I've seen many a fair and a bright sunny morning
Turn into a dark and deludinous day.

Aunt Mary Ann heard the racket and came out on her porch, and I could tell by the way she stood there with her hands on her hips and looked up the hill at me going by, I could tell that she was wondering what on earth had come over me. I thought to myself, right now Aunt Mary Ann is saying to Oly, "Why that's Balis's young un going 'long up there. Swear I reckon he's a-raising him up a right wild girl."

That night after we got supper over and the dishes washed, we all were sitting around in the front room, doing one thing and another. I was trying to get my lessons, but I couldn't to save my neck do a thing but write Cleve Hamilton's pretty name over every page I turned. Dad came stomping in off the back porch with a great log for the fire. He threw it on the fire in just the right place, and a thousand sparkles cracked out and sailed up the chimney.

"Shore is a fall time out tonight. Makes me wish I had a little patch of cane—might near the best stirrin'-off weather I ever seed."

I got a quivering breath and my heart near failed me at the thoughts of a stir-off. I'd make Cleve go, and we would stand in the dark and talk, like the other girls and their boys did. I never said a word, though I felt like if I cleared my throat everybody would know what was in my mind, and they'd start to shame me and make fun.

"I know who's raising cane this year," Mom looked up from the Bible she was reading, halfways smiling, teasing us.

"Hunh. Who wouldn't know that!" Wilmer said. "It's Lee-up-on-the-Branch. I saw that cane patch when the cows broke out of the pasture one day last month, and I had to hunt them up on the left-hand fork. Went all the way up to Lee's 'fore I heard their bells, and I passed a right pretty patch of green cane."

"Don't get too brash now," Dad warned. "Maybe he's a keeping it a secret. Maybe he don't aim to have a stir-off for everybody."

"Well, the secret's out now, I already told a lot of boys about it, and we won't let him stir-off by himself now!" Wilmer laughed.

Sure enough, one day not long after that, Dosh Brashear, Lee's woman, passed by on her way from the store to her house a mile up the branch, and she stopped to talk awhile with Mom like she always did. She said they had gathered in the cane, and tomorrow they would gin it. If all went according to plan, they'd stir-off just after dark the next evening. As she went out of sight at the big cliff in the curve of the branch, she thought to holler back, "We had a right smart patch this year, so you'ns can bring your bucket!"

Next day at school when Cleve came to my seat, I let him know in a round-about way that I was going to a stir-off that night. He said that was funny, he was going to the same one.

"I reckon I'll see you there, then," he said. "If I do, will you talk with me?"

"I been brought up to be civil to everybody, mister."

"Aw, you know what I mean. You just better be there, that's all!"

As I recall those days, it was the craziest feeling I had about Cleve. I liked him and I didn't. I liked him whenever he sat in my seat at school and all the other girls saw us and wished they had him. But I didn't like him when he'd come and butt in on the games we girls were playing at recess, or when he'd catch me drawing paper dolls and laugh at me. I liked for the girls to see him put his arm around the back of my seat and hug a little before I could stop him. It tickled me for them all to see it, but it really would make me mad for him to do that, and when I'd get mad and tell him he better stop I meant it. I couldn't stand for him even to touch my hand. It was a strange thing, in my heart I wanted him to touch me, I would dream day and night about him holding my hand, about how it would be to comb his curly head with my fingers. I would dream and tremble with pleasure, but as soon as he would get near to me and take hold of my hand I would get mad and begin to fight him, say mean things, and tell him to let me alone. Then he'd laugh and call me his little wildcat, but after a while, three or four weeks after he first began to pay attention to me, I began to catch him looking at me when he thought I wasn't noticing, in a way that caused me to be afraid.

The day of the stir-off was a Friday, and school let out early for some reason.

On the way home Sallie suggested that some of us go up early and watch Lee-up-on-the-Branch gin his cane. Mom said I could go, but we must just watch and not get in the way of the work. Pauline and Jewel and Wilmer would come on up after dark. Mom came out on the porch and hollered after us.

"You'ns keep your feet dry now, for it's late in the year and you'll sure catch a cold if you don't. Walk on the rocks whenever the road goes through the water. As I recollect, that left-hand fork road runs along ever so fur right smack dab in the creek bed. Don't sass anybody, and help if they want you to."

I had on my prettiest blue dress, and my hair tied back with a big blue ribbon because Cleve was coming. But I clear forgot about Cleve as soon as we started racing each other up the branch. For a while we tried to see which one could outrun the others, then we played banner. Sallie's baby brother, Cotton, was the banner, and he led us through thickets of blackberry briers and all manner of places like that, and we had to follow him or we'd be out. He walked the footlogs on their tip edges, and he jumped the branch in the widest parts. We did everything that he did until just before we got to Lee's, he bannered all of us girls by doing skin-the-cat on a tree limb. We all had dresses on and couldn't do it.

"There's where at they're ginning! Down there in the big bottom yonder!"

We sailed down that mountainside like we had wings. There was Lee watching the cane juice squeeze out into the pans and emptying out the full ones into the big long stirring-off pan over the pit. They were almost done ginning. There was already a fire blazing in the pit, and two of Lee's boys were feeding the last scattered bunches of cane stalks into the gin.

"Why howdy, chillern. Little early now. Help yourselves to some good juicy cane stalks to suck on, then you can help dig the skimming hole. You've come in fine time for that."

Lee-up-on-the-Branch pointed to a place not far from the pit where he wanted to have his skimming hole dug. We all stood around sucking our cane stalks and taking time-about, digging with the pick and shovel. Everybody was making big plans about who he would push into the skimming hole before the night was out.

"Dig her wide and dig her deep there, feller. You don't want your legs cramped none whenever you get pushed into her tonight!"

"Hunh. Nobody won't have to shove you in, knucklehead. You got such a little understanding, you'll just flounder in 'thout being shoved!"

"Me, I'd like to see Jean here fall in. Like to see that purty blue dress all dripping with them old 'lasses skimming. Wonder would Clevie love her so well then!"

"You don't hush up, Mr. Fred Hall, you going to get into that hole 'fore she gets finished. Smarty."

"Wait'll atter moonrise, we'll see who's first."

The sky darkened and the hoot owls began to holler along the black ridges. If you looked away from the fire, up through the woods to the deep, deep gray sky and the cold pale stars, and heard the owls and other night birds singing their doleful songs, why then it seemed like a mighty scary, lonesome place to be in. Then you looked back quick at the bright blazing fire and the sweet molasses bubbling soft green-yellow bubbles in the big pan, and boys and girls laughing and chasing one another, and lantern lights along the high hill road bringing more and more folks to the party. That was a beautiful sight, and the warm brightness of it folded in around you and kept you from the dark.

It was time to skim the molasses. Lee took the skimmer, a great wooden spoon with a handle four or five feet long, and passed it along the top of the bubbling mass. He dipped off as much as he could of the green jellyish skim which lay on the top, and the boys emptied it, with devilish grins on their faces, into the skimming hole. I began to chew up one end of a cane stalk and spread the chewed end out into a nice brush, to be ready to dip into the pan. That is one of the best tastes on earth. You dip your cane stalk down into the boiling pan, catch the yellow foam on the end of the stalk, wave it in the air until it's cooled down some, and suck it off. Again and again you dip it in, for once you start there's no stopping. It's far better than the finished molasses; the taste of it puts you in mind of fall winds and wood smoke and dancing in the fields and games played in the secret dark.

Lee saw me fixing my stalk and laughed a big laugh. "Here now, here's a little girl going to eat her skimmings green! You put away that stick for at least another hour or two, have to skim another time or two yet fore the skimmings get yellow. Green foam'll make you sick sure."

The young folks heard that and they started to work fixing a place to run a set. They made everybody help.

"Here, let's yank up those old stalks and stomp us down a level place. Here, you little ones, get to trompling, you got nothing else to do, stomp it until it's just like a floor."

"They hain't no music come yet, Wint. Can't run a set 'thout music. Not a solitary fiddle amongst us."

"Shucks, they'll be a fiddle or a banjer or something turn up soon. Anyway, reckon we can play 'Cedar Swamp' right now. Get you a gal and don't be bashful, and mind the skimmin' hole!"

I had been wishing in the back of my mind all evening long that Cleve wouldn't come. It would be no fun at a stir-off, I decided, if I had to stand around and talk to an old boy all evening and not get to run and wrestle with the young uns as I was used to. Besides, now we had been rolling and tumbling about, so that my pretty blue dress was wrinkled and the hem was torn with the briers. My ribbon was gone and my long hair was blown about my face, and I had to keep brushing it back with my hands. I was one of the children—and mighty glad of it—not old enough to court.

But when they commenced lining up for "Cedar Swamp," I wanted to play. I stood with the other littler ones and wished someone would ask me to play, but no one did. Someone whispered, "Where's Cleve at?" and I wanted to die. Now everybody would think he had made it up with me to come, and then disappointed me.

Above the singing voices and dancing feet I heard the clear high sound. Faraway it was, and so faint that the sound of it sometimes got lost, but there was no mistaking what it was.

At last they heard it, too.

"Hush boys, hush a while. Swear if I don't hear that old fiddle a-whinin' down the holler some'ers!"

"Whose bow is it? Chad McDaniel's?"

"Naw, nary a bit like Chad. Hush, there 'tis. More like Cleve's."

"Cleve Hamilton. That's who it is. That young un can really play. What's his tune? Listen. Hush."

"Favors 'Napoleon Crossing the Rockies.' Is it? Listen."

"Can't you fellers hear it thunder?" Dad said. Dad was known to be hard of hearing, but I guess he just had an ear for music. He said, "I can hear plain as day, that chap is playing 'Goin' to See My Truelove.'"

He began to hum and fool with the song, and some joined in:

The days are long and lonesome,
The nights are a-gettin' cold;
I'm goin' to see my truelove
'Fore I get too old.

   O get around, Jenny, get around,
   O get around I say,
   O get around, Jenny, get around,
   Long summer day.

I went up on the mountain
Give my horn a blow,
I thought I heard that pretty girl
Say: "Yonder comes my beau!"

Ast that gal to marry me,
Tell you what she said.
Picked her up a knotty pine stick
And like to broke my head.

I went up on the mountain
Give my horn a blow,
If I can't get the gal I want
Let that ole gal go.

I went up on the mountain
Get me a load of pine,
Loaded my wagon so heavy
Broke it down behind.

Met a raccoon in the road
Mad as he could be,
Quiled his tail and whupped my dog
And bristled up at me.

Well, I heard Cleve's fiddle playing that tune, I began to brighten up. I must have looked better because Jim Hall came right over then and asked me to dance with him. It made me proud to be dancing when Cleve came into the firelight. I was glad I wasn't standing with the little children, looking on.

Then Cleve played for the sets, and it seemed like that fiddle music turned the devil loose among the boys. One of them would be standing beside his girl, patting his foot and clapping and waiting his time to dance out, then the dancing couples would go by him, and next minute, splop! there he'd be up to his shins in the skimming hole, mad and sputtering. I guess they finally had shoved all the boys and one or two of the tomboy girls into that hole before Lee finally hollered out to us.

"Here young uns, run dip in your stalks. Prettiest yellow foam you ever did see. Dip in, dip in there, and eat all you can. Ollie, Abbie, hand me your buckets here. This foam'll settle to more'n half molasses, you'll see."

Aunt Mary Ann said, "Just fill my bucket halfways up, Lee. I know this ain't the last skimming. I'll finish filling it whenever you skim her for the main last time. That's the best foam."

"Why, yes, I guess you will! That last skimmin'll be most all of it pure molasses. Well, I don't reckon I mind giving a good neighbor a quart of molasses. There'll be some for sale in the wintertime, and I'll get a good price out of you for it, lady!"

I had forgot about my feller again, and was down at the foot of the big pan with Cotton and Kathleen and little Amanda, eating 'lasses foam to beat the band. Cleve came up behind me and pulled me by the ends of my long hair up and away from the others. He looked mad.

"Well, do you want to see me or not? Fine way to treat someone. Here you run off and I had to walk up this long dark holler all by myself—"

"You scared of the dark?"

"No, I'm not scared of the dark, but just the same I don't know the road much well, almost fell head fo'most off'n that high bank where the slip is, stepped in the creek up to my knees, kept hearing all kind of strange noises in the woods, seeing eyes looking at me—"

"Wonder the hants didn't get you. Wisht they had!"

"Spiteful! Then I get up here, and there you are dancing with everybody else, and me having to play the fiddle all the time, and then you won't even offer to feed me off'n your cane stalk, you set down here eating like a little pig, and now you stand there laughing at me. I ought to whup you, that's what I ought to do."

We both were laughing then, and I began to like him again. At last he whispered in my ear. "Come walk with me."

"Whereabouts?"

"Over yonder, anywhere, where they can't spy us. Never did like to stand and talk to my girl in front of everybody."

"What's wrong with talking in front of people? They won't care."

"Aw, come on. Look around. Most of the others are off walking and talking out there in the field. What're you afraid of, little baby?"

"I said I'd talk with you, but I didn't promise to walk."

"You're my girl, ain't you? If you're not now, I want you to be my girl. Then walk with me a little."

"Well, just to the edge of the dark there. Now, what do you have to say that's so blessed important?"

"I don't know. You look right pretty tonight, with your hair blowing back wild like that in the night wind—"

"I lost my hair ribbon, running with the others—"

"And your pretty blue dress that I love so well, that fits you so neat—"

"I tore it in the berry briers, playing banner with the children—"

"You look like a little girl, and yet like a woman grown, and the sight of you takes out of mind all the things I had to say to you—"

"Here we are on the edge of the dark. Take me back—"

"No, no, look on out there in the fields. It's not dark out there, it just seemed so when you were by the fire. The full moon is halfway the sky, how can it be dark?"

He had hold of my hand and we stood still. I trembled for a while, but he said not a word. Then he said listen to the wind in the ridges, and the hoot owls calling out bad news, and he said look at the stars and how pretty the moon is, and after a while I stopped trembling. Back at the fire someone hollered out.

"All right, we going to play five-ten. I'll count first and everybody hide, but not more'n a hundred feet away!"

The voice began to chant,

Five, ten, fifteen, twenty,
Twenty-five, thirty, thirty-five, forty—

"Come on, let's hide together. I know a place—" We began to run.

Forty-five, fifty, fifty-five, sixty,
Sixty-five, seventy, seventy-five, eighty—

"Cleve! Stop it, stop, we're way over a hundred feet—"
"Right here. Old fodder stack, nobody'll look for us here!"

Eighty-five, ninety, ninety-five, hundred.

Bushel of wheat, bushel of rye,
All ain't hid, holler "I."

Bushel wheat, bushel cotton,
All ain't hid, better be a-trottin'!

Bushel wheat, bushel clover,
All ain't hid, can't hide over!

We ran stumbling and panting hard to the fodder stack and fell down behind it. We were both laughing so hard we were afraid the counter would hear us, and I couldn't stop laughing at all, so that Cleve clapped his hand over my mouth to keep me quiet.

I had never before been so close to any boy. I sat leaning my back against him, very quiet, and it seemed like I had a hundred hearts all inside of me trying to get out. I didn't have the power to move, to do any more than breathe, but I wasn't resting easy. I kept trying to act to myself like it was Kathleen or Cotton or some of the others there behind me. If it was one of them I wouldn't be shaking and shivering this way, it would just be fun, hiding there in the dark. But I couldn't forget it was Cleve. The hand holding my mouth was the shape and the smell of Cleve's hand, the breath that moved the body behind me was his breath.

Out there in the moonlighted field the counter roamed about in the shadowy places. He'd see someone, and then they'd break in a race for the counting tree. Sometimes the words that rolled over the field would be, "One-two-three for Pauline!" and again they would be, "In free! In free! One-two-three-for me!" Their voices and laughing and the sound of their running came clear to us and seemed very near, but the counter never came over as far as our fodder stack.

I heard the sounds of the game as though they were dream sounds. Everything I could see and hear around me seemed so queer; it was like the whole world was changing away from me, everything was different, nothing was real. This morning I had dreamed of being near to Cleve, now here it was and I didn't like it. It was the feeling inside of me that came along with being alone with him that I didn't like. I didn't know what to do with it. I had never had this kind of feeling before. There was almost something nice about it, but I was afraid and miserable and wanted to cry. I kept having to swallow for no reason, and the sound of my swallowing was louder than the beating of my heart. I knew Cleve could hear, and I was shamed to death. He'd think I was a fool and a baby.

His hand moved away from my mouth, over my face and forehead, and smoothed on my hair. He put his other arm around my waist. I sat there stiff as a board, wanting to holler out and yet wanting to let him hold me; wanting to run away and wanting to stay. I remember that most of my mind was to run, but some stubborn thing or other made me want to stay even against my liking. It was something inside of me that had to know what this strange feeling was, had to find out things everlastingly. So when he turned my face to him, I sat still and waited. He leaned over quick and kissed me on the mouth. I just looked at him right straight for awhile, kind of foolish. I thought I was going to cry sure, I was so disappointed. Everybody'd talked and carried on about kissing and hugging, why there wasn't a thing in the world to it anyway.

"You like that there kiss, honey?" Cleve looked anxious.

"Well, I don't know hardly. You better kiss me again."

He did it different this time, slower and softer. He wouldn't stop. I jumped up and lit out across the fields before he could come to himself. I wiped my mouth hard with my hand. I couldn't wait to get to some water and wash my mouth out good. Cleve was running after me now; I could hear him brushing against the crackly cane stalks, stumbling over the dried clods, cussing mad. I was mad, too. Why had folks led me to believe that love was so wonderful, that a kiss was such a pleasure? I was glad, too, as I ran. Let the boys chase me, or not, I wouldn't care either way. I could be scornful of them all now that I was free of their spell. I laughed out loud at the moon, and all at once I was almost up to the fire and the young uns were motioning me to be careful or the counter would see me.

"Lay low, lay low!" they chanted out. I glanced behind me and saw that Cleve had stopped in the field and was rolling him a cigarette like he never had a thought of running after me. I dropped to the earth and watched the counter look about for me. It was Sallie, and at last she strayed away from the counting tree, and I saw I could make it.

"Come in, come in!" I heard them call. I rose and made for the tree and beat Sallie to it and got in free. She looked around a while longer, then she gave up finding the rest of the hiders. She cupped her hands and hollered.

"Bee, bee, bumble bee, all's outs in free!"

"Why, who else is out? Nobody but Cleve. Now where could he be?"

"Aw, he's not even playing," I said.

Some of the older folks had begun to stir around to go home; they gathered their buckets and their little children and lit their lanterns. They said, "Go home with us, why don't you?" and "Can't tonight, I reckon. You'ns come," to each other, and pretty soon their lights were fading this way and that way through the hills. The fire in the pit was low, almost ashes. Some of the boys were staying around to put it out, and to wash up the stir-off vessels. Over to one side the good-smelling molasses was cooling in a row of big shiny milk buckets. It would taste mighty fine along in the wintertime when all the green plenty of the garden stuff was gone. Dad would take his whole meal on it, just about. He would take a big spoonful of molasses and let it run thick and slow over fresh-churned butter in a dish, then he'd take his fork and mix and stir, make Gravy Horse to eat on his cornbread. Hot cornbread, or biscuits, either one it would go with fine.

The young folks were leaving now. They lingered about the fire long enough for their families to get a head start, and then the sweethearts began to pair off down the holler and through the woods. I got with Kathleen and Cotton and Amanda and wouldn't let them game along too much, for I didn't want to see Cleve. I might have to let him take me home. We hurried along in the dark and we'd catch up with one light after another and pass the sweethearts by. Pauline and Bingham, Helen and Chad, Ernestine and Buford, Sallie and Jerry.

I got to wondering whereabouts Cleve was. My mouth still burnt me, and I knew that if I got in the light too much everybody could see where Cleve had kissed me. I was as sure as I ever was of anything that my mouth didn't look the same. Every time we passed one of the lanterns I'd keep away to the side of the light and turn my head to the dark. What would I do tomorrow when I had to face the light of day, what would I do and say? How on earth could I hide it? That worried me more the farther down the branch we got and I walked quiet. The others were getting sleepy-eyed, and they began to sniffle and fuss and whine for their mommies. What babies! Couldn't even stay awake on their own feet and it not midnight. At last I couldn't stand their trifling little ways any longer. I decided to walk faster and catch up with Mom, then I decided to walk slower and watch for Cleve. Not that I wanted to walk with him, but I was peevish because he didn't seem to be trying to find me.

The fiddle sung out then, far back up in the dark holler, not a dancy tune now. A slow-like tune, a lonesome love tune. Sometimes it sailed clear up to the night sky, and sometimes it sunk down and got lost in the branch waters. All at once I had a frightening thought that the music was a living thing, lost and crying, the fiddle bow making little slides and quavers and trembles all around the tune, like teardrops. Every note of it seemed to light in my breast; I was that song.

The sound came nearer and nearer, and my steps fell slower and slower, keeping time, and as Cleve came up to my side, the words came and sang themselves inside of me.

Awake, awake, you drowsy sleeper,
    How can you lay and slumber so
When your truelove is a-going to leave you
    Never to return any more?

How can you slumber on your pillow
    When your truelove must stand and wait,
And must I go and wear the willow
    In sorrow mourning for your sake?

O Molly dear, go ask your Mother
    If you my bride, my bride can be,
And then return and quickly tell me
    And I no more shall trouble thee.

O no, I cannot ask my Mother
    Such stories of love she will not hear;
Go on your way and court some other,
    I must not trouble Mother dear.

O Molly dear, go ask your Father
    If you my bride, my bride can be,
And then return and quickly tell me
    And I no more shall trouble thee.

Oh no, I cannot ask my Father
    He's a-lying on his bed of rest,
And in his hands is a silver dagger
    To pierce the one that I love best.

I wish I was in some lonely valley
  Where no one could ever hear,
My food would be the grief and sorrow
  My drink would be the briny tear.

Down in yon valley there grows a green arrow,
  I wish that arrow was shot through my breast,
It would end my grief, it would end my sorrow
  And set my troubled mind at rest.

FOOD and LOVE

Back to the Bayou

RICK BRAGG

I loved a Cajun woman once. It was her eyes, I believe. When I was a little boy, just because it is the kind of thing boys do, I would look at the hot sun through a green, sweating bottle of 7Up. The sunlight seemed to freeze in the middle of the bottle, and glow.

She had eyes like that.

I was afraid that coming back here, to her Louisiana, would make me think of Her. And sure enough, every mile, every road sign, tapped me deeper into that green bottle.

The Bayou Teche, seeming more mud than water, did not flow or even crawl, but just lay. Morgan City still existed on a bubble of oil, its conjugal beds left half-empty by men who worked rigs out in the deep blue. Along the Atchafalaya River, blue herons, their beaks like stilettos, stabbed into the dark water and came back out with wriggling silver. Alligators and rumors of alligators haunted Lake Henderson, where gray trees raised stumps of arms into the haze.

All of it gritty, lovely, like Her.

My heart hurt, a little.

And my stomach growled.

The air on the side streets and outside the wood-framed restaurants smelled of crab boil and crawfish and hot lemons. In the roadside stores, big countertop Crock-Pots simmered with boudin, the sausage made from pork, liver, onions, rice, and spices. Iron pots in open-air cook shacks rendered tiny cubes of fatback into golden cracklins, and old men and little children stood in gravel parking lots and ate them like M&Ms. In the evenings, in dives and fine-dining establishments, chefs took the ingredients of their liquid country—the rice, crawfish, shrimp, oysters, okra, duck, trout, crab, catfish, turtle, and drum—and turned them into dishes that tasted better than the mere ingredients should have allowed.

With every bite I felt a little better, as if there were a tonic in the turtle soup— as if, since I had been hexed in the swamp, it was the swamp itself and its people that had to heal me.

They did their best. Descendants of French Canadian exiles who drifted south to these swamps and prairies in southern Louisiana more than two centuries ago, they have long been accused of fusing magic with their food. I ate it in oil towns and shrimp shacks and interstate gas stations, in themed restaurants with stuffed alligators swinging from the ceilings, and in late-night bars where there was more swinging than I care to remember.

I ate to forget.

The smell swirled from underneath the roof of the cooking shed and permeated the air over the parking lot, the smell of a million skillets of bacon all sizzling at once. But it was a witch's cauldron of fatback, roiling, the cracklins bopping up, the size of postage stamps, all crunchy skin on one side and thin layers of crisp-fried fat on the other.

Some people argue that Eddie Goulas makes the best cracklins in Acadiana in his cook shed in Ruth, not far from Breaux Bridge. "I never did like cracklins," Goulas said as he and a few helpers trimmed the lean from big slabs of fatback, diced it, and fed it into the pots.

"I guess I thought if I can make them where I would eat them, they must be pretty good," he said. His face intent, he watched the trimming process, kept an eye on the heat. "It's not hard to do something," he said, "when you ain't guessing."

In the parking lot I ate cracklins from a paper sack. I listened to people speak to each other in French and smiled like an imbecile.

"The food, the music, it's the joy of life," explained sixty-eight-year-old Claude Simon Jr., as he handed me his business card: "Custom Woodwork, Antique Repair, Cowhide Furniture." At the bottom of the card, he has written in a single word: *Traiteur*.

Like his papa before him, he is a treater, healer, someone the Cajuns—the ones who still believe—would ask to heal bellyaches, arthritis, or general malaise with herbs, roots, and prayers. His papa was a grand *traiteur*. Even when he was very old and in a nursing home, people came to be treated.

Sometimes evil spirits invade us, Simon explained, and make us forget to enjoy life. I nodded, my mouth full of cracklins.

Before he left, Simon mentioned that he also does exorcisms.

"I don't charge. It's the Lord's work," he said. "I do accept donations."

I was healed a good bit more in Carencro, about a block from city hall. Here, in a place called Paul's Pirogue, a spirit helped stir the pot.

It was a poor man's dish called catfish court bouillon, just a few catfish pieces smothered in stewed tomatoes, onions, and other good things. Paul's served it with some of the best potato salad, with Cajun spices in the mayonnaise.

I asked the man at the cash register: "Who cooked the catfish?" He told me he had, mostly, but his grandma, who has gone on, might as well have.

"It comes from her—I learned from her," said forty-three-year-old Terry Soignier, who manages Paul's Pirogue. "She lost her first husband in the yellow fever, I believe, of '46. Her name was Lena. My oldest brother had epilepsy, and she would sing to him in French. When she cooked, he was always on her hip."

He spoke about them both, the food and his grandmamma, with such love that I expected to see her standing there. "A black cast-iron pot," he said, thinking back. "Fresh onions. Catfish, pulled from the bayou.

"Not a bad memory at all," he said.

I ordered a shrimp po'boy because I had seen one go by, and I lusted after it. It was deep-fryer hot, the shrimp spiced and peppery and served on the best French bread that I have ever tasted. It did not crumble into dust like delicate, airy French bread, but was chewy, buttery, comforting.

I am sure someone's long-dead grandpapa kneaded that bread.

I walked out feeling loved.

I met the hands that had kneaded the bread, and I was half-right. Phillip "T-Sue" Roberts owns the bakery in Henderson that furnishes Paul's Pirogue—and much of the Atchafalaya Basin—with bread. The recipes go back to his grandparents, Pete and Della Patin, who ran a family bakery in Cecilia from 1934 until 1975. It is not designed to be French bread at all, but just good bread.

Roberts's grandparents gave him his skill, and even his name.

"What does T-Sue mean, anyway?" I asked.

"Little Drunk," he said.

"Oh," I said.

It involved a bottle of Crown Royal. "I was thirteen," he said, "and it was the first time they let me out of the house. It was an adventure."

I told him I reckoned so.

"I danced all night at the American Legion," he said, "whether the music was playing or not."

Someone told on him. His grandfather started calling him, in French, *tee soux*, or "little drunk."

That became T-Sue, and that is what he named his bakery.

I ate a piece of bread stuffed with boudin from Charlie-T's Specialty Meats in Breaux Bridge. I can't write well enough to tell you how good it was.

The waitress was pushing the alligator at Prejean's, the big Cajun restaurant in Lafayette, but I don't like to eat things that are said to taste like chicken when what they really taste like is snake and lizard. Instead, I ate delicious corn and crab bisque, and asked about dessert.

How about *gateau sirop*, the syrup cake?

"I don't like it," she said.

It was dense and dark and tasted of molasses.

"Did you like it?" the waitress asked.

"Yes," I said.

"A lot of the older people do," she said.

The bakery chef's name is Roe Zenon, a smiling but no-nonsense woman who eyed a single fly in her bakeshop like it was a flying gopher. She told me she learned from her mom, Bulia Zenon, who called it spice cake.

Her mom would call to her from the porch, "and the kids in the neighborhood would smell that cooking and all come with me. 'Your momma cooking?' they'd ask me. She always was. Momma would say, 'We always got something burning.'"

The children ate their spice cake with Kool-Aid.

I ate mine with gratitude.

Before I left, the folks at Prejean's made me try the alligator. "We just use the tail meat, not the lung meat, and never from a gator over six feet," said Dean Dugas, the general manager. I didn't know what that meant, but it was good.

Dickie Breaux and Cynthia Breaux, once married but still partners in Café Des Amis, the restaurant they founded more than a decade ago, are still bound. Their love of the Breaux Bridge restaurant, and its food, survived their breakup.

"I believe you and I were brought together to create this thing," Cynthia said to Dickie one night at dinner.

If that is true, then maybe I was left standing in a driveway in Miami, watching taillights fade, just so I could be healed by barbecued shrimp and a slab of white chocolate bread pudding. All I know is, it is hard to be heartsick when you are eating crawfish étouffée served on hot cornbread.

"You have to be raised in the atmosphere of the food," said Dickie Breaux. "We just cook better than anybody else. A Cajun knows he's got it right when, after it's done, you can throw away the meat and just eat the gravy."

The gravy, then. The gravy is the antidote.

That night, I ate the best turtle soup I have ever had. I listened to people who love food talk about how it can hold something fine together that might otherwise have come apart. I knew I couldn't face my bed-and-breakfast on the Teche.

I knew I wouldn't sleep.

So I asked the question millions of men like me have asked.

"Know a good beer joint?"

The dance floor at Pat's Atchafalaya Club was packed with a hundred, more. Geno Delafose wore his squeeze box low, like a gunslinger, singing in French and English as white people and black people and old people and young people danced like it was their last night on this earth. Crawfish corpses littered the tables. The band never took a break. The dancing never stopped. A big woman in a pantsuit looked at me a little too long, and I got scared.

The next morning, a Saturday, Café Des Amis opened for breakfast, but a breakfast like I had never seen. A zydeco band tore up the small stage at the front of the restaurant, and people danced between tables loaded with bacon and eggs.

A lot of the people dancing were the same ones I had seen the night before. One of them, Ted Couvillion, said hello.

"My wife died of cancer two years ago," he said. He vanished into his grief, until his friends dragged him out dancing. Now, every week, he dances and dances his way out of heartache.

I can't dance a lick. But I have two bags of cracklins in the trunk of my car.

Bill

· ·

BRAD WATSON

Wilhelmina, eighty-seven, lived alone in the same town as her two children, but she rarely saw them. Her main companion was a trembling poodle she'd had for about fifteen years, named Bill. You never hear of dogs named Bill. Her husband in his decline had bought him, named him after a boy he'd known in the Great War, and then wouldn't have anything to do with him. He'd always been Wilhelmina's dog. She could talk to Bill in a way that she couldn't talk to anyone else, not even her own children.

Not even her husband, now nearly a vegetable out at King's Daughters' Rest Home on the old highway.

She rose in the blue candlelight morning to go see him about the dog, who was doing poorly. She was afraid of being completely alone.

There were her children and their children, and even some great-grandchildren, but that was neither here nor there for Wilhelmina. They were all in different worlds.

She drove her immaculate ocean-blue Delta 88 out to the home and turned up the long, barren drive. The tall, naked trunks of a few old pines lined the way, their sparse tops distant as clouds. Wilhelmina pulled into the parking lot and took two spaces so she'd have plenty of room to back out when she left. She paused for a moment to check herself in the rearview mirror and adjusted the broad-brimmed hat she wore to hide the thinning spot on top of her head.

Her husband, Howard, lay propped up and twisted in his old velour robe, his mouth open, watching TV. His thick white hair stood in a matted knot on his head like a child's.

"What?" he said when she walked in. "What did you say?"

"I said, 'Hello!'" Wilhelmina replied, though she'd said nothing.

She sat down.

"I came to tell you about Bill, Howard. He's almost completely blind now, and he can't go to the bathroom properly. The veterinarian says he's in pain and he's not going to get better and I should put him to sleep."

Her husband had tears in his eyes.

"Poor old Bill," he said.

"I know," Wilhelmina said, welling up herself now. "I'll miss him so."

"I loved him at Bellau Wood! He was all bloody and walking around," Howard said. "They shot off his nose in the Meuse-Argonne." He picked up the remote box and held the button down, the channels thumping past like the muted thud of an ancient machine gun.

Wilhelmina dried her tears with a Kleenex from her handbag and looked up at him.

"Oh, fiddle," she said.

"Breakfast time," said an attendant, a slim copper-colored man whose blue smock was tailored at the waist and flared over his hips like a suit jacket. He set down the tray and held his long delicate hands before him as if for inspection.

He turned to Wilhelmina.

"Would you like to feed your husband, ma'am?"

"Heavens, no," Wilhelmina said. She shrank back as if he intended to touch her with those hands.

When the attendant held a spoonful of oatmeal up to her husband's mouth he lunged for it, his old gray tongue out, and slurped it down.

"Oh, he's ravenous today," said the attendant. Wilhelmina, horrified, felt for a moment as if she were losing her mind and had wandered into this stranger's room by mistake. She clutched her purse and slipped out into the hall.

"I'm going," she called faintly, and hurried out to her car, which sat on the cracked surface of the parking lot like an old beached yacht. The engine groaned, turned over, and she steered down the long drive and onto the highway without even a glance at the traffic. A car passed her on the right, up in the grass, horn blaring, and an enormous dump truck cleaved the air to her left like a thunderclap. She would pay them no mind.

When she got home the red light on her answering machine, a gift from her son, was blinking. It was him on the tape.

"I got your message about Bill, Mama. I'll take him to the vet in the morning, if you want. Just give me a call. Bye-bye, now."

"No, I can't think about it," Wilhelmina said.

Bill was on his cedar-filled pillow in the den. He looked around for her, his nose up in the air.

"Over here, Bill," Wilhelmina said loudly for the dog's deaf ears. She carried him a Milk-Bone biscuit, for his teeth were surprisingly good. He sniffed the biscuit, then took it carefully between his teeth, bit off a piece, and chewed.

"Good boy, good Bill."

Bill didn't finish the biscuit. He laid his head down on the cedar pillow and breathed heavily. In a minute he got up and made his halting, wobbling way toward his water bowl in the kitchen, but he hit his head on the doorjamb and fell over.

"Oh, Bill, I can't stand it," Wilhelmina said, rushing to him. She stroked his head until he calmed down, and then she dragged him gently to his bowl, where he lapped and lapped until she had to refill it, he drank so much. He kept drinking.

"Kidneys," Wilhelmina said, picking up the bowl. "That's enough, boy."

Bill nosed around for the water bowl, confused. He tried to squat, legs trembling, and began to whine. Wilhelmina carried him out to the backyard, set him down, and massaged his kidneys the way the vet had shown her, and finally a little trickle ran down Bill's left hind leg. He tried to lift it.

"Good old Bill," she said. "You try, don't you?"

She carried him back in and dried his leg with some paper towels.

"I guess I'd do anything for you, Bill," she said. But she had made up her mind. She picked up the phone and called her son. It rang four times, and then his wife's voice answered.

"You've reached two-eight-one," she began.

"I know that," Wilhelmina muttered.

" . . . We can't come to the phone right now. . . ."

Wilhelmina thought that sort of message was rude. If they were there, they could come to the phone.

" . . . leave your message after the beep."

"I guess you better come and get Bill in the morning," Wilhelmina said, and hung up.

Wilhelmina's husband had been a butcher, and Katrina, the young widow who'd succeeded him at the market, still brought meat by the house every Saturday afternoon—steaks, roasts, young chickens, stew beef, soup bones, whole hams, bacon, pork chops, ground chuck. Once she even brought a leg of lamb. Wilhelmina couldn't possibly eat it all, so she stored most of it in her deep freeze.

She went out to the porch and gathered as much from the deep freeze as she could carry, dumped it into the kitchen sink like a load of kindling, then pulled her cookbooks from the cupboard and sat down at the kitchen table. She began looking up recipes that had always seemed too complex for her, dishes that sounded vaguely exotic, chose six of the most interesting she could find, and copied them onto a legal pad. Then she made a quick trip to the grocery store to find the items she didn't have on hand, buying odd spices like saffron and coriander, and not just produce but shallots and bright red bell peppers, and a bulb of garlic cloves as big as her fist. Bill had always liked garlic.

Back home, she spread all the meat out on the counter, the chops and steaks and ham, the roast and the bacon, some Italian sausage she'd found, some boudin that had been there for ages, and even a big piece of fish fillet. She chopped the sweet peppers, the shallots, ground the spices. The more she worked, the less she thought of the recipes, until she'd become a marvel of culinary innovativeness, combining oils and spices and herbs and meats into the most savory dishes you could imagine: Master William's Sirloin Surprise, Ham au Bill, Bill's Leg of Lamb with Bacon Chestnuts, Bill's Broiled Red Snapper with Butter and Crab, Bloody Boudin à la Bill, and one she decided to call Sausage Chops. She fired up her oven, lit every eye on her stove, and cooked it all just as if she were serving the king of France instead of her old French poodle. Then she arranged the dishes on her best china, cut the meat into bite-sized pieces, and served them to her closest friend, her dog.

She began serving early in the evening, letting Bill eat just as much or as little as he wanted from each dish. "This ought to wake up your senses, Bill." Indeed, Bill's interest was piqued. He ate, rested, ate a little more, of this dish and that. He went back to the leg of lamb, nibbling the bacon chestnuts off its sides. Wilhelmina kept gently urging him to eat. And as the evening wore on, Bill's old cataracted eyes gradually seemed to reflect something, it seemed, like quiet suffering—not his usual burden, but the luxurious suffering of the glutton. He had found a strength beyond himself, and so he kept bravely on, forcing himself to eat, until he could not swallow another bite and lay carefully beside the remains of his feast, and slept.

Wilhelmina sat quietly in a kitchen chair and watched from her window as the sun edged up behind the trees, red and molten like the swollen, dying star of an ancient world. She was so tired that her body felt weightless, as if she'd already left it hollow of her spirit. It seemed that she had lived such a long time. Howard had courted her in a horse-drawn wagon. An entire world of souls had disappeared in their time, and other nameless souls filled their spaces. Some of them had taken Howard's soul.

Bill had rolled onto his side in sleep, his tongue slack on the floor, his poor stomach as round and taut as a honeydew melon. After such a gorging, there normally would be hell to pay. But Wilhelmina would not allow that to happen.

"I'll take you to the doctor myself, old Bill," she said.

As if in response, a faint and easy dream-howl escaped Bill's throat, someone calling another in the big woods, across empty fields and deep silent stands of trees. *Oooooooo*, it went, high and soft, *Oooooooo*.

Wilhelmina's heart thickened with emotion. Her voice was deep and rich with it.

Hoooooo, she called softly to Bill's sleeping ears.

Oooooooo, Bill called again, a little stronger, and she responded, *Hoooooo*, their pure wordless language like echoes in the morning air.

Falling for My Husband

BLAIR HOBBS

Beanstalk skinny, I cared more about not eating.
Most flavors left me cold,
but peas, cooked to an institutional drab,
downright offended my fallow tongue.
In heaps, peas showed up on school cafeteria trays
and in my great-aunt's "Crowder Pleaser Salad," a water-logged
mayonnaise and relish mishap she concocted
for her nursing home's special occasions.

Alone, uncooked,
a pea was a stone
or the period at the end of a boring sentence.

My thin smile appealed to a man whose tongue was a meadow.
For courtship, I wore size zero silk dresses, high heels
and peony-pink lipstick. He took me
dancing and we twirled and shook.
We laughed and baptized ourselves with spilled Zinfandel.

He dined me and tried seducing my love-dumb senses
into surrendering to field pea risotto with white truffles,
Texas caviar, and blackberry-glazed quail
on a bed of pink-eyed pea salad.
Although I dismissed his razzle-dazzled legumes with a "yuck,"
he kissed me anyway. Little did I know
that those night-time words he whispered into the hull of my ear—
Whippoorwill, glory, snow, butterfly,
Sweet, and (later) *zipper*—were all names of peas!

One noon, full of buttery sunlight,
this man offered me lunch, sage leaves and lady peas.
Perhaps brainwashed, I took the warm bowl.
Before I knew it, my mouth eased open
above the question mark of steam. I chewed and felt
the tender pearls dissolve across my peppered tongue.
First lips and throat,
then the whole rest of my body sighed awake.

CONTRIBUTORS

Colleen Anderson is a writer, graphic designer, and singer/songwriter who lives in Charleston, West Virginia.

Harriette Simpson Arnow (1908–86) was a writer from Kentucky whose works address the rich culture of the Appalachian area. Her books include *The Dollmaker*, *Hunter's Horn*, and *The Weedkiller's Daughter*.

Marilou Awiakta is a Cherokee/Appalachian poet, storyteller, and essayist. Her third book is *Selu: Seeking the Corn Mother's Wisdom*. She has been profiled in the *Oxford Companion to Women's Writing in the United States*. Originally from Oak Ridge, Tennessee, she now resides in Memphis.

Deb Barshafsky explores the mysteries and delights of Southern foodways from her home base—a 100-year-old bungalow in Augusta, Georgia.

Burkhard Bilger is a staff writer for the *New Yorker*. His book *Noodling for Flatheads: Moonshine, Monster Catfish, and Other Southern Comforts* was a finalist for the PEN/Faulkner Award for First Nonfiction.

Roberta Bondi, from Birmingham, Alabama, was educated in Semitic languages and theology at Oxford University. She now teaches at the Candler School of Theology at Emory University in Atlanta.

Rick Bragg's books include *All Over but the Shoutin'* and *Ava's Man*. In 1996, Bragg won a Pulitzer Prize for feature writing.

Frank Browning ferments hard cider in Kentucky and crafts sweet radio stories in Paris, France. He is the author of *Apples: Story of the Fruit of Temptation* and *The Culture of Desire*.

Marcia Camp's poetry and prose have been published, both regionally and nationally, for thirty years. She now resides in Little Rock, Arkansas.

Sheri L. Castle is a culinary instructor and writer who grew up in the Blue Ridge Mountains and wound up in Chapel Hill, North Carolina. She lives there now with her husband, Doug Tidwell, and daughter, Lily Castle Tidwell.

David Cecelski is a historian and writer in Durham, North Carolina. His most recent book is *The Waterman's Song: Slavery and Freedom in Maritime, North Carolina*.

Billy C. Clark is a native of Catlettsburg, Kentucky. His thirteen award-winning novels include *Riverboy*, *The Mooneyed Hound*, *The Trail of the Hunter's Horn*, and *A Long Row to Hoe*. In addition to publishing numerous poems and short stories, Clark served as founding editor of *Kentucky Writing* and *Virginia Writing*.

Guy Davenport (1927–2005), a writer and painter, was a serious observer of food and customs.

Joel Davis is a mystery to the editors of this volume. He is reported to be a journalist in East Tennessee.

Tony Earley's short stories earned him a place on *Granta*'s list of the Twenty Best Young American Fiction Writers in 1996 and a National Magazine Award for fiction. He is an assistant professor in the Department of English at Vanderbilt University in Nashville, Tennessee.

John T. Edge is a writer and director of the Southern Foodways Alliance at the University of Mississippi. His latest books are *Hamburgers and Fries: An American Story* and *Donuts: An American Story*.

Kelly Norman Ellis is assistant professor of English and associate director of the M.F.A. program in creative writing at Chicago State University. She is a poet whose work has appeared in the anthologies *Sisterfire*, *Spirit and Flame*, *Eclipsing a Nappy New Millennium*, *Boom Girls*, *Role Call*, and *New Sister Voices*. She is a founding member of Affrilachian Poets.

Elizabeth Engelhardt is an assistant professor of American studies and women and gender studies at the University of Texas at Austin. She is the author of *The Tangled Roots of Feminism, Environmentalism, and Appalachian Literature* and the editor of *Beyond Hill and Hollow: Original Readings in Appalachian Women's Studies*.

Diane Gilliam Fisher is the author of *One of Everything* and *Kettle Bottom*. She currently resides in Ohio.

Sarah Fritschner has been food editor of the *Louisville Courier Journal* for twenty-one years and is the author of *Derby 101*.

Jane Gentry lives in Versailles, Kentucky. Her new collection of poems, *Portrait of the Artist as a White Pig*, is forthcoming from Louisiana State University Press.

Nikki Giovanni, three-time National Association for the Advancement of Colored People Image Award winner and Grammy nominee, has enjoyed the first three decades of her career in poetry. She will publish three children's books in 2005.

James B. Goode is a filmmaker, poet, essayist, short fiction writer, and professor of English at Lexington Community College. He has published six books, and his work has appeared in the *Kentucky Encyclopedia*, *Encyclopedia of Southern Culture*, *Encyclopedia of Appalachia*, and *Encyclopedia of the Midwest* and in anthologies such as Robert Higgs and Ambrose Manning's *Appalachia: Inside Out*.

Blair Hobbs teaches applied writing at the University of Mississippi and is a visual artist, the mother of Jess Edge, and the wife of John T. Edge. Her poem "Falling for My Husband" originally appeared in the spring 2005 edition of the *Oxford American*.

Mary Hufford teaches in the graduate program in folklore and folklife at the University of Pennsylvania, where she also directs the Center for Folklore and Ethnography.

Matt Lee and Ted Lee write about food for the *New York Times* and are contributing editors at *Travel and Leisure* magazine.

George Ella Lyon, originally from the mountains of Kentucky, has published poetry, picture books, and novels for children and adults.

Michael McFee's seventh collection of poetry, *Shinemaster*, which includes the poem "Plenty," is forthcoming from Carnegie Mellon University Press.

Jim Wayne Miller (1936–96) was a professor of German language and literature at Western Kentucky University. He was the author of seven collections of poems, two novels, numerous essays, and one play.

Robert Morgan was born and raised in the Blue Ridge Mountains of North Carolina. He earned an M.F.A. from the University of North Carolina at Greensboro in 1968, and since 1971 he has been a faculty member at Cornell University's Department of English.

Naomi Shihab Nye is a writer living in Texas. She has three forthcoming books: *A Maze Me*, *Going Going*, and *You and Yours*.

Tim O'Brien is a singer-songwriter who lives in Nashville, Tennessee. He likes to cook when he's home.

Janisse Ray, writer, naturalist, and activist, is the author of three books of literary nonfiction. She lives with her husband and son in Vermont.

Robert S. Richmond is a pathologist in North Carolina and a shape-note singer in East Tennessee.

Jean Ritchie is a traditional musician, author, and composer. Born in Viper, Kentucky, she now resides in New York with her husband.

Fred Sauceman is executive assistant to the president for public affairs at East Tennessee State University in Johnson City, Tennessee. He is also a board member for the Southern Foodways Alliance.

Sally Schneider is the author of the award-winning *A New Way to Cook*. Her commentaries appear on National Public Radio and in many national publications.

Rebecca Skloot is a freelance writer. Her book *The Immortal Life of Henrietta Lacks* is forthcoming from Crown.

William Jay Smith is the author of more than fifty books of poetry, children's verse, literary criticism, and memoirs and the editor of several anthologies. He served as consultant in poetry to the Library of Congress (a post now called poet laureate), and two of his collections of poetry were finalists for the National Book Award.

Frank X Walker is the author of three books of poetry and is a multidisciplinary teaching artist from Affrilachia. He currently teaches at Eastern Kentucky University.

Brad Watson is the author of *Last Days of the Dog Men* and *The Heaven of Mercury*. He lives in Wyoming and Alabama.

Pete Wells is an articles editor at *Details* magazine. His freelance pieces on eating and drinking frequently appear in *Food & Wine*.

Steve Yarbrough is the author of six books, including *Prisoners of War*, *Visible Spirits*, and *The Oxygen Man*.

Jake Adam York grew up outside Gadsden, Alabama. He is the author of *Murder Ballads*.

ACKNOWLEDGMENTS

Neither this volume of *Cornbread Nation* nor the two that preceded it would be much more than a bunch of remembered good stories gathering moss in the editors' recollections were it not for the hard work and keen attention of Mary Beth Lasseter. For her salary, we owe thanks to the Center for the Study of Southern Culture at the University of Mississippi; for her unfailing sense of humor and grace under pressure, we thank her Mama, Daddy, and fine Southern upbringing.

Fred Sauceman of East Tennessee State University is the unseen hand and heart behind much that is best about this volume on his beloved home place. He was aided and abetted by Rebecca Tolley-Stokes, reference and cataloging librarian at ETSU. To both, I offer my genuine gratitude.

For demonstrating by example what it is to live with meaning and how to be both friend and mentor, I thank John Egerton and his gentle wife, Ann. For shelter from the storm, I am grateful to Mary Hartwell and Beckett Howorth, Jill Buchanan, Deborah Morgenthal, and Greg and Joni Conrad Neutra.

Thanks to my sisters-in-arms, Elizabeth Sims and Marcie Ferris, for their skill in talking desperate unnamed persons off the ledge, and to the brethren, John T. Edge, Lolis Eric Elie, and David Perry, for getting me out there in the first place.

All of us who get to speak our piece here, or at the annual symposium or field trip, owe deepest thanks to the ever loyal, curious, thoughtful, energetic, and loving members of the Southern Foodways Alliance. I just happen to owe them my life as well. To everyone who clapped for Tinkerbell, my deepest gratitude, most particularly to Jamie Estes and Sarah Fritschner.

I have been blessed on occasion to be allowed to speak for the mountain people who shaped my life. This book, more than any other, is for Pap, who laid the foundation, and for Meghan and Todd, who beautifully build on it for the future.

The Southern Foodways Alliance is grateful to the contributors whose works appear herein. Many contributors waived their reprint fees, and we are doubly thankful for that. We have made every effort to trace and contact copyright holders. If an error or omission is brought to our attention, we will make corrections in future editions.

If you wish to submit an essay for inclusion in *Cornbread Nation 4*, please write to John T. Edge in care of the Southern Foodways Alliance, Center for the Study of Southern Culture, P.O. Box 1848, University, MS 38677, or send an e-mail message to sfamail@olemiss.edu.

The following is a list of permissions to reprint the essays that appear in this book.

"Cornbread Nation Anthem" by Tim O'Brien. Created for the Southern Foodways Alliance by Tim O'Brien. The song is forthcoming on the album *Cornbread Nation* (Sugar Hill Records, 2005) by Tim O'Brien. The lyrics are published here for the first time by permission of the author.

"I Offer You a Gift" and "Compass for Our Journey" by Marilou Awiakta. Originally published in *Selu: Seeking the Corn-Mother's Wisdom* (Golden, Colo.: Fulcrum Publishing, 1993). Reprinted by permission of the author.

"Cornbread Communion" by Sheri L. Castle. Printed by permission of the author.

"Two Grandmothers" by Tony Earley. Portions of this essay were originally published in the *Oxford American* 19 and the *New Yorker*, September 6, 2004. © 2004 by Tony Earley. Reprinted by permission of Regal Literary as agent for Tony Earley.

"A Man and His Beans" by Sarah Fritschner. Originally published in the *Louisville Courier-Journal*, July 3, 2003. Reprinted by permission of the author.

"Leatherbritches" by Billy C. Clark. Originally published in *Savory Memories* (Lexington: University Press of Kentucky, 1998). Reprinted by permission of the author.

"Beating the Biscuits in Appalachia: Race, Class, and Gender Politics of Women Baking Bread" by Elizabeth Engelhardt. A version of this essay was originally published in *Cooking Lessons: The Politics of Gender and Food*, edited by Sherrie A. Inness (Lanham, Md.: Rowman & Littlefield, 2001). Olive Dame Campbell's travel journal is located at the Southern Historical Collection, Wilson Library, The University of North Carolina at Chapel Hill; permission to quote the journal is gratefully acknowledged. The author wishes to thank her godmother Imogene Eaker, her friend Bonnie Hayes, her mother Betty W. Delwiche, and her grandmother Iva S. Whitmire for their gracious storytelling and research help.

"A Theory of Pole Beans" by Nikki Giovanni. Originally published in *Love Poems* (New York: Morrow, 1997). Reprinted by permission of the author.

"Where I'm From" by George Ella Lyon. Originally published in *Iron Mountain Review* 10 (Summer 1994). Reprinted by permission of the author.

"Raised by Women" by Kelly Norman Ellis. Originally published in *Tougaloo Blues* (Chicago: Third World Press, 2003). Reprinted by permission of the author.

"Taking Stock of Being Appalachian" by James B. Goode. Originally published in *100 Years of Appalachian Visions* (Berea, Ky.: Appalachian Imprints, 2000). Reprinted by permission of the author.

"Steep" by Robert Morgan. Originally published in *Land Diving: New Poems* (Baton Rouge: Louisiana State University Press, 1976). © 1976 by Robert Morgan. Reprinted by permission of Louisiana State University Press.

"From Oats to Grits, Mutton to Pork: North British Foodways in Southern Appalachia" by Jim Wayne Miller. Originally published in *Savory Memories* (Lexington: University Press of Kentucky, 1998). Reprinted by permission of the author's estate.

"Plenty" by Michael McFee. Originally published in the *Independent Weekly*, June 30, 1999. Reprinted by permission of the author.

"On the Appalachian Trail" by Matt Lee and Ted Lee. Originally published in *Food & Wine*, March 2002. Reprinted by permission of the authors.

"Homesick" by Diane Gilliam Fisher. Originally published in *Now & Then* 15, no. 1 (Spring 1998). Reprinted by permission of the publisher.

"The Dollmaker" by Harriette Simpson Arnow. Excerpt from *The Dollmaker* (New York: Macmillan, 1954). Reprinted by permission of the author's estate.

"Cooked Food" by Roberta Bondi. Originally published in *Southern Changes* 12, no. 4 (September/October 1990). Reprinted by permission of the author.

"Grandma's Table" by Steve Yarbrough. Originally published in the *Oxford American*, Fall 1997. Reprinted by permission of the author.

"Roadside Table" by Michael McFee. Originally published in *Nantahala Review* 1 (2002). Reprinted by permission of the author.

"Affrilachia" by Frank X Walker. Originally published in *Affrilachia: Poems by Frank X Walker* (Lexington, Ky.: Old Cove Press, 2000). Reprinted by permission of the author.

"Holy Manna" by Robert S. Richmond. Originally published in *Now & Then* 15, no. 1 (Spring 1998). Reprinted by permission of the publisher.

"Ramp Suppers, Biodiversity, and the Integrity of the Mountains" by Mary Hufford. Originally published in *Folklife Center News*, American Folklife Center, 20, no. 4 (Fall 1998). Reprinted by permission of the author.

"April in Helvetia: 1995" by Sally Schneider. A version of this essay was originally published in *Saveur* 5 (April 1995). Reprinted by permission of the author.

"A Talk with Adriana Trigiani" by Fred Sauceman. Portions of this interview aired on *Inside Appalachia*, produced by West Virginia Public Broadcasting, November 2004. Printed by permission of the author.

"Two Americas, Two Restaurants, One Town" by Rebecca Skloot. Originally published in the *New York Times* magazine, October 17, 2004. Reprinted by permission of the author.

"The Anthropology of Table Manners from Geophagy Onward" by Guy Davenport. A version of this essay was originally published in *Antaeus*, no. 36 (Winter 1980); it also appeared in *The Geography of the Imagination: 40 Essays* (Boston, Mass.: David R. Godine Publisher, 1997). Reprinted by permission of the author's estate.

"Syrup Boiling" by Janisse Ray. A version of this essay was originally published in *Wild Card Quilt: Taking a Chance on Home* (Minneapolis, Minn.: Milkweed Editions, 2003). Reprinted by permission of the author.

"To the Unconverted" by Jake Adam York. Originally published in *Crab Orchard Review*, Spring 2003. Reprinted by permission of the author.

"Of Possums and Papaws" by Joel Davis. Originally published in *Now & Then* 15, no. 1 (Spring 1998). Reprinted by permission of the publisher.

"A Passion for Bacon" by Pete Wells. Originally published in *Food & Wine*, May 2003. Reprinted by permission of the author.

"Mad Squirrels and Kentuckians" by Burkhard Bilger. Originally published in *Noodling for Flatheads: Moonshine, Monster Catfish, and Other Southern Comforts* (New York: Scribner, 2000). Reprinted by permission of the author.

"The Oyster Shucker's Song" by David Cecelski. A version of this essay was originally published in *A Historian's Coast: Adventures into the Tidewater Past* (Winston-Salem, N.C.: J. F. Blair, 2000). Reprinted by permission of the author.

"The Fruit of Temptation" by Frank Browning. Originally published in *Apples* (New York: North Point Press, 1998). Reprinted by permission of the author.

"A Pawpaw Primer" by Colleen Anderson. Originally published in *Now & Then* 15, no. 1 (Spring 1998). Reprinted by permission of the publisher.

"Going for Peaches, Fredericksburg, Texas" by Naomi Shihab Nye. Originally published in *The Words under the Words* (Portland, Oreg.: Eighth Mountain Press, 1995). Reprinted by permission of the author.

"Tales of Dough and Dowry: Fried Pies in Tennessee" by John T. Edge. Originally published in *Apple Pie: An American Story* (New York: Putnam, 2004). Reprinted by permission of the author.

"The Pumpkin Field" by William Jay Smith. Previously published in *The Cherokee Lottery: A Sequence of Poems* (Willimantic, Conn.: Curbstone Press, 2000). Reprinted by permission of the author.

"Stand Buy Your Yam: The Lure of the Southern Produce Stand" by Deb Barshafsky. Originally published in *Augusta* 25, no. 4 (August/September 1998). Reprinted by permission of the author.

"Farmer's Market" by Marcia Camp. Most recently published in *Working the Dirt: An Anthology of Southern Poets* (Montgomery, Ala.: NewSouth Books, 2003). Reprinted by permission of the author.

"Of Sorghum Syrup, Cushaws, Mountain Barbecue, Soup Beans, and Black Iron Skillets" by Fred Sauceman. Portions of this essay were previously published in the *Kingsport (Tenn.) Times-News*. Reprinted by permission of the author.

"A Garden in Kentucky" by Jane Gentry. Originally published in *Hollins Critic* 26, no. 1 (February 1989). Reprinted by permission of the author.

"Of Fall Days and Harvesting, and Falling in Love" by Jean Ritchie. Originally published in *Singing Family of the Cumberlands* (Lexington: University Press of Kentucky, 1963). Reprinted by permission of the author.

"Back to the Bayou" by Rick Bragg. Originally published in *Bon Appétit*, November 2004. Reprinted by permission of the author.

"Bill" by Brad Watson. Originally published in *Last Days of the Dog Men* (New York: W. W. Norton, 1996). Reprinted by permission of the author.

"Falling for My Husband" by Blair Hobbs. Originally published in the *Oxford American*, Spring 2005. Reprinted by permission of the author.

The Southern Foodways Alliance (SFA), an institute of the Center for the Study of Southern Culture at the University of Mississippi, celebrates, teaches, preserves, and promotes the diverse food cultures of the American South. Along with sponsoring the Southern Foodways Symposium and Southern Foodways Field Trips, we document Southern foodways through oral history collection, archival research, radio journals, and original films.

Established in 1977 at the University of Mississippi, the Center for the Study of Southern Culture has become a focal point for innovative education and research by promoting scholarship on every aspect of Southern culture. The center offers both B.A. and M.A. degrees in Southern studies and is well known for its public programs, including the annual Faulkner and Yoknapatawpha Conference, the Conference for the Book, and Blues Today: A *Living Blues* Symposium.

The fifty founding members of the SFA are a diverse bunch: they are cookbook authors and anthropologists, culinary historians and home cooks, chefs, organic gardeners and barbecue pit masters, food journalists and inquisitive eaters, native-born Southerners and outlanders too. For more information, point your browser to <www.southernfoodways.com> or call 662-915-5993.

SFA Founding Members

Ann Abadie, Oxford, Miss.
Kaye Adams, Birmingham, Ala.
Jim Auchmutey, Atlanta, Ga.
Marilou Awiakta, Memphis, Tenn.
Ben Barker, Durham, N.C.
Ella Brennan, New Orleans, La.
Ann Brewer, Covington, Ga.
Karen Cathey, Arlington, Va.
Leah Chase, New Orleans, La.
Al Clayton, Jasper, Ga.
Mary Ann Clayton, Jasper, Ga.
Shirley Corriher, Atlanta, Ga.
Norma Jean Darden, New York, N.Y.
Crescent Dragonwagon,
     Eureka Springs, Ark.
Nathalie Dupree, Social Circle, Ga.
John T. Edge, Oxford, Miss.
John Egerton, Nashville, Tenn.
Lolis Eric Elie, New Orleans, La.
John Folse, Donaldsonville, La.
Terry Ford, Ripley, Tenn.
Psyche Williams Forson, Beltsville, Md.
Damon Lee Fowler, Savannah, Ga.
Vertamae Grosvenor, Washington, D.C.
Jessica B. Harris, Brooklyn, N.Y.
Cynthia Hizer, Covington, Ga.

Portia James, Washington, D.C.
Martha Johnston, Birmingham, Ala.
Sally Belk King, Richmond, Va.
Sarah Labensky, Columbus, Miss.
Edna Lewis, Atlanta, Ga.
Rudy Lombard, Chicago, Ill.
Ronni Lundy, Louisville, Ky.
Louis Osteen, Charleston, S.C.
Marlene Osteen, Charleston, S.C.
Timothy W. Patridge, Atlanta, Ga.
Paul Prudhomme, New Orleans, La.
Joe Randall, Savannah, Ga.
Marie Rudisill, Hudson, Fla.
Dori Sanders, Clover, S.C.
Richard Schweid, Barcelona, Spain
Ned Shank, Eureka Springs, Ark.
Kathy Starr, Greenville, Miss.
Frank Stitt, Birmingham, Ala.
Pardis Stitt, Birmingham, Ala.
Marion Sullivan, Mt. Pleasant, S.C.
Van Sykes, Bessemer, Ala.
John Martin Taylor, Charleston, S.C.
Toni Tipton-Martin, Austin, Tex.
Jeanne Voltz, Pittsboro, N.C.
Charles Reagan Wilson, Oxford, Miss.